THE
SANTA CLAUS
BANK
ROBBERY

THE
SANTA CLAUS
BANK
ROBBERY

A. C. Greene

ALFRED A. KNOPF/NEW YORK/1972

364.1
G799s

THIS IS A BORZOI BOOK
PUBLISHED BY ALFRED A. KNOPF, INC.

Library of Congress Cataloging in Publication Data

Greene, A   C   1923–
The Santa Claus bank robbery.

1. Bank robberies—Cisco, Tex.   I. Title.
HV6661.T42S33   1927   364.1'55   77–171114
ISBN 0–394–44379–9

Manufactured in the United States of America

Published July 31, 1972
Second Printing, August 1972

For my children: who all, at one time,
believed in Santa Claus.
I never did. I was told it was sacrilegious.

A Note to the Reader

THIS IS NOT MEANT to be a historical recounting of the event known as the Santa Claus bank robbery of Cisco, Texas. It is a human reconstruction. However, with few minor exceptions, everything in this book is based on facts, either from eyewitnesses (if that is fact) or from testimony made later. Even the rather quaint phraseology which crops up in quoted remarks is almost always based directly on surviving records.

In some cases I have put conversation in the mouths of characters when it is obvious no one was present to record it. But these conversations were dictated by the logical sequence of affairs and not whim. We know they must have been made. As for how some of the characters felt privately, this too is drawn from later witnessing.

In a few instances I have changed the names of people, but most of the names come directly from police and court records. At the time there was still a regional flavor to the naming and nicknaming of humans, wonderfully connected to the social or physical environment. Where today, even in Texas, would a public official dare go by such a name as "Tub"?

I have not tried to gather the biographies of the persons involved except as their lives were connected to the robbery or its aftermath. There are facts of personal history about each of the principals which would make fascinating biography but which have no direct bearing on the central episode.

The best place to reconstruct the story of the Santa Claus

A NOTE TO THE READER

bank robbery is through the coverage of Texas newspapers, particularly the Abilene (Texas) *Reporter* and *Morning News,* complete files of which are only available at the Abilene Public Library. Miss Thelma Andrews, the former director, was most helpful, turning over excellent working facilities to me, and her staff performed physical labor on my behalf, hauling the huge, bound files around.

I wish it were also possible to thank the late Max Bentley, who was managing editor of both papers, for the superior job of reporting, editing, and writing his journalists did. Max was that rare editor, in any media, who responded intelligently and unselfishly to the human tides of the daily craft.

I would like to thank Mrs. Paul Weiser, the former Freda Stroebel, for pleasantly answering my questions; Jewell Poe, for giving me another eyewitness recital; Woodrow Harris, for showing me his engraved timepiece (see the book) and describing how he earned it; Mrs. W. E. Bellew, of San Antonio, and Mrs. L. S. Ripley, of Comanche, each of whom furnished unusually valuable personal recollections.

And to Mr. Lloyd London, who really was a vice president of the First National Bank at Cisco, I want to express special thanks for allowing me to use him as a character in the narrative.

A. C. GREENE

Austin and Dallas
1969–1971

THE
SANTA CLAUS
BANK
ROBBERY

1 / A VOICE was singing as the car drove through the winter night. It was a man's voice, singing a hymn. A nasal voice, drawing out the words in a plaintive way:

> *When the ro-o-oll is call 'dup yonn-der*
> *When the ro-o-oll is call 'dup yonn-der*

The sound was that of country churches, unaccompanied singing harmonized by ear: country alto, country tenor, and country bass. It was hot, dry Sunday mornings, the sun and the wind pouring in at the church house windows:

> *When the ro-o-oll is call 'dup yonn-derrr . . .*

It was funerals held around raw holes in the red dirt, sin the climax of living, death the climax of life:

> *When the roll is call 'dup yonder . . . I'll be there!*

Four men were riding in the car; two in the front seat, two in the rear. There was no way to distinguish who the men were or what they did. All wore cheap coats that showed their poor tailoring in their bulky fit. Three of the men wore dark, felt hats and one wore a cap, which was a popular piece of headgear at the time. Two had on heavy, high-topped shoes and two wore pointed-toed oxfords, but there were no odd, identifiable items of dress, and there was no uniformity.

The man who was singing sat in the front seat beside the driver. His name was Marshall Ratliff. He was twenty-four years old but had a mature face with careless good looks that hinted at recklessness and experience. The driver, who never took his eyes off the dirt highway before him, was Robert Hill. He was also young—in fact, he was the youngest man in the car—and he was handsome, but his rounder, softer face looked more pouty than recklessly attractive.

In the back seat were Louis Davis and Henry Helms. Davis was tall and rawboned, with big hands and a reddish complexion. He was the only one of the four who did not wear a tie but instead had his white shirt buttoned at the collar. He was in his late twenties but looked older. His face was open but unexpressive, as if he were not given to many opinions.

Helms, at age thirty-two, was the oldest and seemed even older than that. He looked down a lot, or "studied the ground," as people said, and his face had a dark cast to it. Most people, meeting him for the first time, instantly took Helms to be unfriendly, and some even thought he looked dangerous. He had been sleeping but Ratliff's singing had gradually wakened him, and now he stirred and asked, "Marshall, what the hell you singing for?"

Ratliff looked back over the seat: "I'm just trying to keep me and ol' Bob from goin' to sleep. Didn't mean to wake you up."

"Can't you sing something besides a goddam church hymn?"

Ratliff laughed, "That's what comes easiest, Henry, you know that the same as I do. Way we was raised; lots of churchgoin' and razor-strappin'."

Helms blew his nose and grunted, "Might as well sing away, I guess. Sleep alone ain't goin' to get rid of this head I've got anyway."

The car's headlights were jumpy as the big sedan moved over the dirt road. It was open, lonesome land with very few houses or lights to be seen anywhere, and it had been more than an hour since they had seen another automobile.

The car they were driving was a dark blue Buick, with less than two thousand miles on the odometer. It had gray plush upholstery with wood trim, and a folding footrest for the back seat passengers. The rear windows were equipped with roller shades, and there were cut-glass vases for flowers on the side posts. Altogether, it was a much finer automobile than any of the four passengers could have aspired to purchase, or all four of them together. So it had been stolen.

THE DRIVER, still keeping his eyes on the road, spoke up: "You know, driving this Buick here is traveling in the style I was borned for, I have come to realize."

Everyone laughed. Helms said to him, "Now Bobby. You wasn't borned for this kind of horsepower. You was borned to gaze across the south end of a northbound mule."

Hill nodded. "Well, I reckon I've done some of that, too. An' by some, I mean enough to last me the rest of my life."

The time was beyond midnight and the date was December 23, 1927. Most people failed to realize that civilization had made some jolting changes in 1927—changes that were tilting the world toward being a vastly different place. Lucky Lindy had flown alone across the Atlantic, ending the New World's isolation in a very personal way. And trans-Atlantic telephone service had begun, putting Europe and America in each other's lap. The first talking picture had been released by Hollywood, and that was the end of "the sticks" forevermore, but even more portentous, the first television transmission in America had been made that year between New York and Washington. A watershed year surely—except that history still hasn't quit measuring it off.

But the men in the car were not thinking in terms of historical epochs and watersheds and new ages of man. They were concerned with a purpose and the means of achieving it. They probably would have remained solely concerned with that purpose had you been able to convince them that epochal events had indeed taken place that year which separated 1927 from all other years. Essentially, they were men of ambition.

They were looking for an opportunity to improve their lot, and they had decided it was an opportunity they would have to make for themselves. They were driving south, this December midnight, from Wichita Falls, Texas, toward the smaller Texas town of Cisco, where they believed an opportunity existed. Cisco was on the edge of the fabled Ranger oil field which had opened up that part of the world to its superabundant mineral wealth. At the top of the boom, thousands and thousands of men came rushing in to seek a fortune, and a good many of them succeeded. Now, although the boom days were over, it was still a fair territory.

But the men in the car were not headed for Cisco to challenge mother earth and the odds of the oil business. They were going there for a very special kind of employment, a get-rich-quick job with easy hours, high risks, and big returns.

They were going there to rob a bank.

"IT WAS OLD MAN Ewell that got me started on banks," Ratliff said. "He lived by us out in Jones County. Old sonofabitch never hit a lick of work but he always had plenty of money."

He shook his head, recollecting old man Ewell. "I was no more than a big kid. But one day the old man told me all about his money and where it come from."

Ratliff stopped and asked Davis, "You haven't heard this, have you?"

Davis said, "No, I don't suppose so."

Ratliff said, "Well, old man Ewell and his brother robbed a bank when they were young and got away with it. That was all it took to put him on easy street the rest of his life. He said it was the easiest way to make money there was."

Helms said, "Well, I got to admit, if you're looking for money there ain't a much better place to start than in a bank."

"Of course not," Ratliff said, "and besides, the money don't belong to the bank. They're just keeping it. And every dime of it's insured. The banker don't stand to lose a nickel. You take a smart banker and poke a gun at him, he won't argue. He'll just shovel it out till you yell quit!"

Bob Hill spoke, "If the banks are so proud to get helt up, how come they're offering that five thousand dollar reward for killing a bank robber?"

"Don't pay any attention to that reward," Ratliff said. "You notice, it ain't the real hold-up men that get shot. It's some ignorant sonofabitch that gets set up for killing by the laws."

Helms said, "I reckon it's always running a risk, but it's the only way a man like me can ever get any kind of a start. I sure can't do it workin' for the other fellow. They got people like us all figured out. They're always goin' to make more off you than you do."

Ratliff laughed, "That's why we got a right to even the odds, Henry. One big one. And this is the one."

Louis Davis had his eyes closed but he was not asleep and he had not been sleeping. He had been sitting in the dark listening and thinking. He was the stranger. Henry Helms was the only one of the men he knew and Davis didn't feel like saying anything, even when the rest of them were all joking. He wasn't afraid of them; in fact, he liked them all. But he knew he wasn't like them. Not right now, at least. The other three were all ex-convicts, and he had never been in any trouble with the law. Marshall Ratliff, Bob Hill, Henry —they had all been to Huntsville, in the state pen.

Henry was the reason he was along. They had planned on using another man, another ex-con, but he had come down with the flu a couple of days ago, just as they were ready to move. So Henry had come to him. Henry was kin to Davis by marriage, and he knew Davis was hard up for money, already with a big family and just in his twenties. Henry had talked Davis into joining by telling how simple the job would be and how big its rewards. He had agreed without too much argument. It had come to that with Louis Davis. He just had to get more money.

But these men were not friends of his. They weren't like him and he knew it. And they knew it. And he couldn't help being afraid. Not of them, but of where they were taking him. The road.

ROBERT HILL WAS afraid of Davis. The country boy, they called him. He made Bob Hill uneasy. Because he was stiff and awkward. Because he was quiet and didn't ask questions. Because he'd never been in trouble with the law. Not because he was a country boy. They were all country boys. They'd all grown up on farms; plowing, hoeing, pulling cotton, cursing. Getting away from the country was what had got them in trouble.

But they weren't going back. They couldn't go back, not even Davis, the country boy. You couldn't make it any more in the country.

If this thing panned out, Robert Hill was going to the big city. He liked sidewalks and running water in the house, and a kitchen that didn't always smell like a coal oil stove.

And he wanted to live some place big enough so he could tell everybody there to kiss his ass.

Bob Hill was the freest one of them. Henry Helms was married and had a bunch of kids, and so was Davis. Even Marshall Ratliff was tied to his family. But Bob Hill was alone, and had been all his young life. And if this panned out, things were taking a different turn.

HELMS SPOKE: "Marshall, you talking about that old man and his brother holding up a bank and all, seems to me like I met somebody else and his brother down behind the walls who had held up a bank, too. And they didn't do so hot out of it."

Ratliff laughed, "Fine boys. Pillars of the community. I knew 'em both real well. Especially the one named Marshall and the one named Lee."

"How come they got caught then?" Helms asked.

"There was two reasons, brother Helms. One a redhead, and one a pee-roxide blonde."

Helms laughed, "Well, I just hope you remember that yourself, brother Ratliff, when the day comes we've got some money and you decide to let the good times roll."

The bank was in Valera in Coleman County, Marshall said. The women were in Abilene. He and Lee were sort of laying-out there, after holding up the Valera bank, figuring to be safe. Then one day, here drives up Sheriff O'Bar and a carload of deputies. Lee thought it was a competing bootlegger had turned them in, but Marshall always figured it was the girls. Anyway, they got caught.

"You and Lee were lucky to get out as quick as you did," Helms said.

"Hell, I don't call two years quick. That and all the money it took."

"Where's your brother now?" Davis asked.

There was silence, then Ratliff laughed. "Lee's back in jail. Can't seem to steer clear of the law. They keep after his ass."

Marshall shook his head: "But hotdamn, I feel good. We're all goin' to get rich—and godamighty—ain't it about time?"

2 / IT WAS THAT back door and that alley that Marshall Ratliff kept thinking about after he got out of Huntsville and was beating around West Texas looking for work.

You walked in the front door, put a gun on the teller and made him open the vault, then you slipped out that back door with the money, got into your car you'd parked in that alley, and before anybody knew it, you were halfway to Oklahoma.

The bank at Valera had been simple to take. He and Lee were gone-ass before the laws even knew about it. If they'd just not screwed around in Abilene all that time and give Sheriff O'Bar a chance to hear the gossip.

So after Huntsville, Marshall kept thinking of what they had done wrong and how it could be done right. But Lee, his brother, said thanks, but no more bank jobs for him. Too many people got their feelings hurt. Ever-goddam-body that had a dollar bill on deposit thought it was his hoard you were trying to get to. Drop that bank business from your mind, Lee advised.

Out of the pen, Marshall rambled around trying to get a job or keep one. They didn't like to hire an ex-con, even as a roughneck. Then, when he landed up in Wichita Falls looking for work, he had run into Henry Helms. Helms was an ex-con, too, and Henry also liked the sound of that back door.

Then there had come Bobby Hill. Bobby had been sent up from Eastland County, where him and Lee were from, so they had naturally fallen in with him behind the walls. When Bobby got out of prison he took the name Bobby Catcher and went to Cisco and stayed with the Ratliffs' mother, Rilla Carter. She and Bobby had moved out to the oil camp of Crane and tried to run a cafe, but before long Bobby had come to Wichita Falls to join Marshall and Lee.

At first the three of them were in a big rooming house with half a dozen other oil field workers, but Henry Helms said he knew a place that was, in his words, "more comfortable." A woman named Midge Tellet had a sort of boarding house —she took in boarders when it suited her—and it wouldn't bother her that they had been crosswise with the law. Henry said he had known her for several years. There would just be them and she and her husband, Freeman, who was an electrician, and their daughter.

So they got a room with the Tellets, under another name, just in case. But Midge Tellet turned out to be safe as well as likable. She talked a lot but she didn't tell things she shouldn't. She just chattered. Besides, she had a lot of wit to her, and her dark eyes would sparkle when she told a joke on herself. She was a little woman, almost pretty, and very trim. She wore her reddish hair bobbed, and she liked mannish clothes. She had a pair of half boots like the roughnecks wore in the oil fields, and she would put them on with some khaki pants that she had cut down to fit her.

But her daughter was interesting, too, although Bob Hill was careful never to say anything about it. The girl, Rheba, was fifteen years old but she acted like a grown woman. Like a lady, really, because she kept her dignity and didn't have that easygoing way with men her mother had. Rheba liked to sing, and Marshall had a fair voice and would sing with her anytime she hinted. They sounded nice together, didn't they? Midge asked her husband Freeman. But Freeman got up and left the living room without answering yes or no.

"Well, fuck him," Marshall said, watching Freeman depart. They had been drinking homebrew since early afternoon because it was Saturday. They were all a little high except the girl, who did not drink any of the beer.

Midge Tellet said to Marshall, "Now look here, big boy. You don't talk that way around my daughter, you hear?"

"Listen, Midge, I forgot Rheba was here . . ." Ratliff looked miserable. The girl's cheeks were red. Bob Hill suddenly couldn't stand it. He got to his feet and said, "I'm going to bed," and went upstairs.

The next morning Marshall apologized to the girl and she said that was all right. But Marshall told Bob, "She was just letting me off easy because she thinks she can't expect anything any better than that from us."

"Well, she can't. And she might as well get used to it if she plans to stay in this house," Hill said.

Bob Hill had been introduced to the Tellets as a friend of Helms and the Ratliff boys (who went under the name of Chaney), but Hill's prison record was not mentioned. One evening Midge and Bob were eating supper alone when she said, "Bobby, you're a good kind of guy. You can make yourself a good future here. And you ought to do it."

"Not me," Hill said.

"Yes, you really should. Rheba likes you, and she's awful sound in her judgment, even if she is young."

She continued, "You know . . . I wasn't much older than Rheba is now when she was born."

Hill continued to eat.

"You're a good-looking guy. Got quiet manners. And you know, you're a lot smarter than Henry or the Chaney boys are."

Hill looked up, but didn't reply.

"I don't have anything against any of them," she said, "but . . . well . . . they're bound to get back in trouble again. The way they go around telling everybody how they hate the law."

Bob Hill shook his head, "Marshall's got a good heart. But people won't let him alone."

"Bobby," she said, "I know that him and Lee are ex-cons. I knew it when they moved in here. I don't hold it against them. But you're different. Rheba thinks so and so do I."

Hill stood up and pushed his plate away from him.

"I'm going away. Going away and never coming back. I don't like this damn country."

Midge put her hand on Hill's. "Bobby. Can't you see that Rheba's going to amount to something? She'll better herself?"

"You're wrong about me, Midge," Hill said. "I got no future either."

"It's not too late for you, Bobby. You're young. You just need some good help . . . somebody that's thinking about your good—"

"Midge," he said, "quit kidding yourself. You might as well find it out from me. I'm an ex-con, too. Just like Marshall and Lee. I got out just a little while before they did. That's where I met them, at Huntsville."

Midge looked stricken. "Oh, Bobby, I never knew that. I never dreamed . . ."

"I was railroaded. A tailor shop hold-up I had to take the blame for. The jury was bound to get me behind the walls."

She shook her head, "They didn't tell me."

"You should have known. You think anybody but another ex-con would run around with them all the time? It was that or starve to death for company."

She said, "They just told me you were an orphan that knew their mother."

"I am an orphan. I've been on my own since before I was ten years old. I got absolutely nobody. But I'm an ex-con and that's the only thing that will ever count."

Bobby waited for her to say something more, one thing . . . anything. Something with softness in it. But she didn't say it. She looked sad and patted his hand and said, "I never suspected a thing. I never suspected a thing at all."

Midge never brought the subject up again.

MARSHALL CALLED HIM out to the car one afternoon and told him Lee had been picked up on a robbery charge. Hill shook his head: "The damn fool. He hasn't even been out a year."

"He's no fool, Bob. Just unlucky. Lee's a good man, even if he is my own brother, but he gets unluckier as he gets older."

"If you start unlucky you don't get any unluckier," Hill said.

Marshall frowned, "Well, I don't know. I'd depend on Lee for my life. He's steady as a two-ton boulder. For instance, I've got something working in my head right this minute that would excite the hell out of Lee."

Hill shrugged, "Well, I bet he'll get ninety-nine years this time, if they've got anything on him at all. So you may as well keep your big idea."

But Marshall said it didn't have to have Lee, and he outlined the bank job, telling about the back door and the alley, and how he knew the people in the bank. Hill thought of his talk with Midge, and how this was something he ought to run from, but he also thought of how much he hated everything in his life, and that he might as well play the part life had given him to play.

Even Marshall was surprised when Hill stopped him and said, "All right, big boy. You can count me in. I'll take Lee's place, because it's plain as day what you're trying to ask me."

Ratliff looked at him with a grin, "Naw, Bobby. We'll

have to get somebody else for Lee's place. You see . . . I'm countin' on you for a place of your own."

A WEEK LATER they met with Henry Helms.

"The three of us might pull it off, but I'd like one more man," Ratliff said.

Helms rubbed the back of his neck. "You figuring on a clean split of the take, or do you want a bigger piece for yourself?"

"Henry, I wouldn't offer anybody less than I'd get. We split everything top to bottom."

Henry said in that case he had a man in mind. It wasn't a friend, but it was a good man, a pro. And a man who knew guns and wasn't afraid of them.

"You planning on everybody carrying a gun?" Hill asked.

"Look, Bobby," Ratliff said, "we're all going in the bank, so we've all got to have a gun. I don't plan on us having to use them, but there ain't no way I'd do it without guns. This business of holding up a bank with a bottle of water for nitroglycerin or an empty paper sack that's supposed to have a weapon in it—you better read about that in the detective magazines. Me, when I go to hold up a bank, I don't want anybody thinking I'm bluffing."

"And I don't want to work with a man who's scareder of a gun than the fellow he's holding it on," Helms said.

Hill shrugged, "Forget it. I didn't mean anything. I'll do it. I ain't scared of a gun."

Marshall told Helms not to contact his man until they were ready to move. "If he's a pro he won't be hard to sell," Marshall said. "It's too sweet a set-up."

But they were never to see the pro. And that was their first mischance.

. . .

Freeman Tellet thought he saw more and more happening between Marshall and Rheba.

"I don't like what's going on," he told Midge. "It may be innocent enough on her part, but I don't like the looks of it."

"The girl's got more sense than you give her credit for," Midge said. "You don't have to worry about her."

"It's not her that worries me. It's them two. They're going to give us trouble over Rheba if we don't do something about it."

"You're better off leaving things alone," Midge said.

"I'm going to take her over to stay at my sister's for a while," Freeman said later.

"You could cause more trouble doing that than leaving her here," Midge said. "I told you—she's got more sense than you give her credit for."

"I think it's a father's duty to see to it his daughter is kept out of trouble," Freeman said. So Rheba had been taken to stay with her aunt.

Midge was surprised, the first night they came in from work, that neither Bob nor Marshall mentioned the girl not being there. The men had their minds on something.

After supper, they got Midge alone and asked her if she would mind helping them. "We've got something working," Marshall said.

She sensed the possibilities in the request.

"Now boys, I can't afford to get involved in anything that's, well, outside the law. Freeman and me, we've never . . ."

Marshall quieted her. "This is strictly legal, Midge. Least-ways, I reckon buying a few groceries and stuff is still legal in the state of Texas."

"You know as well as I do buying a few groceries isn't all you have in mind, Marshall Ratliff."

"And some bandages. Stuff I'd just as soon not too many people knew I was buying."

Her eyes widened in curiosity. "What're you planning, big boy?"

"I just need a roll of bandages and some iodine, in case anybody cuts a finger on the job."

She considered. "Just so it don't involve me buying guns and ammunition."

Marshall grinned. "Don't worry about that. But don't you go trying to lift that green sack I got in my bedroom, either."

THE NEXT AFTERNOON, while Midge was out Christmas shopping and Freeman was at work, Marshall, Bob, and Henry met at the Tellet house.

"Your friend be here this afternoon?" Marshall asked Helms.

"He can't make it today," Helms said. "He's so sick with the flu he can't stand on his feet."

Marshall looked alarmed. "But we've got to have him."

Helms nodded, "Don't worry. He'll be ready when the time comes."

"But we're ready now. I'd like to roll out of here Thursday night. We've got to get this job off before Christmas."

"Before Christmas?" Bob asked.

"Use your head." Ratliff showed an edge of temper. "There's more cash in a bank just before Christmas than any other time of the year. We ought to hit it about Friday noon. If we wait until next week we cut our take by 50 per cent."

Helms closed his eyes. "And you're sure we need four men for it?"

Marshall said, "Now boys . . . just this one time, don't argue. Take my word or let's drop it. I've been planning this for a long, long time. There's got to be four to take care of whatever we might run into. It's got to be four. Your sick friend will have to get on his feet."

But the pro couldn't shake his sickness, so Wednesday night Helms told Marshall he had someone else. An in-law named Louis Davis who had a family, was out of a job, and was desperate for money.

"He's strictly straight, but you can depend on him," Helms said. "He ain't never been involved before, but once he says he'll go in, he'll go in. He's that kind."

Marshall closed his eyes and shook his head. "Goddam, I hate to take a greenhand. I wish to God we could have us a real seasoned man."

"Another thing," Helms said, "he's got a married sister living down in that part of the country. Out to theirselves. I know 'em pretty good. Her husband don't care much for me, but he wouldn't give us any trouble."

That night they met Louis Davis. "Sure wish I had more time to weigh things," he told them, "but you say we might get as high as ten thousand apiece, and I just quit thinking. That's more money than I can make in ten years, the way I'm going now."

He said he would tell his wife he was going south to look for a job; that he was getting a ride with some men who knew the country down there. If she got suspicious from Henry being along, he'd hint they might do some bootlegging.

"She won't like it but she'll believe it," he said.

At first he didn't like the idea of stopping at his sister's place but decided because it was so far out in the country, it wouldn't hurt anything. The only other thing he asked about was, if something happened, would his wife get his share?

"She gets it regardless," Marshall said. They shook hands, standing around the kitchen table. Davis and Henry Helms left. Hill and Ratliff, after the two were gone, agreed that Davis would do. He was inexperienced, but he had that steadiness about him that makes a man trust another man.

"The best people come from the farm," Ratliff said.

"But they don't generally leave," Hill said.

Ratliff grinned. "Could I take that to mean you'd like to go back?"

"Hell no, I wouldn't. But I ain't one of the best people, neither."

IT WAS NOTHING but nerves that got them to drinking on the very afternoon they were planning to pull out for Cisco.

Ratliff had come into possession of a quart of powerful prohibition whiskey given the local name of Electra Lightning from a rowdy, little oil boom town where it was reportedly run off. They sat around the back end of a filling station that was run by a friend of Henry's and consumed it. Helms drank more than Marshall did but he didn't drink it as quickly. Hill stayed fairly sober and he didn't like it that the others showed signs of being drunk.

"How the hell you two think you're going to feel tomorrow when we'll have that job facing us?"

Ratliff laughed. "Come on, Bobby. Get down off your high-horse."

Helms said, "Besides, I operate better with a load on. Ask anybody's worked with me."

"I can't," Hill said, "they're all behind the wall."

"Listen to that," Ratliff said, "Bobby's gettin' mean."

"I say let's quit drinking right now and get something to eat so we'll be sober. We got a hard night facing us."

They arrived at the Tellet house about dark. They hadn't picked up a car yet. That would be the last thing they did. When they walked in the house, Midge was sewing on a Santa Claus suit. Freeman, sitting beside her, got up and left the room without speaking when they entered.

"What the hell's got into him?" Marshall asked.

"He thinks he's too good to stay here and talk to us," Hill said. "Bunch of jailbirds."

"Oh, you know better than that, Bobby," she said. "He's just jumpy because you boys have been drinking."

"What else you told him?" Helms asked.

Midge got solemn. "Honest to God, Henry, I've not told him a thing. You know I'd never tell Freeman nothing he wasn't supposed to hear."

"There's nothing he'd like better than to see all three of us throwed in jail," Henry said.

"Or dead," Ratliff said, looking at the doorway Freeman had disappeared through.

Midge said, "Freeman don't know anything unless one of you all told him. I don't even know myself what you're planning."

"You know more than you should," Helms said. "You bought the groceries. You might even say you're in it too."

She looked at Helms and said, "Now Henry, don't talk to me that way. Have you ever had cause to regret me knowing anything?"

"He's been drinking," Hill said.

Helms shrugged, "I just meant . . . you're an accessory before the fact in case Freeman starts getting ideas."

"He won't," she said. "Free isn't that kind of a man, even if he doesn't like a person. He's fair."

Marshall looked at the clock on the mantel. "Where's Rheba? Ain't it time she was gettin' home?"

Midge went back to her sewing, quickly. "She's spending the night with her aunt. Free's sister."

Marshall frowned. "I ain't seen her since—when was it? Sunday or Monday night, come to think of it."

"Freeman thought that maybe during the holidays she'd like staying with her aunt . . ."

"Like hell. He's scared of me, a goddam jailbird. Thinks she's too good to be around us. Scared one of us'll rape her."

"Don't talk that way, Marshall. It's not right and it's not true. You've never been anything but gentlemen to Rheba."

"Well where is she then? Why'd you let her go off? I had in mind to spend some time with her. Might be my last chance . . ."

He went to the doorway and yelled, "Hey, Freeman. Come in here a minute."

There was no answer.

"Maybe he's out in the garage," Midge said. "He told me he wanted to put some alcohol in his radiator."

Marshall let out a laugh. "That little piss ant can't hold enough alcohol in his radiator to keep it from freezing."

He yelled again, "Hey, piss ant. You back there hiding somewhere?" He cocked his head and listened. There was no sound.

"Hell, I'm goin' to go find him."

"Leave him alone, for God's sakes," Hill said.

"I'm jus' goin' to see where he is. Have a little talk with him. 'Bout eavesdroppin'. List'nin' in on the big boys . . ."

"He don't have to eavesdrop," Hill said, "he can hear everything you're thinking."

Ratliff looked hard at Hill. "Say now, Mr. Hill? Don't you appreciate my style?"

"I'm not appreciating or dis-appreciating anybody, but

you're talking too damn loud for your own good."

Helms laughed, "The trouble with you is, you ain't drunk enough."

They heard the kitchen door open and slam as someone came in from outside. Midge said, "I'll bet that's Free." Marshall called, "Hey, Freeman. That you?"

Freeman's voice came from the kitchen, "Yeah, it's me."

Marshall called back, "How about comin' in here a minute. I got somethin' I want to ask you."

Freeman appeared at the door wearing a coat and hat. "Been getting ready for the cold weather," he said, grinning.

"You better drink that stuff instead of pouring it in that Model T," Helms said.

"I got plenty of the drinking kind already," Freeman said.

"I don't notice none of it being put out for company," Marshall said.

"Aw, you boys ain't company. You're homefolks."

Marshall walked to face the other man and said, "If we're homefolks then how come you're scared to leave Rheba here with us?"

Freeman said, "Nobody's scared. She's just over to my sister's helping her with her Christmas tree."

"Well why ain't she over here helping with her mother's Christmas tree?" Marshall asked.

"Just circumstances," Freeman said. "I didn't know we needed any help with our Christmas tree."

"Well you know it now," Marshall said.

Freeman looked startled. "What do you mean, Marshall?"

"I mean, go get the girl. That's what I mean."

Freeman glanced at Midge, "She's all absorbed with what she's doing, Marshall. She don't want to come."

"You're lying and you know it," Ratliff said. "That tree's been up a week and you know it. You took her over there to keep her away from us."

Freeman shook his head, "She won't want to come—"

Marshall interrupted, "You tell her I asked her to come. Nice and pretty. She'll come."

Freeman stood in the doorway. "I just don't think it would . . ."

Suddenly Henry Helms pulled an automatic pistol from his pocket and waved it toward Freeman.

"You heard him . . . now git from here!"

As Freeman jumped back, Henry turned the muzzle of the gun toward the floor and fired. Freeman jumped almost a yard and Helms fired again on the other side of him. Midge had come to her feet, spilling her sewing on the floor, and Hill tried to grab Helms, shouting, "You crazy drunk bastard . . . put up that gun . . ."

Helms grinned and fired twice more as Freeman yelled, "Don't shoot me . . . don't shoot me . . ."

Marshall Ratliff was dancing around laughing and yelling. Hill grabbed Helm's arm and twisted the automatic from his hand.

"Christamighty, you want every cop in Wichita County to be on our ass?"

Freeman was pressed against a wall, the flooring around him ripped in bright yellow slivers of fresh wood where the bullets had plowed.

Helms pulled his arm away from Hill, who now held the gun. "All right, Bobby. Give me back my gun."

"Not unless you've got your senses back, I'm not."

"It's okay," Helms said. Then frowned, "You do that another time and I'll use a gun on you."

Hill, still furious, said tightly, "Goddam if I'm going to let some drunk bastard get me jailed again over nothing. I didn't like that sonofabitch place at Huntsville."

"I done more time there than you done," Helms said.

"Well quit clowning, then."

Freeman said, "I'll go get . . . Rheba."

Ratliff said, "I'll go with you to make sure."

"Make it snappy," Hill said.

Ratliff and Freeman went out the kitchen door. Helms said to no one in particular, "I knew when I met that sonofabitch I'd have to take a shot at him some day."

WHEN RATLIFF and Freeman got back to the house with the girl, Ratliff said to Midge, "Say, I thought of an idea while we were driving over there."

"I'll bet it's a dandy. Like all your fine ideas tonight have been," Midge said.

"Naw, this one is about something else. Doesn't have anything to do with what we've been doing here."

"In that case I might listen," she said.

"Well," Ratliff said, "I need that Santa Claus suit you've been working on."

Midge said, "I'm making it for Freeman. He's going to be the Santa Claus for his family this Christmas."

"I'll have it back in time," Ratliff said. "Besides, if I didn't I don't suspect he'd say anything."

"What's up, big boy? Are you just teasing or do you really want this suit?"

"You got the rest of it . . . like the whiskers and things?"

"Everything but the pants. They're cut out but not sewed."

Ratliff said, "You reckon I could get into that coat? I'm a good deal bigger in size than Freeman is."

"What do you want with it?" Midge insisted.

Ratliff smiled, "Well, let's put it this way: if you'll let me have it for just a little while, it'll be a mighty big help. And I mean it."

She considered, "All right. I guess I don't have to know

what for, do I? But you've got to have it back here before Christmas. And I wouldn't say nothing about it to Freeman if I was you. I'll explain to him later."

While Freeman stayed in his bedroom, Midge and Rheba fitted the coat to Ratliff.

"I can sew the pants tomorrow," the girl said.

"She's good with sewing," Midge said, "makes most of her own clothes."

"Sorry to disappoint you ladies, but I can't wait," Ratliff said. "I need to take this coat with me tonight."

Rheba laughed, "I'd like to see you playing Santa Claus. Can I go with you?"

"This here's a party for grownups, baby doll," Ratliff told her.

"I'm as grown up as you are, Bill Chaney," she said, calling him by the name he had used when he first moved to the Tellet house.

"You still ain't ready for this party," he said.

"Oh . . . you and Daddy. You make me so mad. You're both silly."

Bob Hill suddenly spoke up. "I've got to run an errand. You want to join me?"

Ratliff took off the coat. "That's right. I forgot . . ."

THEY WERE OUTSIDE in the dark: Hill, Ratliff, and Helms.

"That suit's a good idea," Ratliff said. "Ain't a soul in Cisco will know me with it on. It beats hell out of a bandana over my face."

"The suit's all right," Hill said, "but this clowning around you've been doing isn't. If we're going, we've got to get started right now."

Helms said, "What's the matter, Bobby? You got your tail in the crack permanent or just because you're nervous?"

"It's a long way to where that car is we've got spotted," Hill said, "and once we get it, we've got to move out of town."

Ratliff shook his head in agreement. "You've got a right to be sore, Bobby. We've done screwed around too much. I'm still feeling that white lightning, to be frank. But I promise you, we won't do it again. I'm all right now. The night air's feeling good."

GETTING THE CAR turned out to be easier than planned. Helms had noticed, riding the streetcar every day, that the owner always parked the Buick outside his house early in the evening. When Helms and Hill got there, they were prepared to jump the ignition, but the keys were in the car. They didn't even have to push it out of the driveway. Nobody was in the house and no one seemed to be moving on the whole block. They just started up the motor and drove away.

Helms lived on the edge of town in the direction they would have to take to get to Cisco, so Hill dropped him off and said he and Ratliff would come pick up him and Louis Davis on their way out.

The gas gauge on the Buick showed a full tank, for which Hill was glad. He didn't like the idea of driving up to a lighted filling station in the stolen car.

It was a nice car, the nicest he had ever driven. It was exciting to push the gears smoothly through their pattern and feel the car move away so quickly. If he came out of this with as much money as Ratliff had said, he would pay the eleven or twelve hundred it took to get a new Buick, he told himself. Or maybe even go a few hundred higher and get a Packard. Not that he was all that particular. Bob Hill had never owned a car, or even a bicycle. He'd driven somebody else's Model T, or some old, heavy truck that gave you the piles from bouncing your ass into the seat so hard.

The dark streets were broken by lighted windows where he could see trees in the living room, or families decorating or wrapping gifts. Everybody but him, Bobby Hill, was having a good time at Christmas. Nobody particularly wanted him around. They wanted Marshall Ratliff around, but not him. A man ought to make up his mind about Christmas and either spend it with somebody, even a whore, or not let it get to him.

After this he was going to start over; after this job. All his life it had been Bobby Hill against the world. With a little money he could buy a life of his own.

He was back at the Tellet house in less than an hour from the time he and Henry had left—the car caper went that smooth. He pulled the Buick up in the driveway next to the kitchen door. Things looked quiet. If the neighbors had heard that idiot Helms's shots they must have thought it was Christmas fireworks. On the other hand, pistol shots weren't all that big a curiosity in this part of town, with the oil field workers and all that lived here. It was pretty tough.

Midge and the girl saw the car but asked no questions. The two men stowed the food and supplies on the floorboard of the back seat. Ratliff asked Midge, "You get that doctor's name from Henry?"

She nodded, "I've got everybody's name. Henry's wife and his folks up in Oklahoma. Except your mama. I don't have hers."

"I don't have it neither, and I hope it ain't needed," Ratliff said.

Midge took each of the men in her arms, Marshall Ratliff

first, then Bob Hill, and kissed them lightly on the cheek. She was near tears. "Let me know . . . I wouldn't want to miss . . ."

Marshall laughed and patted her shoulder. "Gal, I wish there was some way you *could* miss."

She said to Hill, "What about you, Bobby?"

He shrugged. "I'll see you in the funny papers."

They drove the stolen car away into the rapidly chilling night.

LOUIS DAVIS SAID his sister's place was out on an oil lease south of Moran. Moran was a little town about halfway between Albany and Cisco. The lease house was located quite a few miles off the highway and sat off to itself. Davis said his sister, Doris, and his brother-in-law, Rob Englin, wouldn't mind them spending the rest of the night there at the house before they drove on to Cisco, but nobody was to say anything or make the least hint they were planning to break the law.

"Doris's scared to death of that kind of trouble," he said.

The four had picked their way down from Wichita Falls through Seymour and Albany so they could avoid as many towns as possible—especially the larger ones such as Graham and Breckenridge. So far their luck had been exceptional. They had not met another car or passed one on the highway since a few miles out of Wichita County. Even Bob Hill was feeling optimistic about the trip.

"Think I'll buy me one of these Buicks with my money," he said.

"We'll all drive Pierce-Arrows this time next week," Ratliff said.

After they passed Seymour, Ratliff had given them the details of the job. He described the bank building to Davis and told him about the people who probably would be there.

"Just so there's no shooting," Davis said.

"I don't think we have a thing to worry about," Ratliff said. "I've heard Alex Spears say himself that he wouldn't risk a hair on his head to be a hero in a hold-up."

Henry Helms said, "Even if there was to be some shooting, we can take care of that. Me and Marshall. There won't be no call for you to get in it."

Davis said, "Well, it's not that I'm a coward . . . it's just that I don't want for there to be any plans already made to do a lot of gunfire and me not knowing about it."

Ratliff said, "I give you my word, Louis, we don't have any plans to fire a single shot. I'm hoping to God myself that nothing like that happens. If I thought it would . . ."

"I don't want to sound distrusting, but . . . well, I guess it's my nerves," Davis said. "I got this deep feeling that, well, it's a deep, uneasy feeling."

"Louis, you've got every right to feel uneasy," Ratliff said. "I know how you feel. I've been there too, buddy. First time, and with people you hardly know. But I want to give you my word and Bob and Henry's word; we're in this four for four. You get my meaning? Four for four and not one for one."

None of the others said anything. Ratliff cleared his throat and continued. "We ain't talked none about this, but we've all got to face the possibility that they take one or two of us and give us the third degree. In that case just remember this: every man's life in this car depends on whether or not anybody sings. And don't forget this, neither. If they get anything on us, they've got to prove it unless we break down and confess. Don't admit a damn thing, anytime. Make 'em prove it."

There was silence for several moments, then Henry said

quietly, "And don't never let nobody tell you them sonsof-bitches can't play rough. I pissed blood for a week one time up in Hardeman County, they whipped me so hard."

There was silence. Then Ratliff let out a yell and said, "Godamighty. We're sittin' around like a bunch of under-takers at a funeral and we're all fixin' to get rich. We've got to cheer up!" He began to sing a hymn again.

THEY GOT TO the Englin lease between 2 and 3 A.M. Davis went to the door of the house while the others stayed in the car. He knocked several times before a man's voice asked who it was.

"Robbie? It's me. Louis." The door opened. The man inside said, "What in the hell are you doing showing up here this time of night? Come on in."

Davis entered the dark room and the man lighted a coal oil lamp. He was wearing long underwear and had on a purple wool bathrobe.

"What brings you down here, Louis?" Robbie Englin asked his brother-in-law.

"Bunch of us on our way south and we got tired of driv-ing," Davis said. "We need a place to sleep until daylight."

Englin looked toward the door. "You're welcome to what we've got. How many of you are there?"

"Four altogether. Me and a couple of fellows from Wichita . . . and Henry."

Englin scowled. "Henry Helms?"

"Yeah."

The man shook his head, "Hell no, Louis. Not Henry Helms. I won't have him setting foot on this place."

"Listen, Robbie, just until daylight. Henry's not all that bad."

Robbie shook his head again. "Till no time. You can't tell me anything about Henry Helms. He's not setting foot on my place."

"But Rob, this is a quick trip. Just a few hours?"

Englin was adamant. "Henry Helms is bad news, Louis. He'll get you in trouble, you have anything to do with him. What are you out running around with Henry Helms for in the first place?"

"Well, we're going down a few miles south of Cisco. A fellow down there Henry knows has some goods we can make a little money off of."

"A fast trip to Huntsville, if you ask me," Englin said. "I expect I can name your 'goods' if it's anything Henry knows about. Bootleg liquor, or worse."

"Well Rob, if it is I ain't the first."

"Nor the first for Henry, neither . . . first trip to Huntsville." Robbie put his hand on Louis's arm. "Louis, you better stay with us, or you'll be another of Henry's jailbird friends."

Davis said, "Rob, you've known me since I was a boy. I ain't been no angel maybe but I ain't done much I wouldn't share with you. But I got to have money. I've got to have it. There ain't no more plums on the plum tree."

"This isn't the way to do it, Louis. I don't know what Henry's fixin' to lead you into, but I wish to God you'd drop out now. Being broke's better'n being in jail—and jail is exactly where everything Henry Helms has ever done has led to. I've known him fourteen years."

Davis hesitated. "Rob . . . just once. This one time. It's all I'm asking."

Englin looked at him. "You mean you know what you're fixin' to do?"

Davis almost whispered, "Rob, don't make me say nothing else."

Englin shook his head sadly. "Louis, I'd damn near ruther

you'd kept lyin' as to admit you're into something so bad you know about it."

"I didn't say it was—"

"Oh shut up, Louis. Don't . . . don't . . ."

Robbie looked toward the bedroom door. "I don't want Doris to know. And I don't reckon you do neither." He sighed and shook his head. "All right. You can spend the rest of the night. Except for Henry Helms; I won't have him in my house. And you can tell him so. I ain't scared of him, even if he's got a gun in his hand."

Davis said, "Rob, you still got your tent? I think it would be better if we all stayed outside in the tent."

"It's in the shed. Do whatever you like, except for Henry."

Davis told the others the Englin house wouldn't hold them so maybe some of them ought to sleep in the tent. Helms seemed to understand that he wasn't wanted. He stopped Davis abruptly in his explanation: "I savvy, Louis. You and me can sleep in the tent. I guess the others won't hurt Robbie none."

They went to the shed and found the canvas tent and set it up beside the car. It was a bright, crisp night and the tent was plenty of shelter.

It was still gray-dark when Louis Davis heard Rob Englin start up his truck and drive off. None of the others seemed to have waked. Louis got up quietly and went into the house where his sister was in the kitchen.

"Well, Louis honey. Robbie told me you showed up here last night. You get any sleep at all?"

"I feel fine. It wasn't no feather bed, but it was comfortable."

"You ready for breakfast?" she asked him.

"Sure am," he said.

"Rob mentioned there was four of you; reckon they're ready to eat?"

Davis looked at his sister. "One of 'em's Henry."

She put down the skillet she was holding in her hand. "What are you doing with Henry?"

"We're heading for Gorman or some place to the south, sis."

"With Henry Helms?"

"Henry has a way to make some money."

"You be careful what you get talked into, honey. You've got that wife and those babies to think about."

"That's why I've got to have some more money, sis. We just keep fallin' behind."

"If it was anybody but Henry . . ." she said.

"Henry ain't all that bad, sis. You've just lived around Rob too long."

"I ain't by Henry the way Robbie is, I'll grant you, but I know Henry draws trouble. He can't seem to keep out of it."

"Well, it's just a job, sis."

She shook her head, "You know good and well it's not just a job. It's something you're not proud to admit, I can tell."

"Well, maybe a little white mule from the shinnery . . ."

She studied him sharply, "I don't expect Henry thinks that's much of a job. Henry considers himself beyond bootlegging."

Louis shrugged, "Listen, if they decided to crack down on everybody that's run a little booze for his friends they could fill all the jails in West Texas."

She shook her head, "Just don't tell me any more. I'd just as soon not know." She went to the kitchen safe and looked inside. "You reckon I got enough eggs for your crowd? I don't keep chickens any more."

"I guess we'll eat whatever you fix. We ain't proud." He watched her. "Just so there's enough for you, too."

"I ate with Robbie when he got up" she said. "I fixed coffee and some biscuits. He'll be back about nine and we'll have another bite then."

"We'll be gone by then," Louis said.

"I expect you'd better," she said.

DAVIS HELPED Doris clean up the dishes after they had eaten. She had been careful not to say much to Helms besides hello. The others went out to the car and waited for Louis. When he had finished in the kitchen he put on his overcoat because the morning was staying pretty cool.

"Well," he said to Doris, "I guess I'll be seeing you tonight sometime, if we come back this way. I don't know exactly how we'll go back to Wichita."

She kissed her brother goodbye. "Try and get back by here. Wilburn and his wife are coming in on the train to Moran this afternoon. He'd like to see you."

He waved goodbye again after he had joined the others at the car. She watched his tall frame fold itself into the sedan and saw the rear door slam. He had always been thin and sort of gawky.

She told herself she guessed she would always think of him as a little boy no matter how big he got; a little boy running to his big sister.

The blue Buick picked up speed and kicked up dust in the bright, chilly air, and she watched it go down the lease road until it turned toward the south and disappeared.

"Tell old Wilburn hello for me if I don't get to see him."

Louis had said it to her as he left the house. She said later she hadn't dreamed it would be the last words she would ever hear her brother say.

3 / IT HAD BEEN a warmish season. Some of the Cisco merchants, in fact, had complained about the weather being too springlike this close to Christmas. They said they liked to see a good drizzly freeze as near Thanksgiving as it could get. It put people into the mood for Christmas shopping.

But to tell the truth, in 1927 Christmas shopping was going on about as good as the merchants could have wanted. Cisco was doing fine. It had just completed what it advertised as the world's biggest, hollow concrete dam out north of town, which created a blue-water lake like you couldn't find anywhere else in that part of Texas. A group of investors was putting up a nine-story hotel catty-corner from the old, red brick Mobley Hotel where Conrad Hilton had started in the hotel business a few years before. Good farmlands surrounded the town and the crops had been heavy. And the oil fields to the east were still paying well. The Ranger field, fifteen miles away, had slowed down considerably from its boom days of 1920 but Cisco, and the rest of Eastland County, was still making good money off it.

The three Eastland County towns were strung out along the Texas & Pacific Railway exactly ten miles apart: Ranger to the far east, Eastland in the middle, Cisco on the west side of the county. Ranger had the fame and the gaudy reputation, Eastland was the county seat—but Cisco was the city. It had a tone to it the other towns lacked—or claimed they didn't want. Cisco had managed to take a lot of the cream off the Ranger oil boom without catching the dregs. The businessmen liked to say theirs was white-collar money.

Cisco had about eight thousand people, Chamber of Commerce count, in 1927. In that part of the nation at that time, this was enough population to make it a major center; big enough to offer the farmers a good market and their wives some fancy shopping. On the other hand, it was small enough for a person in town to know just about everybody he saw on the streets, even folks from Dothan, Nimrod, Scranton, and the other, smaller places in the south end of the county who came to Cisco to shop.

Avenue D was called "Main Street" by everyone in Cisco although that wasn't its official name. It was the main thoroughfare. It started at the T & P and the Katy railroad tracks, on the north end of downtown, and ran south through the business district, becoming the Rising Star road out at the south end. Cisco's business section was mainly from Third to Fourteenth along Avenue D. It was a wide street, paved with red brick, and its most important commercial intersection was at Sixth where the Cisco Banking Company had an imposing building with tall stone columns up the front.

In the next block south, at number 704, was the First National Bank. It had been giving the Cisco Bank more and more competition during its ten years of operation. But right now, both banks were more worried about a statewide problem than they were about each other. The problem was armed robbery. Texas banks were being held up at an astonishing rate—three and four a day—particularly little banks in those one-horse towns where the robbers had only a constable or maybe a town marshal to contend with. They could steal a fast car, drive in and stage the hold-up, and be a hundred miles gone before anybody outside town got the news. None of the hold-up men seemed to care that under a state statute, robbing a bank was a capital offense.

Earlier in the fall of 1927 the Texas State Bankers Association had made a desperate, dramatic announcement. It would pay, the Association thundered, five thousand dollars to anyone who killed a bank robber caught in the act, "but not one cent for a hundred live ones." It was a gesture born of and worthy of the frontier society that had spawned most of the Texas bankers of the day. It was the kind of retribution, the old-timers said, that the criminal mind could understand and would waver in the face of.

Of course, it didn't take long for some citizens to figure out ways of luring other less shrewd citizens to their deaths in a manner calculated to look like the thwarting of a bank robbery. From the first, some people, even lawmen, saw the danger in such a reward and one sheriff had already spoken out against what he called "a sordid head price." But the Texas public mind of 1927 was not turned to benevolent inspection of criminal laws, and the newspapers, which formed the bulk of public opinion, automatically supported any action of the bankers; so in December of 1927 the "dead robber" reward, as it was called, was still considered a creditable move. The irony of the whole thing was, however, that the huge reward for dead bank robbers wasn't stopping—or even slowing down—the bank robberies.

In Cisco, Alex Spears, cashier of the First National Bank, had led a drive among the merchants to buy the police special arms—shotguns and high-powered rifles—to cope with possible hold-ups. It was a sort of civic Christmas present to Chief G. E. (Bit) Bedford and his police force—as well as a subtle reminder to the police as to what was expected of them in the way of priorities.

The First National Bank was in a one-story brick building which sat on the west side of Avenue D near the middle of the block. About twenty-five feet wide, the building had originally been constructed for use as a retail store. There were two display size windows across the front and four smaller windows along the alley which ran along the north side of the building.

As you entered the bank from the front door the offices of the president and the cashier were to your left. They were open cubicles formed by waist-high marble walls that separated them from the lobby area. The tellers' cages were also on the left beyond the cashier's office. The bookkeeping room was separate from the rest of the bank, running across the rear of the building, with a door that opened into the lobby. An outside door in the bookkeeping room opened into the alley.

The alley was paved and was used as a street. Cars drove through regularly and pedestrians made a sidewalk of it when there were no cars. It was handy, cutting through the middle of the long block from east to west. For example, you could come in the front door of the bank, make a deposit or withdrawal (there was very little banking by mail in those days), then go out the rear door into the alley and be right in front of the City Hall, almost. It was on Sixth Street, only a few steps across a vacant lot from the alley. The police station was located in the City Hall, too. Although it was kept thumb-latched, this informal use of the bank's alley door was common. So was the custom of parking in the alley.

Parking was beginning to be a real problem in downtown Cisco. Main Street was so wide that, for years, drivers had parked their automobiles in a line down the middle and there was still plenty of room for traffic to flow along either side. But recently this had become too big a headache to allow, and Chief Bedford started sending a motorcycle patrolman up and down the street, making people move their cars when they tried to leave them parked in the middle of the street.

"People have to understand that things have changed," the chief told the Cisco paper when some of the merchants protested that his actions discouraged shoppers. "There's too many of them [cars] to let them park just any old way they want to."

But he still allowed parking in the paved alleys and, at Christmastime, he instructed his policemen to overlook some of the parking infractions. Christmas, after all, was when the town's merchants made their money.

So that more or less is how things were on Friday, December 23, 1927, shortly after the noon whistle blew at the Cisco & Northeastern roundhouse, and Santa Claus, in his red coat with snowy whiskers and a smiling, red-cheeked mask, stepped through the front door of the First National Bank.

4 / THEY LEFT THE Englin house with Bob Hill behind the wheel. They kept south for a few miles and drove the country dirt roads as Ratliff gave instructions.

"We'll join the main highway from Moran into Cisco. It'll bring us into town directly from the north," he said.

"They're liable to spot this big car, ain't they?" Helms asked.

"There's lots of traffic between Moran and Cisco," Ratliff said. "Besides, Buicks ain't all that scarce around here. You've got to remember, there's lots of oil money in this county."

"What about you in that suit?" Helms asked.

"Well hell, Henry, you don't think I'm going to sit up here like I was in a Christmas parade, do you? I intend to get down on the floorboard soon as we get to the highway. And I can sure as hell duck if we see somebody comin'. I ain't all that dumb."

"Forget I asked," Helms said. "Go on with your instructions."

"Well, you all let me out over by the Katy tracks between East Fifth and East Sixth. There's a line of loading docks there so there won't be but a few people around, especially at noon."

After they let him out near the loading docks they were to drive around to the west end of the alley that ran by the bank, and they were to park the car as near to the bank's back door as possible. The alley was one-way going east so they wouldn't have to worry about someone coming from the other direction.

"When I go in the bank, chances are they'll all look at me. You can sort of slip in," Ratliff said.

"Bobby, you can come right along behind me and take whoever's in the offices—probably Alex Spears. Henry, you can cover Jewell Poe. He's a big tall guy that's usually in the first cage. I want those two with a man apiece on 'em because if there's a gun in the bank, they'll have it."

Ratliff continued, "Louis, you keep an eye on the door. If somebody comes in, you cover 'em and keep 'em still. I'll collect the money from the cages and from the vault. Spears or Poe will open it. I happen to know, it ain't a very complicated lock."

"What about the customers?" Hill asked.

Ratliff didn't answer for a second, then said, "I don't anticipate more than one or two. We can cover them when we cover Spears and Poe."

"I sure don't want there to be any shooting," Davis said.

"Best way to avoid shooting is to look like you're ready to do it first, Louis," Ratliff said. "You start shaking or look like you're bluffing and somebody'll start trouble. Don't shake and keep your gun out and they'll keep respectful."

Ratliff grinned around the car: "If we do it right we ought not to be in the bank any longer than it takes to cash a check."

Hill said, "Hell, Marshall. I've never cashed a check in a bank!"

"Not one that was writ by me, neither," Helms said. And they all laughed.

By then they were within sight of Cisco and within minutes of the robbery itself, and they had made three critical errors, or mistaken assumptions. First, nobody had remembered to get gasoline for the car. The Buick had left

Wichita Falls with a full tank but two hundred miles later the gauge showed it to be almost empty. Perhaps the booze and excitement of the night before caused them to overlook it; perhaps they were used to driving smaller cars that got better mileage than the big Buick; perhaps Hill was not accustomed to looking at a fuel gauge, many cars of the time had none— or perhaps they were simply unfamiliar with automobiles to the extent that the need didn't occur to them. None of the men owned a car.

Their second error was in the assumption that only two or three persons would be in the bank. This, too, may have come from their unfamiliarity with banking and business in general, because the noon hour during Christmas season has always been a busy time for most banks. This error was compounded by the further assumption that people would always respond the way they wanted them to at gunpoint. This, too, may have been a sociological flaw traceable to their own backgrounds: they certainly would take orders at gunpoint.

The third error was probably the most serious, and the hardest to understand. Why would anyone think that wearing a Santa Claus costume on the streets of a town the size of Cisco would be a workable disguise, a disguise that would allow someone to fall back into the crowd, so to speak? In any town, even a metropolis, the sight of that red suit, that smiling, whiskery face, was an instant magnet.

Especially for the children . . .

RATLIFF HAD RIDDEN into town crouched on the rear floorboards. The Buick left the main street and Hill said, "There's not half a dozen people back here. Just some parked cars."

Ratliff, in the Santa Claus suit, slid out the back door as Hill halted the car beside a loading dock. Then the Buick drove to the end of the dock and turned back toward the main part of the business section.

Ratliff straightened up and began walking rapidly toward Avenue D and the bank. He left the deserted tracks and entered East Fifth. Almost immediately, the first kid spotted him.

"Hello Santa," the little boy said. The boy's father, just getting out of a car, spoke too. "Hi old-timer" he said. Ratliff said, "Merry Christmas," in what he tried to squeeze out as a different sound from his natural voice.

"Santa . . . Santa . . ." another child's voice, then another, came at him. "Goddam," Ratliff muttered under his mask, but waved a gloved hand at the children.

He turned the corner of East Fifth onto Avenue D and even more kids began to notice him. Some merely waved, or hollered, "Hello Santa," but several of them began following along. "You working for Garner's?" one boy asked, mentioning a department store in Cisco. "Where's your candy?" another child asked.

"Hey Santa, ain't you givin' away nothing?"

Three boys of about age ten followed closely at Ratliff's heels, teasing him to give them something.

"You ought to talk to John D. Rockefeller," Santa told one of the boys.

"Who's that?" the boy asked.

"He's the man that's got all the money, that's who it is," Ratliff answered. "Might give you some if you're good."

"Aw, you're not a real Santa," a little girl said.

"Leave him alone, honey," her mother said.

"Why isn't he riding in his sleigh, if he's real?" the little girl insisted.

"He's going to go eat," her mother said. "Even old Santa has to eat dinner. Isn't that right, Santa?"

Ratliff was walking as fast as he could, but he nodded

and replied, "That's right, ma'am. Old Santa's got to get fed."

"You hear?" the mother asked her little girl, "Santa's going to go have a nice lunch."

"He's not a real Santa," the girl said again.

The mother looked Ratliff over and frowned, "I don't see any sign on you. Who do you represent?"

"You'll find out pretty quick," Santa told her. At least, when she was asked about it later, she thought that was what he had said.

5 / ALEX SPEARS WAS CHATTING with Marion Olson, who was home for the holidays from Harvard Law School. Alex stayed in the bank at noon while Charlie Fee, his father-in-law and the president of the bank, went home to eat.

Jewell Poe, in the first cage, was the only teller on duty. He had just taken a deposit from Oscar Cliett, manager of the Cisco branch of the Radford Wholesale Grocery Company. Oscar, leaving the bank, leaned over the low marble wall to say something to Alex.

Vance Littleton and Freda Stroebel, two bank employees, were in the bookkeeping room, using the noon hour to catch up on their posting. It had been a brisk morning.

Two girls, Laverne Comer, age twelve, and Emma May Robinson, age ten, were walking toward the front door. Laverne had raised some calves with her older sister and they had deposited their profits in a joint account. But when Laverne wanted to withdraw her part of the money so she could buy Christmas presents, she was told she must get her sister's signature, too. As her sister was one of the persons Laverne wanted to get a secret present for, she was trying to think what she could do.

Three other men came into the bank behind Santa Claus, but nobody noticed them at first because everyone was watching the costumed man. Alex Spears smiled and said, "Hello, Santa Claus." Santa didn't speak, and Spears wondered, momentarily, who it could be. Spears had been cashier since the bank opened for business in 1917. He knew everybody in town, and whoever it was should have spoken, even if he was wearing a Santa mask.

Then Spears saw the guns, and he realized a hold-up was about to take place.

One of the three men behind Santa Claus stepped up to Poe's cage and shoved two pistols in the teller's face saying, "Stick 'em up!"

Poe, who had been watching Santa Claus and hadn't noticed the other men, thought it was some sort of joke connected, perhaps, with the man in the costume. Poe smiled and asked the gunman, "What do you mean?"

The guns shook under his nose and the gunman didn't smile when he said, "I mean business, big boy."

That convinced Poe. He raised both hands, feeling, for the instant, foolish doing so. It was just like the movies.

Santa motioned for Poe to leave his cage. "Get that vault opened," he ordered. Poe looked at Spears who said, "Go ahead." It was the first the bankers realized Santa was part of the hold-up.

Santa said something to the gunman that sounded like, "Let's get it," and was headed around behind Poe's cage, where the vault was, when the front door of the bank opened and in walked two females. And they quickly put an end to all the plans the four men had made for a swift, smooth bank robbery.

WE ALL KNOW six-year-olds like little Frances Blasengame. She spotted Santa Claus from across Avenue D, just before the costumed man walked into the First National Bank.

"Mama," she said, "there's Santa. You promised me I could have one last wish. You promised."

She tugged at her mother's hand and started across the street.

"Oh, Frances," the mother tried to resist.

"You promised, Mama. You promised if we saw Santa I could have my last wish."

"But I meant in a store. Not out here on the street. We can't cross against the traffic. Besides, Santa's busy. See? He's going in the bank."

"But you promised. You said if we saw Santa . . ." The little girl had her mother to the curb by now.

"Oh . . . all right . . ."

The mother and the little girl cut through the traffic and crossed the street there in the middle of the block. When they walked into the bank, guns were already out and showing.

Mrs. Blasengame shook her head, her eyes wide, "Oh my Lord!"

She grabbed Frances's arm and started to back out the front door but there was a fellow standing there with a pair of pistols. She hadn't seen him when they walked in. So she began pushing Frances in front of her toward the rear of the bank where the back door was, while the little girl began crying, "They're gonna shoot Santa Claus . . . they're gonna shoot him!"

Another gunman, standing midway in the lobby, waved his gun at Mrs. Blasengame and yelled, "Get back there, lady. Get back," but she didn't stop. She kept pushing Frances:

"Hurry up, honey—hurry up!"

The two stumbled toward the rear and someone yelled, "Shoot, goddam it. Shoot."

LOUIS DAVIS WAS CONFUSED. He looked at his gun; he looked at Hill. He couldn't tell who was yelling and if they were yelling at him or at everybody who had a gun.

The woman and her little girl came right by him and he

yelled, "Come back here, lady," but neither seemed to be hearing him. He would have tried to catch them with his hand, they were so close, but he had a gun in it. "Shoot . . ." he heard.

"I can't," he explained aloud. "I might hit . . ."

Mrs. Blasengame and the little girl got to the bookkeeping room and no one had tried to stop them except by shouting. The mother pushed Frances through the door and said loudly to Vance Littleton and Freda Stroebel:

"They're robbing the bank."

The two clerical workers, in their room separated from the bank business area, had only the moment before heard the shouting. Mrs. Blasengame's cry was the first they knew of what the noise signified.

Davis, finally breaking the immobility that had seized him, came running toward the room, still yelling, "Lady, get back here!" But Mrs. Blasengame and Frances had reached the back door, the one that opened to the alley, the mother still shoving the little girl in front of her. She had trouble getting the door open because it swung inward and she was pushing outward.

"Wait, honey," she said to Frances, jerking her daughter back, "let mother open the door."

She finally got the door open only to discover the outside screen was latched. The mother, with the child before her, threw herself against the barrier. The screen door hook was ripped from the frame and the woman and the little girl went flying out into the alley while the gunman behind them was still yelling, "Come back here . . . get back here . . ."

She ran up the alley and across the vacant lot to the police station, bursting through the front door of the station, hollering, "They're robbing the bank! They're holding up the First National!"

Chief Bit Bedford came out of his office on the run.

"Who said so?" he yelled.

Mrs. Blasengame waved her arms at him. "I said so. I just got out of there. The whole place is full of men with guns. There must be seven or eight of them. They tried to capture us. Me and Frances."

It didn't take more than three or four minutes before the word that the First National was being robbed was all over downtown Cisco, and nearly every man there was either running to get himself a weapon or was headed toward the bank with a gun in his hand.

DESPITE THE FLURRY of yelling at the woman, most of the men inside the bank, robbers and victims alike, didn't realize what had happened. Mrs. Blasengame had disappeared from the lobby and their attention was on what they were doing, presuming (we must presume) that someone else had taken care of the situation. Hill, covering Spears and Olson, had yelled at Mrs. Blasengame but had not stopped holding a gun on the two men. He was pale and nervous and his head jerked from side to side as he continually looked about, each jerk of his head causing the pair of automatics in his hands to sweep back and forth.

"I hope those things're on safety," Alex Spears said, thinking aloud more than trying to be funny. When he said it Hill looked down at his weapons as if he had never realized before that there were guns in his hands.

Poe and Cliett were being guarded by Helms, who stood back, away from the tellers' cages. Helms had also included Vance Littleton and Miss Stroebel in the range of his guns when they had come out of the door of the bookkeeping room, although there had been several seconds when Miss Stroebel thought she could simply have walked out past

Davis—the gunman was so dazed in his reaction. But Littleton, who was much older than the twenty-four-year-old young lady, whispered to Freda, "Don't be crazy. Put your hands up."

Santa hadn't shown a weapon. He had quickly searched Spears and found him unarmed, then stepped into Poe's cage and got a small automatic which was lying on a shelf just beneath the teller's window. He stuck the gun in his waist and said to Poe, hoarsely, "Now get the vaults."

"I can't open but one safe," Poe said, "the other one's on time lock."

"All right, get going," Santa said.

While Santa and the teller were at the vault, Helms confronted Laverne and Emma May, who had been cowering against the north wall, holding hands. He motioned with his head for them to step around beside him, but he didn't point his gun at the girls. The girls walked with both hands raised high over their heads, although no one had ordered them to do so.

"How old are you?" Helms asked Laverne. She was too frightened to answer and he didn't repeat the question. Helms herded them into the bookkeeping room and as he did, Freda Stroebel looked closely at him, directly in the face. She said later her curiosity about what kind of man a bank robber might be overcame her fear. It was the first thing that had happened inside the bank that seemed to upset Helms. He shook his head and said, almost angrily, "Don't do that. Don't look at me."

There was so much tension in the lobby that it almost hummed, but Oscar Cliett, the wholesale grocer, had a personal problem that took his mind off the robbery even though it was in progress. After Helms had put the little girls where Davis could cover them, too, he took the few steps necessary to put him directly by the entrance gate to Spears's office. Cliett, who was a few feet from the gunman, suddenly blurted out, "Move over."

Helms swung toward Cliett almost as if he would shoot him.

"What?" he asked.

"Move over."

"Why?"

Oscar, his jaw full of chewing tobacco, pointed, "You're standing in front of the spittoon."

Helms looked down at the spittoon, then back at Cliett. "Spit on the floor," he told the grocer.

Cliett did.

In the vault Poe was handing out money and paper. He pretended to overlook two bags of currency which, he knew, amounted to several thousand dollars, and he kept hoping Santa Claus wouldn't look in the drawer of his teller's cage where there was five thousand more in cash. When Poe began handing out money, Santa pulled from under his red coat a tow sack with idaho potatoes printed across it. It had been the padding for his belly.

"Put it in here," he told Poe.

Poe didn't try to keep track of how much he was taking from the vault. His mind was racing with thoughts of the two sacks of currency and the drawer full of cash. He stuffed checks, bonds, currency, paper into the potato sack until all the valuables in sight were gone. He was about to toss in several rolls of nickels when Santa said to him, "That's it," and then yelled loudly to his companions, "Let's get out of here!"

Not more than two hundred and forty seconds had passed since he had walked into the bank. And then . . .

As Santa and Poe turned from the vault back to the lobby, Santa looked up and saw a face peering in through one of the front windows. Hill and Helms also saw it, and the shock caused one of them to react without thinking. Someone fired a shot. The bullet drilled a hole in the window facing, just above the head of the person outside. There was sudden, heavy silence inside the bank as the noise of the shot ballooned in the air, then dissolved. Everyone looked at Santa in fear, assuming he had fired his gun. While they were looking at him, an answering shot came from outside. The gunmen looked at one another, stunned, realizing the robbery had been discovered.

Hill raised his pistol and said quickly, "I'm going to warn them we're armed." He fired four shots into the ceiling. Once again the noise of the blast ballooned, then dissolved away into a heavy, suspended silence inside the bank.

Then from outside came another reply. But this time it was not a single shot. It was a burst from front and sides, a fusillade that broke windows and sent bullets ricocheting around the interior. Freda Stroebel screamed and the two little girls, huddled in the bookkeeping room, started crying. One of the gunmen shouted for them to get under a big table, below the level of the windows. Miss Stroebel and the girls dropped to the floor quickly, and Vance Littleton immediately crouched there under the table with them.

Santa began trying to move the other customers and bank people toward the bookkeeping room where there was more protection than in the lobby area with its big front windows. Davis was covering the front of the bank and Helms edged his way cautiously along the wall toward the back door so he could shoot from it and cover their escape. Somebody yelled, "It must be the police," and Santa shouted back, "It must be every damn body in town." He was very nearly right.

· · ·

WHEN MRS. BLASENGAME CAME screaming into Chief Bedford's police station that the bank was being robbed, it was as if everyone in town was waiting to hear that particular piece of information. The chief grabbed up one of the new shotguns the merchants had bought him and told two of his officers, George Carmichael and R. T. Redies, to take positions in the alley at the rear of the bank.

"I'm coming in from Main Street," he told them. "You cover me and I'll try and get at 'em with this shotgun."

"If there's as many as she says there is, we'll need help," Redies said.

"We can get all we want," the chief said. "Lot of the boys have just been waiting for the chance."

He was correct. When the three policemen came out of the station at a run, carrying their weapons, the sight set the town off. Men on the sidewalks yelled, "What's happening?" and the reply from all over was, "Bank robbery! First National!" The excitement spread faster than the police could run.

Clerks in the hardware stores snatched rifles and shotguns off the racks and passed them out to customers. Businessmen who kept pistols on their premises rummaged through their desk drawers looking for ammunition and cursed when they couldn't find any but ran off toward the bank anyhow. All work in the downtown area stopped. The post office was temporarily located in a building behind the bank, opening onto the same alley. Postmaster J. W. Triplitt and his assistant W. P. Coldwell got out the two big-caliber service revolvers Uncle Sam had issued the post office years before—neither weapon having ever been fired since. Coldwell crept out in the alley and got behind a thick utility pole that shielded him from the bank's back door but allowed him to see that opening. He was part of an ambush of a dozen armed men, formed in minutes around the front and rear of the bank. No one realized that the blue Buick parked in the alley was to be the getaway car.

Nobody said anything about the five thousand dollar reward for dead bank robbers either, except that later one man remembered thinking that if Mrs. Blasengame's guess as to how many bandits there were was right then there'd be enough to go around. But the money must have come to mind in a lot of cases. The announcement had drawn a lot of attention—and five thousand dollars was a staggering sum. Very few persons in Texas made that much money in a year's time, much less a few seconds of legal gun-shooting.

There was also an air of gaiety, plus a justifiable tone of rectitude to the excitement: here was a bunch of criminals caught dead to rights inside the bank in the very act. It was exhilarating and outrageous at one and the same time, so that several Cisco men who wouldn't ordinarily have been able to shoot at a live target were redhot to pump a few rounds into the beseiged bank or its illicit contents.

Bit Bedford, though, wasn't going after thrills or the reward money. He was going after lawbreakers. Bit was one of the last of the old frontier lawmen—he and George Carmichael, who had served with him for years. Bit was brave in a stolid, patient way which he didn't see as bravery. It was just a form of reality. "I go where the law sends me," he said.

Bit had once been sheriff of Eastland County, and in the days of the Hogtown boom at Desdemona, the meanest in Texas oil history, he'd been the chief of police who finally straightened things up. Bit, alone, had stood in front of a mob on the streets of Desdemona one night and dared the hellraisers and the gamblers, the pimps, bootleggers, and jitney extortionists to make their move. Some of Texas's toughest, most sordid ruffians were there but he quieted the riot without cocking his gun. There was this to be said about

Bit: you knew by looking at him that if he decided he had to kill you—he would.

INSIDE THE BANK, the ambush going like fire now, the two little girls and the bookkeepers stayed under their table while a stream of shell casings bounced and spun off the floor and rolled under the table with them. The gunmen inside were firing wildly through the windows of the bank.

"Where in hell did they all come from?" Helms asked as he ducked and fired.

"It's that damn reward," Santa shouted. "They're all after that reward."

Davis, who had come running from the front, said half in a sob, "My God, I thought we wasn't going to have nothing like this."

"You think somebody ordered it special?" Hill said. "You don't have to aim at nobody. Just keep 'em away from the car," he added.

Santa reached under the table and started pulling out the four who were protected there.

"The only chance we got is right here," he yelled. Littleton, on hands and knees, said to Hill, "You can't make it. Why don't you give up?"

Hill growled, "Your ass'll get shot off right along with ours. Those people out there don't care who they shoot."

"I'm staying right here behind this brick wall," Littleton said.

"Like hell you are, big boy," Hill told him.

Then it occurred to Littleton that if the hold-up men used them as shields, the way the mob was shooting, it wouldn't matter who stepped through the door first; they would get it. The ambushers were firing at everything, not just the robbers. And the choice to go or stay was not his.

"Oh," Littleton said solemnly, aloud. "I see."

The four gunmen were doing a fair job of keeping the alley clear, firing rapidly from windows and the back door. But they had to move, and they knew it.

"Get everybody in the car," Helms yelled. "In a hurry."

Santa grabbed Freda Stroebel and crisscrossed his arms in front of her, a pistol in each hand.

"Go on," he ordered the hostages. "Go on. When they see who it is, they'll stop shooting."

The others hesitated. Someone yelled out again, "Get going."

Alex Spears looked around at the others and made a lunge out the back door. He was immediately hit in the jaw by a bullet. He fell back, grabbing his streaming face and moaning, "I can't go. I'm bad hurt."

"Hell, you're not hurt; you're just grazed," one of the robbers said, putting a pistol in the banker's ribs.

"Get in the car. Everybody."

It was ridiculous, of course, to order everyone in the car. At most, the sedan could carry seven or eight persons jammed onto each other's laps—and there were sixteen persons in the bank. But whether they could get in the car or not, the numbers protected the hold-up men. Using their guns, pushing the others, the bodies came tumbling out the back door, some terrified, screaming bank employes, some robbers. Spears pushed open the screen and staggered into the alley with his hands raised and blood gushing from his jaw. "Get in the car," someone yelled at him, but instead of getting in the Buick the banker darted along the wall and rounded the corner of the bank into a narrow passageway at the rear and thus was the first hostage to reach safety.

After Spears, everyone came pouring out almost at once. Young Olson, the Harvard law student, was hit by a bullet and tried to retreat into the bank, but the gunman behind him grabbed Olson and shoved him into the car: "Lean back against that seat and shut up or I'll kill you," he said.

Inside the car a strange calm visited the college student. "I'm shot. I've got to go to the hospital." Saying this, he slid across the back seat of the Buick, opened the door on the other side, and got out. He made it up the alley to safety but he spent two weeks in the hospital. The slug that wounded him was found in the watch pocket of his trousers where it had passed through his body.

Santa came out pushing Freda before him and firing over her shoulder. He pitched the potato sack full of loot into the Buick's front seat and yelled, "Get in!" at her. But the young woman ducked away and around the same corner into the passageway where Spears was.

Oscar Cliett got a bullet in one heel as he emerged from the bank and couldn't make it very far. He drew himself up behind a small pole, although he was a heavy-set man, and somehow survived the crossfire at the corner of the bank building.

Sometime in that confusion Jewell Poe made it to the safety of the north-south passageway, too.

The girls, Laverne and Emma May, were caught in the milling and shooting, not knowing what to do. One of the gunmen grabbed them and said, "Get out on the fender," thinking it would stop the ambushers from shooting. But the girls refused. They stood crying, with bullets flying around them, and the robber only had time to shove them into the car, Laverne in the front seat and Emma May in the back.

When Santa Claus came through the door, Bit Bedford and George Carmichael both advanced. Chief Bedford's new shotgun jammed and he turned to a preacher who was crouched behind Garner's Department Store watching the fight, and shouted, "Get more men and block the street so that car can't get out." Then Bit cleared his gun and, making a six-foot-four, two-twenty-pound target, came pumping around the east end of the alley and fired a blast. Just as he fired, the big man staggered and went to his knees. He was reaching for a six-shooter strapped to his leg when he collapsed and fell back, face upward, to the bricks.

Alice Moore had driven her new Pontiac downtown to her husband Dewey's drug store, which was across Avenue D from the First National Bank. Some man came running out into the street and stopped her, telling her to get out of the car and follow him.

"Not here . . . right in the middle of the street," she said.

"Right now. Come on. They're shooting at the bank robbers. You're right in the middle of trouble."

"But somebody might hit my new car." The man opened the door and grabbed the young woman, pulling her out, "I don't have time to argue. Come on."

She ran toward the front of Garner's, where she saw several men huddled. Alice suddenly woke to the extreme danger she was in as bullets came flying down the alley toward her. Instinctively, she pulled up her fox fur wrap around her ears as if protecting herself from the cold. She looked down just in time to miss stepping on the big man when he collapsed and rolled over.

"My God—it's Uncle Bit."

Alice had been a girlhood friend of Bit Bedford's daughter and the chief was like a member of her own family. After that she seemed to float, without moving her legs and without seeing or hearing anything else. She floated out of the alley, into the shelter of the front of the department store building, her eyes all the time on the fallen man. It was hours after the shooting had ended that her husband told her the new Pontiac, as she had feared, got a big bullet hole in it, right where it could have hit the driver.

.   .   .

THE BANK WAS EMPTYING fast. Davis came out by himself, without any hostages in front of him, and had taken one step into the alley when a shotgun blast hit him. He spun back but then staggered to the car and fell in. Littleton and Hill were the last ones out. Putting a pistol over the bookkeeper's shoulder, Hill pushed him along. The shooting of Bit Bedford momentarily stopped the firing, and Hill made it around the front of the Buick to the driver's seat, but Littleton, instead of staying in front of Hill, had hit straight up the alley and escaped.

At the west end of the alley, policeman George Carmichael, seeing his chief start to rush the car, had also gone toward the Buick. A shot from the bank door hit him in the head. He whirled, lurched against the wall of the bank building, and slid down in a heap upon the alley pavement.

Helms, Hill, and Ratliff made it to the car somehow, although in the confusion they all just seemed to be there suddenly at the same time. Ratliff was in the back seat with Louis Davis, who had passed out as soon as he fell into the car. Hill was behind the wheel and Helms beside him in the front seat. Laverne Comer was held hostage in the front and Emma May Robinson in the rear. The four men were operating more from reflex action than by any predetermined idea of what to do next. They did not know what had wrecked their plan for robbing the bank and getting away, and it is doubtful that they had time to even try and figure out where the sudden, furious mob appeared from.

Alex Spears, as soon as the bandits were in the car, ran from his hiding place to where George Carmichael had been gunned down. The banker grabbed up the policeman's pistol and was about to fire into the car when he saw the head of Emma May in the rear window and realized there were hostages being held. He dropped the gun and ran up the alley to join the others and warn them that there were hostages in the Buick.

There was still an air of adventure and high thrill about the whole affair. R. L. Day, a cafe operator, came around the east end of the alley with a shotgun he had taken from a hardware store rack, just in time to see Hill slam the door getting into the car. Day ran up to the door and shoved the gun in Hill's face as the hold-up man was frantically trying to get the Buick started and in gear. Day pulled the trigger but nothing happened. He pulled it twice more with no results. It was an automatic weapon and he didn't know how to make it fire. He was still pulling the trigger in exasperation as the car started and lurched out of the alley. Then Day turned around, yanked the trigger one last time, and blew a hole in the side of the Garner Department Store building.

As the Buick started moving out, Postman Coldwell stepped into the alley from behind his pole and hit a back tire with one or two of the steel-jacketed bullets he fired. The car careened so badly, making the turn from the alley into Avenue D, that a rear door flew open and Emma May, who was sitting on Santa's lap, almost fell out.

Despite the flat tire the blue sedan gained speed as it headed south. A dozen men began pursuing it on foot, firing as they ran. C. A. Nosek had Chief Bedford's pistol, A. A. Hutton, an oil man, took up Carmichael's pistol where Spears had dropped it, and others came running from stores and side streets as the weaving escape car ran the gauntlet of fire.

Inside the car Ratliff fired and from time to time Helms threw out handfuls of roofing nails which were supposed to puncture the tires of any motorized pursuers. Ratliff had clubbed a hole in the rear window of the car and was firing through it while Helms shot from an open window.

Davis was huddled silent in the back seat, his wounds

having put him in shock. The big sedan was unwieldy, lurching and swaying as it went. Some of the time it was actually traveling on the left-hand side of the street, creating panic in several drivers who were approaching the center of town on Avenue D, not knowing of the hold-up, and suddenly facing a runaway automobile careening down their side of the roadway. One pedestrian, standing on the curb as the fleeing car went past, received a powder burn on the face— a gun from the car was fired so close to him.

On the sidewalk a blind fiddler had been playing for the Christmas crowd farther down the street from the bank. When the shooting and commotion broke out into the street, not knowing what was happening but hearing the tumult coming nearer, he began wildly scraping away on *Soldier's Joy*, and continued, seated on a small canvas stool in the middle of the sidewalk, all alone, fiddling as fast as he could while bullets from pursuers and pursued whipped and sang around him, his frenzied music audible even to the men in the getaway car.

As the Buick outran the foot posse, it picked up motorized pursuit. Just as the area around the bank had become, in an instant, an ambuscade, so did the call for cars and the chase spread over the south side of Cisco. Within seconds after the escape car broke out of the alley, there were other vehicles being driven toward points of possible interception. Communications, however, weren't always clear. Two boys, at home when a friend phoned them the news, got shotguns and climbed in their stripped-down roadster to go help. When they neared Avenue D they saw the Buick roaring along but took it to be one of the pursuers, so they fell in behind and merely followed it from a couple of blocks' distance. L. L. Hooker had been in the barber shop when news of the robbery reached him. He jumped out of the chair, half trimmed, and went to the hardware store where he worked to get a rifle from stock. He got to the bank just in time to see the Buick spinning off south. He ran on foot for a block then saw someone he knew in a car. He climbed in and they gave chase. Policeman Redies was also running after the Buick and was picked up by a motorist. Guy Dabney, vice president of the Cisco Bank, joined the chase at Ninth Street, by chance. He had been at home for lunch when he was called and told that the competing bank was being robbed. He and a nephew, Carl Mauldin, got in a car and were intending to go to the First National when they saw the speeding Buick and figured out it was the bandits' vehicle.

The battle was still a game. The chase, like the ambush, was high spirited and boisterous, a big, civic play party that was spiced up by bullets—bullets zinging overhead and off brick walls, and bullets squeezed off at the impersonal targets of an automobile and an unknown number of faceless men simply called "the bandits."

But inside the car the gravity of affairs was settling on their consciousness. Not only was Davis lifeless, Santa had been hit in the chin by a bullet, and the blood was gushing. Steering the car with a rear tire flat was a strain on Bob Hill, but he had it under control, and despite the increasing number of motorized pursuers, the Buick was pulling away. Then he made the discovery of the lack of gasoline.

"We've got to get another car," he shouted.

"Not till we get to another town," Santa shouted back, thinking he meant the Buick was too hard to steer with the flat.

"We've got to. This one's showing empty. We're running out of gas."

The impact of the news didn't even allow anyone in the car to think about who might be to blame.

. . .

At Fourteenth Street and Avenue D the Ellis Harris family was driving in from the little town of Rising Star to do some last minute shopping. Woodrow Harris, who was fourteen, was at the wheel of the family's brand-new Oldsmobile. His grandmother, Mrs. Sarah E. Graves, was in the front seat beside him, and his mother and father were riding in the back.

"There's Santa Claus waving for us to stop," Woodrow said.

"It's some kind of a Christmas stunt," Mrs. Harris said.

The boy braked the Oldsmobile to a halt and almost before exclamations could be made, the Harris family was looking down gun barrels.

"Get out of that car," someone ordered. Nobody in the car moved. "I said get out! Let's get moving."

Helms was over on the side of the car where Mrs. Graves, who was eighty years of age, was sitting. When he yelled at her, she simply turned and looked the other way.

"Get 'em out, Henry," Santa shouted. "The road's filling up behind us."

"Get out of the car, lady," but the old woman sat without making a motion. Bob Hill ran around to her side, opened the door, and lifted Mrs. Graves bodily from the seat, putting her outside on her feet. Mrs. Harris started screaming then. Helms grabbed her: "Shut up that noise," he yelled. "If you don't shut up I'll shoot you."

Mrs. Harris stopped, looked at him, and said, "You'll just have to shoot me. I can't stop." She went back to screaming.

Santa Claus was at Woodrow's side of the car and told him, over a pistol, "I'll take over." Woody answered politely, "Yes sir," and while Santa stood over him, locked the ignition, slid from under the wheel, and walked away with the key in his pocket. Laverne and Emma May were standing on the sidewalk and Woody stopped and asked them, "What's going on?" The scared girls couldn't reply, so Woody ran behind a nearby house where the rest of his family was taking shelter. The Harrises still couldn't figure out why Santa Claus was mixed up with a bunch of thugs like these.

Santa and Helms began shifting things from the crippled Buick to the Oldsmobile. Davis had to be shouldered over to the new car. He was laid in the back seat and the money sack thrown in with him. The girls were shoved into the front seat.

By now the posse, drawn up a block or so away, was firing heavily at the robbers as they darted from one car to the other. Hooker, with the high-powered rifle he had gotten from the hardware store, hit Hill in the left arm and the force of the bullet spun him completely around, but he continued to return the posse's fire.

"We're all set, get in," Santa yelled. They piled into the Oldsmobile and Hill tried to start it. "Where's the goddam key?" he asked.

"Let's get the hell away from here," Helms growled.

"The key—I can't start it without the key."

"Jump the ignition," Santa yelled. But there was no time to try. "Besides," Hill said, "this sonofabitch has some kind of a lock on the gearshift. You got to have the key."

"Jesus God!" Santa yelled.

So they piled out again, Santa firing rapidly at the posse and herding the two girls in front of him, the others coming behind. Somebody asked about Davis and Santa said, "Leave him. He's nearly dead."

"They'll kill him out of spite if he's alive," Helms said.

"He's got more chance than with us," Santa replied.

They got back in the Buick with its flat tire and gas gauge showing empty, and they managed to pull away again, although the bullets were hailing around them. Some members of the posse who joined the chase later said they hadn't known the girls were in the car until a law officer warned everybody against shooting blind into the Buick, and that was the way the robbers managed to escape a second time. That, and some blistering rapid fire from all the gunmen who were still on their feet.

In the getaway car there was not much conversation. While Santa kept a gun watch, Helms hurled out more of the roofing nails.

"We can't get far," Hill said. Nobody answered. Nobody mentioned Davis, either. But someone remembered another matter:

"Hey, who's got the money sack?"

Even Hill turned around from driving to look at the others. There was no need for anyone to say it. They had left the loot in the back seat of the Oldsmobile with Davis. From now on, no matter what happened or how, they were working without pay.

As THE BUICK LEFT the scene, the pursuers came running or driving up to the Oldsmobile. The Harrises came from behind the house just as a man was yelling, "They left one here." He was aiming a pistol at Davis when Mr. Harris yelled, "Now don't you shoot that man. Look at him, so near dead he's passed out."

Someone else yelled, "Hell no. Let's get a rope and drag him back to town with this car!"

"You're not using my car to drag anybody to town, not even a crook," Mrs. Harris said. The gathering men looked at her and dropped the idea.

Officer R. T. Redies took charge, there at the Oldsmobile,

finding two pistols and three cartridge belts, plus the sack marked IDAHO POTATOES with the bank loot in it. The sack contained 12,200 dollars in cash and 150,000 dollars worth of paper. Alex Spears looked it over and said he thought that was everything the robbers had taken. "I guess they never even got a look at it after they stole it," he mused. When someone said he supposed the bank would close, Spears put a teller in each cage and announced they would stay open to make up for the time lost, it being so close to Christmas— then he went off to have his wounded jaw dressed.

A crowd jammed the bank, of course, looking at the bullet holes and the blood, and trying to count the number of shots fired in the exchange. Someone made a semi-official estimate of two hundred, but almost everyone who had been there said that wasn't half enough. Cisco milled like an anthill downtown.

The wounded bandit admitted his name was Louis Davis. He said he was a family man from Wichita Falls where he worked in a glass factory. He claimed he didn't know the names of his companions. They had just picked him up at the last minute, he said. Another man, a professional safe-cracker, had been supposed to come but he got the flu real bad. When the police asked Davis who the professional was he said he had no idea, that he knew next to nothing about the job and the people he had been with, only that he needed money so bad that he joined without any questions when he was promised a chance at a few thousand dollars. Then the country boy passed out again and they couldn't bring him to, so the interrogation had to be held off for a while.

Bit Bedford, without knowing it, started a troublesome new rumor. The wounded chief, out of his head from time to time, told Harvey Olman, Cisco's motorcycle patrolman, that he was gunned down by a woman.

"I wasn't shot by a man," he whispered from his hospital bed, "it was a blonde-headed woman. I was looking her straight in the eye when she shot me."

Harvey immediately informed everyone to start a search for a blonde-headed female killer. It plagued the posse because no one who had been at the bank could recall seeing any females other than Freda Stroebel and the two girls. It might have been that the chief saw one of them being used as a shield and thought she was a part of the robbery gang —but even this was hard to accept. Freda Stroebel was a very dark-haired woman and neither of the girls was of a physical size to be confused with a grown woman. The chief insisted on what he had seen as being the case.

Following the seizure of Davis and the loot, Cisco began counting up its casualties. Besides Chief Bedford in the hospital, George Carmichael was there in serious condition. Alex Spears's jaw was painful, but not crippling. Marion Olson's wound was more serious than he had first thought (he ultimately spent six weeks in bed), and Oscar Cliett would limp for a month on his bad heel. Brady Boggs had been hit in the leg, some time during the exchange, and Pete Rutherford in the thigh. R. L. Day, of the erratic shotgun, got creased in the scalp. Except for Bit and Uncle George, nobody was sure which side had fired the bullets that did the damage—and it was too embarrassing to guess out loud.

The fighting had seemed to go on for hours. For instance, Tom Whitehead, the Cisco newspaperman, said he was two blocks away when the shooting broke out. He ran to the west end of the alley, peeped around the corner and saw the employes, the customers, and the robbers all piling out of the bank. He then ran to the nearest telephone and called in an eye-witness story to the Fort Worth *Star-Telegram*, and still had time to get back for most of the auto chase. And yet, when people looked at their watches afterward, they found it had all started only fifteen minutes before.

Everyone downtown waited for the word that the rest of the robbery gang had been caught. In fact, most of the men who had come back from the scene at the Oldsmobile were of the opinion that their capture had been only a matter of running down the crippled Buick within the next block or two. They expected the remainder of the posse and the hold-up men to be coming in any minute.

But the minutes passed and nobody showed up with the good word that the men had been taken—though everyone said there was nothing to worry about, they were as good as in jail, and for that matter, as good as tried and convicted. The Santa Claus bank robbery, bizarre as it was, was about concluded.

LAVERNE HAD BEEN WARNED not to look, but when she heard Santa groan, "I've got a bad chin," she had to see. She turned just as Santa pulled his mask from his face, then somebody else hit her in the head with a pistol, growling, "Turn around here." It wasn't a real hard lick, but it hurt. However, it might have been worth it, because Laverne was pretty sure she recognized who Santa Claus was.

The gunman keeping watch out the back window reported they were clear of pursuers.

"Wonder what happened?" one asked.

"Maybe the roofing nails have slowed them down," the driver said.

They drove down the dirt road for a mile and a half.

"Let's try and make it as far south as we can," Santa Claus said. "Those little hills would be the best place to hide."

"We ain't going to make it much further to any place," the driver said.

They came to a big farm, with neat fences and a large barn.

"How about taking this place?" Helms asked.

"Shit no," Santa said, "Let's get the hell away from here. This is Congressman Lee's model farm. It's so well known they'll all be here in a minute."

Hill swung the Buick directly south on a rutted lane.

"This ain't much of a road," he said.

Santa watched, sitting on the edge of the rear seat. "We should get onto a better road somewhere off in this direction." But eventually the rutted lane became nothing more than a wagon track that followed the fence row.

"This ain't no road at all," Hill said. It was getting rougher and rougher. After a few hundred yards the trees closed in and the lane became so narrow that the limbs scraped the sides of the car. Several places were so rutted out that the Buick hit high center every few feet.

Less than a mile of that and Hill turned the car into the thicket, crashing the way through the brush, trying to find some kind of clearing. Then, tangled in brush and small trees, it stopped its forward progress. After backing up and unsuccessfully trying to ram through a half dozen times, Hill said, "Goddam. This is the end of the line."

Santa said, "I guess we hoof it from here."

Getting out of the car, one of the bandits told the girls to bring a satchel from the back seat. It was so full of ammunition that both of them could scarcely lift it. Laverne whispered, "It's the gold they stole." She had been silently praying that Ratliff would not realize she knew who he was.

Santa turned to the girls: "Now I want both of you to get back in that car and lie down on the floor. Keep your hands over your eyes and don't look. If you do we'll shoot you."

The girls sank low in the car but had the courage to peek through their fingers in time to see the men disappear into the mesquite and scrub oak. Santa was limping, Laverne noticed.

Even after the robbers had left the girls were afraid to get out of the car. For a long time there was no sound. Neither said a word, but they hugged each other fearfully when, suddenly, they heard a noise coming from the opposite direction from that taken by the bandits. They weren't sure whether it was someone coming to rescue them or whether the robbers had changed their minds and had come back to take them with them.

It was the posse, but for a moment the girls were almost as endangered by the rescuers as they had been by the bandits. The first three men, Nosek, Dabney and "Daddy" Keyes, saw a foot in the car's rear seat and thought it was one of the hold-up men lying in wait. The three men were raising their guns to shoot when the girls cried out.

The stolen Buick showed what it had been through, as the posse went over it. There were blood stains on both front and rear seats. Bullets had drilled the rear end and all the glass except the windshield. The front bumper had torn loose and was jammed up under the front axle. Two slugs were found embedded in the back seat and the top was slashed, either by bullets or tree limbs.

The robbers had left a good part of their supplies: four loaves of bread, a canteen of water, a can of coffee, and a sack containing what was left of the roofing nails. Laverne's new Sunday dress that she had worn to town shopping had been ripped by a bullet and she had never known it, but she and Emma May had not been hit. The whack on the head from the pistol had only raised a small knot.

"I think I know who he was," Laverne told one of the posse.

"Who, Santa Claus?"

"Yes sir. I think he was Marshall Ratliff."

The rest of the posse was coming up now and one of the first three told a police officer what the girl had said.

"Marshall Ratliff? How do you know?" she was asked.

"Because I know him," she said. "My mama bought the Manhattan Cafe from his mother. Mrs. Carter. He used to eat with us for a long time after Mama bought the cafe."

The men in the posse nodded their heads. "That's why he wore that costume," one of the men said. "Everybody in town knows Marshall Ratliff. If they'd have seen him walking along the streets, they'd have known right off he was up to something."

The policeman talked to Laverne about the identification of Santa Claus, then warned her, "Don't say nothing about who you think it is. If it is Ratliff we might get a chance to trap him if he don't know we know who it is."

The girl nodded solemnly, "I won't say anything. I was scared to death he was going to know I'd seen his face and know who he was. I was afraid he might shoot me, because I know he knew me, once we all got in the car. He couldn't help remembering who I was."

What the posse and the police didn't know was that the bandits were only three hundred yards away as they were talking to the girls.

DESPITE THE PRECAUTIONS to the girls and the secrecy of the police, it didn't take long for the people of Cisco to hear that Santa Claus was really Marshall Ratliff. There was a general wave of "I could have told you's" with the news.

What is there about some boys—born with a curse and can't stay out of trouble? Marshall Ratliff was like that. Spoiled by his mama, some people said, although Mrs. Carter hadn't really done much for her boys that any other mother wouldn't have done.

There was an unreal recklessness in the way Marshall viewed life, the way he had always lived. A recklessness that went beyond irresponsibility. People had been predicting a bad end for Marshall Ratliff since the days when he was a schoolboy, although a few people admitted he could be fun; he was a fair singer and liked to joke and if you were his friend, he was generous as all get out.

But he couldn't keep out of trouble. Only a year before, after he and his brother Lee had robbed the Valera bank, he'd been granted a pardon because some Cisco people had appealed to Governor "Ma" Ferguson to give the boy another chance. And Alex Spears had signed his bail bond in the original Valera case. People tried to help him, but after he got out of Huntsville he had come back to West Texas and gone straight to bootlegging, the stories all said. Now, if he *was* in this bank robbery, it fit the image.

It made sense that he was, too, if Davis was from Wichita Falls. Ratliff was supposed to be working there.

It didn't take long for the authorities to spot Wichita Falls as the place where the bandits had come from. A check of the license showed the Buick was stolen from Wichita County. Eastland County Sheriff John Hart talked to the Wichita officers and they decided one of the men might be Henry Helms, a thirty-two-year-old ex-convict who was an in-law of Davis's. Helms was a family man, with four, soon-to-be five children, the Wichita officers reported. But he had a record from boyhood. His father was the Reverend J. C. Helms, now of Oklahoma City, but who was familiar in the Wichita Falls area. So Henry was one of those men who, once off the rails, never made it back on.

Davis was known as a good worker, the officers reported. He'd lied to the Cisco police about not knowing who he was with during the hold-up, they figured, but he didn't have an arrest record. The Santa Claus robbery, they reported, was his first experience with crime.

And his last.

Louis Davis died that Friday night in Fort Worth where he had been carried for safety. He never regained consciousness after his brief questioning earlier in the afternoon.

Bit Bedford, who had not been believed critically wounded at first, grew steadily worse through the afternoon, and expired in Cisco at 7:45 P.M. There were a good many people in Eastland County who had known Bit Bedford through a long part of his career and who just couldn't make themselves believe it could have happened the way it did. For a man who had passed through so much danger facing the real gunslingers of the frontier days to die at the hands of a bunch of lowdowns like Marshall Ratliff and his gang— it didn't seem possible.

By Christmas Eve nobody in Cisco, Texas, felt much like playing Santa Claus.

6/ THEY PLUNGED INTO the brush; Helms leading, Ratliff next, and Bob Hill making a slow third.

"Let me get out of this goddam thing," Ratliff said, after they had gone a hundred yards or so from the abandoned car. He worked his way out of the gay, red Santa Claus coat, rolled the mask up in it, and pitched the bundle under a bush. He and Helms took an overcoat apiece from the satchel and divvied up the ammunition. Ratliff asked Hill if he needed any bullets but Hill's eyes were almost shut, and he was swaying. He didn't answer.

"Hell, Bobby's pretty bad hit," Ratliff said.

"You reckon they'll find out who we are?" Helms asked.

"Sure. Louis will tell them, if he lives long enough. They'll get it out of him."

"I figure Louis is as good as dead already," Helms said.

Ratliff hesitated, "One of those girls . . . Laverne . . . she knows me. Her mother bought our cafe in Cisco."

"Jesus," Helms muttered, "if she seen you when you took off that Santa Claus face . . ."

"I don't know. I think she'd have showed some sign of it if she'd have seen me." He shrugged. "Well, they're bound to find out pretty quick anyway. Knowing who we are a day or two sooner won't change things much. And as long as we're alive and ain't been caught, I ain't going to start worrying about something that might not have happened in the first place."

He looked at the overcoats. "It ain't really cold enough to wear these."

"With night coming on we may need them," Helms said. Then added, "We've got to move out, Marshall."

Ratliff touched Hill. "Bobby, you all right?" Hill nodded yes. Ratliff started to retrieve the Santa Claus suit then stopped. "I don't guess that makes much difference. Nothing about it says where it come from."

Helms took the lead. The land was rough, all breaks and draws full of brush and small trees: cedar, mesquite, scrub, and post oak. They had, without planning it, picked the best place in Eastland County to escape a pursuit.

No one spoke while they worked their way through the underbrush, running low when they came to a clearing, beating back the limbs that lashed and stung their faces when they had to stand upright. Helms and Ratliff were panting painfully when something warned them to look back. They looked just in time to see Bob Hill slip to earth, unconscious.

Ratliff went back to him and grabbed his coat sleeve, drawing back his hand with blood on it.

"Goddam. He must have bled a quart. Look at my hand."

He turned Hill over and felt for his heart. "Still alive. Maybe he's just fainted." He looked down at Hill. "Reckon we'd better go on without him?"

Helms shook his head. "We leave him here they'll sure as hell find out who we are."

"Hell, Henry, they'll do that anyway."

"Maybe not before we can get out of this part of the country. If we could make it back to Wichita Falls, I got friends there and we can get help."

Ratliff looked at Hill, "Well, Bobby ain't exactly like Louis Davis."

Helms said, "Okay. We've got to take a chance anyway and get to the Englin place. Might as well try to get Bob on his feet along with us."

Ratliff said, "Give me that bunch of bandages. Let's hope

we've got enough of a head start to do something for him. I ain't heard anybody coming after us yet, have you?"

Ratliff opened the satchel and got out the scanty first aid equipment. They stripped off Hill's coat and looked at the wounded arm. They decided the bone wasn't shattered even though the flesh was discolored and torn.

"That must have been a goddam thirty-ought-six hit him," Ratliff said.

They poured iodine in the wound and the burning of the medicine brought Bob Hill's eyes open. Finally they wrapped the arm tightly with gauze and tied it with strips. It was the best they could do.

"I must have passed out," Hill said weakly. "We been here long?"

"Been here long enough," Ratliff said. "If you can't stand on your feet—we'll just have to . . ."

Hill shook his head. "Help me up. Once I get moving again I can keep going . . . I'm thirsty as hell."

Helms raised a hand. "Listen, I hear somebody."

The sound was unmistakable. It was people. The posse had formed again and was sweeping along making no attempt to muffle its movements. Even Bob Hill moved quickly as they pushed into the brush again.

"Jesus, I wish we had a car," Ratliff wheezed.

"I don't hear any hounds," Helms said, "I just hope to God they don't get the hounds on us until we can get clear of this shinnery."

"If we can make it into night we'll have a chance," Ratliff said.

The sounds of the pursuers would disappear, then come back. The country grew hilly; medium-sized elevations whose slopes were almost as dense with vegetation as the valleys. Ratliff felt they should bear east for the Leon River bottoms, but Helms had an idea he liked better.

"We've got to be where the posse ain't looking," Helms said. "We'll be better off laying right back toward Cisco, if we can double back and miss the posse."

Ratliff said, "I think maybe you're right. They'll be lookin' for us in the rough country, not back from where we started."

So THEY BEGAN to cut north, moving always to their left, edging back toward town. At one point they thought they had completely lost the posse and were feeling a sort of weary elation, when a sudden crashing in the underbrush seemed to be coming directly toward them from the direction in which they were headed.

"We can't do a damn thing now but hide and pray," Ratliff said. Hill was staying on his feet but had spoken very little throughout the chase. The three men pulled themselves into a clump of cedar trees, lying flat on the ground, and waited. The noise passed close by, but they could not see who or what was making it. They heard no human voices but it was more than the sounds a few animals might make. They waited so long that Ratliff thought Bob Hill had fainted again, but he had merely gone to sleep.

Helms was the first to speak out: "I haven't heard anything for several minutes."

"I wonder what that could have been. You reckon it was some of them on horseback?" Ratliff asked.

"More than likely. They were coming mighty close, who-ever it was," Helms said. He looked at Hill, "We've got to chance it again."

Ratliff shook Hill gently, "Bobby . . . Bobby . . . you all right?"

Bob Hill looked at Ratliff from under his lids, "Yeah. I guess I am. How long we been here?"

"Something like thirty minutes, I figure. You've been asleep. I thought you'd passed out again, at first."

"You feel like traveling?" Helms asked.

"I reckon I better. You sure as hell can't stay here with me if I don't," Hill said.

They pulled themselves to their feet, cautiously. Helms motioned that he would scout ahead. He came back after a little time and signaled for them to follow. The edge of the sun was touching the tops of the trees to the west. They had been running for four hours, but it seemed like days. As for the robbery and the battle at the bank—that was somewhere in the past year or more. That other day, that day when they were in Wichita Falls, making plans, thinking of the money, that was another life; and a life none of them could believe he had lived.

They didn't know it but they were safe for the night.

FROM THE BEGINNING it was more like a mob than a posse. They had come driving up, rifles ready, to the abandoned Buick and found the girls cowering on the rear floorboards. The girls had pointed to where they had seen the robbers enter the brush, but that didn't mean much. The men could have gone south or east, either one, and would be just as hard to find. Both directions were away from civilization and equally wild.

There was considerable milling around as more men arrived, but there was no one to organize and direct until Deputy Sheriff Cy Bradford, one of the first lawmen on the scene because he had not stopped back at the Oldsmobile, took charge.

"We'd better fan out," he ordered. The posse spread out in a line with a man every ten yards or so. The hunters plunged into the underbrush, more than a hundred angry citizens. It wasn't long before someone stumbled into Ratliff's Santa Claus costume and gave the cry. Most of the others abandoned the search temporarily to run and have a look at the bloody, red flannel coat. Later in the afternoon they found Bob Hill's coat, bloodsoaked, with a bullet hole in the sleeve, where the three fugitives had forgotten it when they heard the posse moving nearer. But both times, finding the trace of the fleeing men halted the pursuit rather than pushed it forward.

Gradually the lawmen of the area took control of the search, although plenty of civilians remained out in the brush. Sheriff John Hart was in command, and he assigned Deputies C. D. Paine, Lee Reid, Milton Newman, and Bradford to take cars and go down every wagon track and trail that went off into that piece of wild country. The search was not coordinated, except for direct contact, because there were very few telephones in the area and no major roads; and at that time there was little or no radio equipment in use among law enforcement agencies of the area.

However, word of the hold-up and escape was spreading over the several thousand square miles of central West Texas. The Abilene *Reporter,* the Fort Worth *Star-Telegram,* and the Wichita Falls *Times* had all managed to get stories of the robbery in their Friday afternoon editions. Telegraph operators along the T & P and the Katy railroads moved bits of information between train orders, but there were dozens of little communities and hundreds of isolated farms and ranches that did not hear about the crime for hours, or even days.

Much of the first information was exaggerated, even before the deaths occurred. Harvey Olman's report that Bit Bedford said his assailant had been a blonde woman found plenty of takers. It spread fast, and was just what the search needed to keep enthusiasm high.

"You take men like them, they have to have women at all times, their lust is so inflamed. Young women, the younger the better. The hard, glittery kind that use their soulless beauty to inspire crime and degradation."

This explanation was made by the Reverend Tom (Pud) Proctor of the Primitive Bible Church, who had joined the hunt equipped with the Colt's Peacemaker he said his preacher father had carried into the pulpit with him back in the outlaw days. Along with him were his sons Finis and Speed. Speed claimed he had had a knife fight with Ratliff one time on a drilling rig at Pueblo. He waited to be sure his daddy was out of earshot, then admitted the fight was over a woman named Sudie from Breckenridge.

"From the sound of the blonde that shot Bit, I'd say they were the same woman," Speed declared.

Some of the civilians got to thinking that the blonde woman ought to be taken alive at all costs, even if killing her might qualify a man for that five thousand dollar bankers' reward. The concerned men were working together at the south end of the drive and one of them said he knew, pretty well, who the blonde was. "And I'll tell you something else; if she's who I think she is, she's a goddam good-lookin' woman. Be worth that reward to take her alive—with a couple of hours head start!"

But, of course, there was no woman, despite the ardent memories of the posse members. The chief's statement presumably was made from the confusion of the bandits firing from behind their hostages or his injury-clouded brain. Eventually Cisco's Mayor J. M. Williamson had to issue a formal statement denying the existence of such a woman, although Harvey Olman kept pointing out those were Bit Bedford's dying words, and he should know who shot him if anybody did. A great many uneasy citizens felt the same way about the woman, based on the chief's famed integrity. For others it was just hard to give up the idea that a good-looking blonde woman (for by then her beauty—unmentioned by Bedford—had become as firmly established as the color of her hair) was out there waiting to be brought to a form of male justice.

The casualty list was growing, by fact and by fancy. Sheriff Gib Abernathy, of Palo Pinto County—one of eight sheriffs who had joined the search by Friday night—was added to it when his gun accidentally discharged, blowing away two fingers and badly wounding him in the leg.

Darkness fell with the posse unable to find the fugitives or more clues. By then there was also some furtive talk as to whether or not the bankers' reward would any longer be paid. Some of the zeal went out with the question for some citizens at that point. And shortly after dusk one of those infamous Texas northers blew in, changing a mildly sunny day to a bitterly cold night. Several of the posse declared the bandits would suffer more left out in the weather than snug in the jail, so they took it as their moral duty to pull off the hunt at least until daylight returned.

RATLIFF, HELMS, AND HILL REMAINED uncaptured more from luck than from their skill at eluding the posse. Half a dozen times they had been close enough to hear the would-be captors and once, for a painfully long period, they had lain hidden listening to someone beating the bushes.

The three men knew the general direction in which they were traveling, but not where they were. Ratliff discovered that his leg had also been hit, and the pain was growing worse and worse. Hill, although still moving, was obviously a hospital case.

Ratliff announced, "We've got to get us another car or we're dead ducks. We're wasting our time on foot. The only reason we ain't been caught now is because there's so many of them they don't know where they're looking."

Helms gave a short laugh. "I don't know . . . Bob and I might be able to pull it. They don't know us in Cisco."

"They know me. Some of them do," Hill said. "You know, they railroaded me from this goddam county."

"Some of the police and the sheriffs know you, but they're all out looking," Ratliff said. "Everybody in Cisco knows me on sight." Then they looked at each other: disheveled, clothing torn and dirty, with blood stains on them, and Ratliff laughed aloud.

"Oh hell no, nobody would recognize any of us. Just look. They couldn't spot you two."

Helms shook his head, but didn't smile.

"But it's get a car or do nothing at all," Ratliff said. "We can't surrender, even if we wanted to. I seen Bit Bedford go down."

"Who was he?" Helms asked.

"He's the chief of police. That big man at the end of the alley. Had a shotgun. He went down and never moved until somebody drug him off."

"Goddam, if he's dead we might as well commit suicide," Helms said. "That posse'll shoot us to pieces if we try and surrender."

"I wonder what they done to Davis?" Hill said.

"Probably lynched him," Helms said.

"Let's get something straight," Ratliff said, slowly. He got to his feet as he spoke.

"I ain't giving up. You ain't giving up either."

Hill spoke without looking at Ratliff or Helms. "We're all going to die. You know that?"

Ratliff said, "Hell no, I don't know that. And you don't neither, Mr. Big Boy. I ain't died till I'm dead, and I'm a young buck now."

"Don't tell me you've got a plan to get us out."

"No, I ain't got no plan to do anything but keep moving and look for a hole. But that's a lot more plan than giving up."

Hill shook his head: "Goddam it, I didn't say I wanted to give up. I didn't say nothing about surrendering or letting them take me."

Helms said, "No he didn't, Marshall."

Ratliff raised a hand: "Nor did I say he did. But the first thing we've got to get together on right now is that we're going to make it. If any of us decides we're not, then we won't. We got to keep running, keep believing we'll find a hole."

"We're in pretty bad shape," Hill said.

"I agree with that," Ratliff said, "but here we are, alive and free. That's not the worst thing that could have happened."

Helms nodded in agreement: "You're right. We can't think about what we might have done or what we ought to do. We'll just have to do it and hope it works."

Bob Hill said slowly and painfully, "You know you don't have to worry about me. You're the only friends I have. My only kinfolks. It won't be me that gives up."

Ratliff said, "Okay, Bobby. Henry. We don't look back from here on in and we don't never let 'em buffalo us about each other." He paused, "It's kind of worth it, maybe. At least we've got . . . we've got . . . something."

Nobody spoke, nobody looked at the other. Ratliff spoke again: "All right. I think we're five or six miles from town. Let's you two go see if there's some nice polite feller's left his car parked out handy for us." He looked at Bob Hill, "Bobby, if you don't feel like you can make it, I'll go. You know that."

"I'm better off than I was. The cold air is helping," Hill said.

"Okay," Ratliff said. "Get a closed car if you can," and he couldn't resist adding, "And for God's sakes, be sure it's got gasoline in it."

HILL AND HELMS CREPT into town wary for signs of a trap, but they were safe. Nobody expected the robbers to return to Cisco. And as it turned out, it didn't matter whether they were strangers or not, nobody saw them.

They got to the southeast edge of town and hadn't gone two blocks when they saw a Ford touring car parked on the dark street in front of a small frame house. There were no lights on in any of the houses around. The car was theirs for the taking.

"It's an open car," Hill whispered.

"Shit on that. It's wheels," Helms whispered back. "It can outrun a man on foot."

They pushed it as far as they could—Hill was coming near to fainting again—then got in it and started it and drove off without creating any disturbance.

Ratliff waited in the wooded area out of town where they had parted. The two men in the car drove by once and made the signal they had agreed on, then came back by again as agreed, in case they had been captured and made to tell their signal, then, the third pass, stopped, and Ratliff came out to the road.

"Get in," Helms said, behind the wheel.

Ratliff looked at the car, "Godamighty, did you have to pick a red one?"

"Get the hell in here and let's get moving. This ain't a red car and you know it."

Ratliff grinned, "Hell, Henry, I'm just so glad to see any kind of a car that I thought I'd make me a little joke."

They drove west, getting as far from where the posse was

as they could, although they wanted to go north. They didn't dare use the Bankhead Highway so they stayed on the county roads and section line trails. It was first light before they reached the pasture north of Putnam where they had planned to hide out originally.

"I'll tell you what we'd better do," Ratliff said. "We'd better hole-up here. This cedar brake will be about as safe a place as we can find. We can sleep, and it'll be good for all of us."

"Sleep hell," Hill groaned, "I'm too hurting to sleep."

"All right, you stay awake and watch. They might use airplanes, once they find out we've got a car."

Helms stretched out under a clump of brush and went to sleep right on the ground. Ratliff, his leg getting stiff, stayed in the back seat of the Ford and Hill slumped over in the front seat.

"Reckon it'll be safe to go back to the Englin place?" Hill asked him.

Ratliff, who had stretched out and had a hat pulled down over his eyes, said "I don't know. But unless we want to starve to death we've got to try it. We left all our groceries in that Buick."

"Maybe they won't find out about Mrs. Englin being Davis's sister."

"If he don't tell them they might take several days to find it out," Ratliff said. "What I'm worried about is getting to Wichita Falls. We don't stand a cut dog's chance if we don't get the hell out of here. They're going to shoot on sight, and there's so many of 'em they could all be blindfolded and still kill us."

"What about the Tellets? Can we get help there?"

"Shit," Ratliff said, "Midge Tellet's all talk. Besides, that husband of hers would like to see somebody get my ass since he's not man enough to do it himself."

"It's Helms he hates."

"He hates me, too, on account of that girl. So afraid she's going to fall in love with a jailbird." Ratliff moved his leg, groaned and fell asleep.

It was now Christmas Eve, Hill mused to himself, and it was freezing, and Henry Helms was the only healthy man in the bunch and there sure as hell wasn't any Santa Claus to help 'em out. The misty pain of his arm forced sleep on him as he mused.

7 / WHEN HE FIRST awakened, Bob Hill couldn't remember where he was or the day of the week. For one of those unexplainable moments he thought he was back working for Stith Morgan on his farm in Coryell County and he was a boy again. Then the pain of his wounded arm brought him back to the reality of the cold pasture where they were hidden, and to the irrevocability of what they had done.

He saw Helms breaking some sticks with a rock. The sound must have been what woke him up.

"What are you fixing to do, Henry?" he called.

"I'm making a little fire. I tell you, I'm freezing my ass off. I think I've got a chill."

"It's pretty risky, isn't it? The smoke in this open country."

"I'm using mesquite limbs. Mesquite don't smoke much."

Hill looked around. "Well, it's still daylight. I guess you can't see the smoke too much."

He got out of the car and joined Helms by the tiny flame. There was no question but that it felt good, grand, to his pain and hunger and coldness of body.

"Reckon we ought to wake Ratliff and let him get warm? This goddam fire is the best thing I ever felt in my life," he said to Helms. Helms turned to the car and yelled, "Hey, Ratliff. Wake up." The man in the car moved his head. "Wake up, Santa Claus. It's nearly Christmas."

Ratliff stirred himself in the back seat of the open car and looked over the side, out at them.

"Put out that damn fire," he said.

"Come get warm first, then we'll douse it," Helms said.

Ratliff sat up, groaned, and felt himself, "Godamighty, it feels like I've been shot in every place on my body." His fingers touched his jaw and he flinched.

"Get out here and get warm. It'll make you feel better than anything else," Helms said.

"I wish to hell we had some coffee," Ratliff said.

It was getting dark now. They had slept the entire day. No lights could be seen on any side of them and no cars had passed on the narrow dirt path that ran to the south of the pasture at a distance of a mile or so.

"What do you think about trying to make it to the Englins?" Helms asked.

"Pretty risky," Ratliff said. "I take it Rob Englin ain't too interested in your welfare."

"Don't worry about that. He'll do something. He sure won't deliberately get us in trouble."

"We've got to have food," Hill said.

"I think we'd better go there while we can," Helms said. "They're bound to find out that Doris is Louis's sister pretty quick."

Ratliff considered, then shook his head in resignation and agreement.

"Okay. We've got to get food and we sure as hell can't get any sitting out here in the middle of a cow pasture."

"It's sooner or later," Hill said.

"You mean food, or something else?" Ratliff asked.

"I mean food. We've already gone over anything else."

"Okay. But I just want to make sure that a few hours of sleep hasn't changed your mind."

Helms said: "With that reward out for us, we can't give up if we want to."

"Maybe the reward don't count any more," Hill said.

"Some of them bastards would as soon shoot us whether there's a reward or not," Helms said.

He scooped up dirt and spread it over the coals of the fire, and when he had extinguished it he stood up and said, "When do you want to start moving? We'd better do all our driving at night."

Ratliff looked around. "I guess it's dark enough now, for that matter."

While Ratliff returned to stretch out in the back seat of the Ford, Hill and Helms checked the gasoline with the stick, which hung on the driver's side of the car.

"We got enough to make it?" Hill asked Helms.

"Make it to where? Where are we fixing to make it to?" Helms did not smile.

"Henry, you think we can't?"

"I think when we left that money sack on the back seat of that car it was a damn poor sign. A whole lot of the fun went out of it."

"The money wouldn't make any difference right now, anyway."

"It would make a hell of a difference in the way I felt. I didn't come on this job just to get experience."

Ratliff moved, then spoke, "We've come this far, and it's a lot further than I'd have given us this time yesterday. If it wasn't for Bit Bedford, I'd start feeling sassy."

"Bit Bedford, dead or alive, won't make that much difference," Helms said. "We shot up too much of the town. One more dead cop ain't going to cook us any doner."

Ratliff disagreed, "No, Henry. It's Bit Bedford I mean. He wasn't a bad old man, chief of police or not. I'd hate to think I done it."

Helms blew his nose, and said, "Hell, I'd as soon shoot a law as another man, if it was just one or the other. In fact, if you get right down to it, a law has more right to expect it. He knew what he was doin' when he let 'em pin that star on him."

"You better keep that attitude to yourself, big boy," Ratliff said. "You go to spouting off like that where you can be heard and you'll catch more hell than the Devil himself."

Helms said, "You forget something, Marshall. I'm a hell-fire preacher's son. I been catching hell all my life, ever time I started to draw a breath. I've heard of hell so long I think maybe it would be a relief to get there. To say, 'Well, here it is and there ain't nothing worse, so I might as well settle in.'"

"This conversation ain't making good sense," Hill said. "One of you crying over the fact that his fine old policeman friend that was merely trying to cut him in two with a pump gun got stopped before he did it, and the other one demanding to go to hell."

Ratliff grinned and spat out on the ground, "I expect you're right, Bobby. Why don't we skip the palaver and haul out of here."

Helms drove because of Hill's stiff arm. They pulled out of the pasture and went south on a lonely dirt road that took them near the little town of Putnam. They were half-heartedly looking for some good luck: a filling station where they wouldn't be recognized, some food they could steal, or a store they might hold up. Hill was very much opposed to doing anything else that would bring attention to the part of the country where they were holed-up.

"As long as we've got 'em thinking we're down there in the far south end of the county let's leave it that way."

Helms was sour as he drove, "I wasn't exactly serious about holding up a store. I might be hungry enough to do it this time tomorrow." He paused, "Which reminds me. This time tomorrow will be Christmas."

Ratliff said, suddenly, "Let's get the hell away from here. We're seeing too many cars."

"I don't want to get to the Englin place before midnight," Helms said, "and we're going to play hell killing that much time."

It was later than they thought. They got to the Englin house at two o'clock Sunday morning. They were fairly sure nobody had followed them. They'd kept to the dirt roads and wagon paths, opening wire gates to drive through big pastures, fording creeks, doing things to throw off anybody who might get a notion to track them. They'd stopped at a windmill once to get a drink, but they'd stopped the car a good piece back and walked so there would be no tire tracks on the ground around the trough to arouse some farmer's suspicion.

"It'd be hell if we got caught because somebody thought we were rustlers," Ratliff said.

They got a scare when they first saw the Englin house. It was all lighted up and there were two cars parked at it. Ratliff didn't want to try the place, but Helms said he knew Doris Englin would have found some way to make a sign if anything was wrong.

"You got a lot more faith in a woman's foresight than I do," Ratliff said. "How would Doris Englin know we'd be coming here?"

"And what kind of a sign do you think she could make?" Hill asked.

"All right," Helms said. "Look at the windows. All the shades are down tight. If it was an ambush she'd have one or two of them pulled out of line to let us know something was wrong."

"Hell, I don't believe that," Hill said. "I just think we've got to take the risk to get food, and I think you've got to go up, Henry."

"I don't mind going to the door, but you know how Rob feels about me . . ."

Ratliff said, "We'll wait with the motor running. If you get the least whiff of trouble, you come at a lope for this car."

Helms went to the house and the other men saw the front door crack light, then open wider. Then they heard Helms whistle an okay. They met him in the dark outside the house.

"It's all right. There's kinfolks here, down from the Plains. Her boy Wilburn and his wife. They're all sitting up, talking. They're here for Christmas."

Suddenly Hill remembered: "My God, it's Christmas."

Helms said, "Something else. Louis is dead. Doris told me. He died Friday night. So did that chief of police."

Ratliff said softly, "Goddam. That's our luck. Both of 'em dying." He sucked air in through his teeth and half closed his eyes. "Goddam," he repeated.

"What do you think about going in? You think it's dangerous?" Ratliff asked.

"We might as well. They know something's up. The other people. Doris said she'd keep everybody in the bedrooms if we wanted to come in."

"We might as well," Ratliff said. "I'm weary. Might as well do whatever we please from now on."

"I wonder who hit him?" Hill asked.

"It don't matter. We'll burn if they catch us," Helms answered.

"I didn't shoot anybody," Hill said. "I swear to God."

"You're not in front of a jury, Bobby. You don't have to convince us," Ratliff said.

"I shot over their heads, even the guys that were shooting at me. I deliberately aimed over their heads. Don't you remember, there in the bank when I fired those warning shots?"

"You can't take no comfort in that, sonny boy," Helms said. "You're in this as deep as anybody else. They're not going to let you off with anything lighter than the chair."

"I think the posse shot everybody, that's what I think," Ratliff said. "They were shooting each other. I know it was the bastards at the bank got Louis."

Bob Hill felt his injured arm and flinched. "Goddam. I wish I knew . . ." He frowned, "It's not that I'm trying to get away with anything, it's just that I really did try to keep from shooting anybody."

"We better quit talking about it," Ratliff said, "or we'll begin putting the blame on each other. We're all to blame, and we're all three in as deep as each other. We've got to keep from thinking there's a difference somewhere. We've got to quit talking about it so much."

Helms and Hill looked at each other, then at Ratliff. Both agreed with a grunt.

"And let's quit being so fucking grouchy," Ratliff continued. "Let's have some goddam understanding. We've been through a whole lot together."

"First time I find something to laugh about, I promise on a stack of New Testaments, I'll let you both know," Helms said.

Ratliff laughed then. "Shit yes. Soon as we eat I'll lead us in a gospel hymn to chase the blues away."

DORIS ENGLIN MET THEM at the front door and embraced each of the men. Tears were in her eyes. She looked tired, and well beyond her forty-five years. The house was silent, but the three men were acutely conscious of the others who were in the next room while Doris was with them.

"Doris . . . we're awful sorry about Louis . . ." Helms started, then halted.

"Yeah, Mrs. Englin . . . he . . ."

She shook her head. "I'm past the hard part, for a while. I'm just sort of numb now."

"He was alive when we seen him last," Ratliff said.

She put her hand to her mouth and closed her eyes. "I went to Moran about noon Friday to meet Wilburn and Gracie on the train. I was sitting there in the car enjoying the sun—it was nice and pretty outside—and this strange woman came up to me and said, 'Oh, there's been a terrible fight in Cisco. They trapped a bunch that was holding up the bank, and they had a regular battle. A whole host of people killed and a bunch more hurt.' It made me uneasy . . . knowing . . . well, somehow I connected it with Louis and . . . you all . . . right off, and I figured I'd better get back here quick as I could."

She stopped: "I guess you boys would like a little something to eat, wouldn't you?"

"We ain't had anything since Friday," Ratliff said.

"Doris, you said nobody had been out here to question you . . ." Helms said.

"They haven't been yet, but you know they will." She shook her head again, "I can give you what we've got. I cooked three chickens and dressing, so you can have that. I'll fix coffee. Might not be a very good idea for you all to stay here too long."

Helms said, "It's a wonder they haven't already set a trap here."

Ratliff said, "When did you find out about Louis . . . I mean, that he was dead and all?"

"Well, the woman in Moran had said one of the bandits was caught and wounded. I came back here and talked to Robbie and he told me then that you, Henry, had said you were going some place south of Cisco for a load of whiskey to take back to Wichita Falls. Then this morning, yesterday morning I guess it is by now, Uncle Dan Moore, that lives out here on a lease, he came over and told me it was Louis Davis that was killed. We went to Cisco in Uncle Dan's car, but I found out Louis had died in Fort Worth, so I didn't get to see the body."

While Mrs. Englin put out food for them, Ratliff sat in one corner of the living room reading about the robbery in the Abilene *Morning News*. He had refused to take off the old felt hat he had pulled on while riding in the open car. Suddenly he put down the paper and exclaimed: "Well goddam. We were cheated to begin with."

"What do you mean?" Helms asked.

"The paper says there wasn't but 12,200 dollars in that sack of cash, and that all that bundle of papers and stuff wasn't worth anything. Alex Spears says there was a hundred-fifty grand's worth but it couldn't be peddled for a dime."

"That's what *they* say," Helms said. "I bet we could have got something out of it. Newspapers always try and make it look like there's no profit in a job like this one."

"Yeah, it really pays off, doesn't it?" Hill said. Ratliff and Helms looked at him.

"Well, splitting twelve grand would have given us four apiece," Helms said. "Where I come from, that's pretty good pay for an afternoon's work."

Hill stopped him: "You're forgetting about Davis and his share. If it had worked, that would have cut the take down considerably . . . " Doris Englin had come back in the room and was crying again.

Hill said, "Mrs. Englin . . . I'm sorry you heard me poppin' off like that. You know we wouldn't none of us have had anything happen to him if there'd have been anything we could have done about it."

She wiped her face on a corner of her apron. "I'm all right, Bob. Louis knew the risk he was taking. I could tell that from the way he acted when he left here Friday morning."

They ate the meal as quickly as they could. She fixed

them more coffee and cut some cake for them, then filled a sack with food. She apologized for not giving them more, but with four other people staying there, she said, she had to keep a certain amount in the house for the next meal. It was a long way into town.

She helped Helms dress Hill's bad left arm and Helms asked Ratliff, "Do you think we ought to try and cut that bullet out of your leg? You can feel the slug."

Ratliff refused, "I've stood it this long and I'll stand it now to the end."

He stood up on his feet and stretched, "My God, it sure feels good indoors. But we got to get moving."

They left the house without seeing the other people, except Robbie. He came out and shook hands very solemnly with everyone, even Helms. The Englins told the three fugitives not to worry about the visit or about the other people in the house.

"What if the laws ask you about us coming here?" Helms asked.

"I guess I better just tell the truth," Doris Englin said. "If the laws ask me I'll just say yes, you were here but you left and I couldn't do anything about it. We don't have a telephone and nobody has told me not to give you anything to eat. I'll tell them I don't know what you planned except to keep moving, and I don't know where, which is the plain and simple truth."

Helms nodded, "I guess that's the best thing to do, being kin to Louis and all, they'll know in reason we'd be bound to come here."

They said they were going to try and break out of the net, but didn't say in what direction. They said also that they might come back sometime, and arranged for her to adjust a window shade in a certain way if there was danger. She agreed to that but warned them, "You know that if something did happen to Rob and me, I can't take the risk of being real open."

Helms finally said, "I know it's a lot of trouble, but there's one other way you could help us . . ."

"What is it, Henry?"

"Well, if you could get in touch with Nettie. Ask her to call Mrs. Tellet. Nettie knows her. There's a doctor might come down here and fix up Bob and Marshall. My dad would pay for it. If you bury Louis in Wichita Falls you might see Nettie."

"That's where the funeral will be," Doris said, "but a doctor will charge a lot, taking that risk and coming all the way down here."

"This one might do it," Helms said. "He could just come out here and meet us. He wouldn't have to do the work here, just meet us."

"I'll tell Nettie, other than that I can't be sure."

"Yes, that's all I ask," he said.

It was still dark when they drove off, although a certain grayness was hinted along the eastern edge of the earth. Christmas Day. They decided to go back to the pasture and pull the car in among the cedars and the mesquites and spend the rest of daylight.

It was easier to do in 1927 than it would have been even a few years later. There were very few miles of paved road in that part of the country—twenty miles from Ranger to Cisco was bricked but nothing west of there was paved, outside the city limits of some of the larger towns. Even the Bankhead Highway, the finest national east-west transcontinental road across the South to the West Coast, was only about 30 per cent paved, in its entirety.

And there weren't many automobiles, especially out in the country. You could drive for hours on the back roads without seeing another motor vehicle. As for airplanes, the rare ones that flew over that area generally followed the rail-roads, which were the most reliable landmarks from the air that could be found in that thinly populated country. There were telephones in the towns, even towns no bigger than Moran and Putnam, but very few of the farms and ranches had them. One little fence-pole telephone line ran through the country north of Putnam, connecting a few of the bigger ranches. None of the law enforcement agencies had radio equipment and the only telegraph line northward out of Cisco followed the Katy Railroad up through Albany. Private traveling was done more by train than by automobile or bus, so eluding a posse was somewhat easier.

Of course, some of these facts also worked against the fugitives. Because there were few cars, the passage of a single vehicle attracted more attention, especially one with three men in it. And because there were fewer cars, there were fewer places to buy gasoline. It was easy to alert all of the filling stations to the possibility of the fugitives stopping for fuel. The three knew this, and they expected that if they had to drive much they would either have to steal gasoline from parked cars or steal other cars with full tanks. They decided they couldn't take the risk of being spotted trying to get gas at a filling station.

On top of that, they were practically broke. None of the men had started out with more than a dollar or two in his pockets. Helms and Ratliff kept lamenting their own lack of foresight in not "just reaching into that potato sack just one time and grabbing out a handful of bills."

"We could have pulled out four or five hundred bucks," Ratliff said. "Enough, at any rate, to keep us running, once we got through this net."

On the whole, they couldn't afford to think about their mistakes. Their best hope was to lay out long enough so that the posse would get discouraged and quit. If it ever did.

There was always the bankers' reward money. If the association let that stand, the posse might keep looking for them all winter. Five grand a head would be a whole lot more money than most possemen could make at an honest job.

EVEN AFTER they had identified the dead bandit, the law officers had not known about Louis Davis's sister living so near the scene of the hold-up. When he died in Fort Worth the night of the robbery, all their attention had been turned to Wichita Falls, his home.

Mrs. Englin's trip to Cisco, in hope of finding out more about her brother's death, had been taken cautiously. She had been ready to identify herself, but when she discovered the body was in Fort Worth, she returned home. It had been a coincidence that her son and his wife had gotten off the train at Cisco instead of Moran, as had been planned. The young couple heard about the robbery at the time it happened but hadn't known that a kinsman was involved.

Another reason the officers had left Mrs. Englin alone was that they were not sure who else was involved in the robbery. Ratliff they were fairly certain of, but not Hill and Helms. It took them a while to begin sorting out the threads and seeing where they led.

Mrs. Englin waited tensely after the three fugitives had left. Her husband and children pleaded with her to go to bed and at least get some sleep, but she said she wasn't sleepy. She was trying to make up her mind what to tell the officers when they came. She suggested they all go on and have their Christmas tree. "We've got to stop thinking about it. The worst is over for us—Louis." But she was not so composed, and certainly was upset, not only about the death of her brother, but the role she had had thrust on her. She in truth felt a certain amount of rancor and blamed the other three men for Louis's death. They were hardened criminals who had led an inexperienced, an ultimately innocent man, to his death. His own weakness notwithstanding, his need for money and his acceptance of the risk, they were the parties who cost her her baby brother, her dearest one. She would never turn them in and she would never refuse them what aid she could conscientiously summon up . . . but never, either, could she forget. Forgiving would be easier than forgetting.

She sat and thought while the rest of the family entered into the traditional exchanges of the season. The officers surprised her by coming as soon as they did, on Christmas Day. For some reason, she had imagined they would pause on Christmas morning, to stay home with their families, perhaps. But at 11 A.M. a car drove up and two men in business suits got out. One eyed the house while the other one knocked at the front door. For an instant, all Doris Englin could think of was if she could adjust the shade, as they had planned. But she didn't dare run over now and do it, with the officers standing at the front door.

"All right, let me do the talking and everything," she told the others. "Just you go on with your Christmas." There were wrappings scattered about the living room from the presents they had opened that morning, sad though it all was.

One of the men introduced himself and his companion and said they were from Cisco. They asked the routine questions: if this was the Englin residence, and if she was Louis Davis's sister, and she affirmed them.

"We're sorry to have to bother you on Christmas Day like this, ma'am, but we'd like to ask you some questions."

She stepped back from the front door and said, "Come in. It's sort of torn up from our Christmas tree, but it's warm."

One of the Cisco policemen stood, the other sat down in a chair, and Mrs. Englin sat, too.

"Could the other people . . . could they go somewhere?" she asked.

The policemen looked at the others carefully. "That's my son and his wife," she said.

"I guess so," the one who seemed to be in charge told her. "So long as nobody plans to drive off."

"No, I just mean go into another room. They're not involved in anything."

The officer gave them permission to go to the bedroom, and they did. Then he asked:

"Mrs. Englin, what we want to know is have the fugitives contacted you?"

She spoke without hesitation: "No. They have not."

The seated detective asked, "What did you know about the robbery?"

"Just what I heard in Cisco and read in the papers."

He shook his head, "I mean, had they told you their plans?"

She hesitated, then spoke. "My brother, Louis Davis, came by here early Friday morning. He said they . . . he . . . was going down about twenty miles south of Cisco to see about a job."

The officer interrupted her: "Who was with him? Who did you mean by 'they'?"

"There were some men, I suppose. I didn't see anybody but him. He talked like there were some others."

"You sure a fellow named Henry Helms wasn't with him?"

"He wasn't in this house," she said.

"Isn't he some kin to you?"

"He's my husband's brother-in-law. But my husband won't let him on the place. There's bad blood between them."

The policeman shifted around, "Mrs. Englin, what kind of work did your brother do?"

"He was working in a glass factory. He's been doing the same work up in Bristow, Oklahoma. He's never been in any kind of police trouble."

"He come up with any money sudden like lately?"

She shook her head, "Why, no. He's a family man, just lives from hand to mouth. We don't any of us have any money to speak of, but Louis the least of all."

The detective pulled out a piece of paper and glanced at it.

"Mrs. Englin, we have reason to believe this same gang might have robbed the bank at Carbon a couple of weeks ago and the Bangs bank back in November."

She shook her head, "Oh no. Louis wasn't involved in any of that. I know he couldn't have been."

The policeman looked up at her, "Well, ma'am, he was involved in one hold-up." She lowered her eyes.

The policeman who had been doing the questioning got to his feet. "Are you going to be around here this week?" he asked.

"I'm going to Wichita Falls for my brother's funeral."

"Oh . . . I'm sorry, I forgot about that."

The officers went to the door. "We want you to be sure and stay in touch with us. We'll probably want to talk to you some more."

She stood in the doorway, watching their car until it was out of sight in the gray, Christmas noon. Then she turned back into the room, collapsed in a chair, and started crying. Her husband and her son came in the room and stood by her chair until she controlled her tears. No one said anything.

She wiped her eyes and looked up. "I've got to go to Wichita."

Robbie asked, "When? Tonight?"

"Right now. As soon as I can get ready."

Wilburn and his wife and Mrs. Englin's daughter, who

had also arrived for a Christmas visit, insisted they would go with her. Wilburn would drive, and although it was a tight squeeze for them in the Ford coupe, she decided she wanted them to go. Robbie and George Barns, a cowboy from up in the Panhandle who had driven down with the daughter, would stay. Robbie would miss the funeral but his job as an oil field pumper was a daily thing that had to be done without fail. Besides, he was anxious to stay out of things.

Doris called him aside. "Robbie, they may come back. The boys, I mean."

"I know in reason they will," he said. "They don't have no other place to go to."

"Well, what will you do if they do?"

Rob Englin shrugged. "Try to get shed of them as quick as I can."

"Will you help them?"

"Not so's you could call it that. Might give 'em some bread and eggs. Coffee, maybe."

She took his arm. "Rob, don't start anything, please."

He put his hand over hers. "Doris, they're going to get us in trouble. I've said it all along. If Louis had have listened to me there wouldn't have been any of this to start with."

"We're already in trouble," she said. She leaned over and kissed her husband. "I'm sorry, Rob. It's my fault, not yours."

"It's mine for not shootin' that sonofabitch Henry Helms as soon as he set foot on this property." He shook his head, "What if the police come back here?"

"I'm in Wichita Falls at the funeral. They can have the Wichita police come check up on me if they want to. I guess I've got a right to go to my own brother's funeral."

"What else you plannin', honey?"

She looked at Robbie painfully, then made a gesture of denial. "Nothing, honey. I'll maybe see Nettie. You don't worry about anything else."

He looked at her closely. "Doris, I heard you lie to those officers."

"I know I did," she said, "and I may regret it. I said I was going to tell the truth, but when he asked me like that and I faced telling him . . . I just couldn't. I thought of those three poor boys, and I couldn't."

"Doris, those three boys, as you call 'em, are grown men. Not only that, but they're hardened criminals. They led your brother into a trap and got him killed. They're dangerous criminals. They could get us all in trouble, and we don't need to be there."

"All right, Robbie. You're right. But I'm going to do one more thing. It's not helping them, but it's the last thing I'm going to do. Then I'm going to go to Cisco and come completely clean about everything, and take my punishment."

They squeezed into the little Ford, with Wilburn driving and his wife sitting in his sister's lap. They left by noon so that they could be in Wichita Falls with hopes of some daylight being left them.

THEY ARRIVED IN Wichita Falls at dusk. They went first to the home of Mrs. Englin's and Louis's brother, then drove out to see Nettie Helms. Nettie Helms was pregnant, and was terribly nervous and upset. She was afraid the police would arrest her and throw her in jail, because of Henry, and the kids would be put in the detention home or the jail. But she finally told Mrs. Englin how to get in touch with Henry's father, the Rev. J. C. Helms of Oklahoma City. She also mentioned Mrs. Tellet's name, whom Doris had forgotten about.

Mrs. Englin called Midge Tellet on the telephone and talked to her guardedly about how things were. The woman was enthusiastic when she found out Mrs. Englin had been in contact with Ratliff, Helms, and Hill.

"Listen, Mrs. Englin, don't worry. The Helmses will help. I can help, too. There's this doctor's name. He'll go down there and patch 'em up."

"Find out how much money . . ." Doris began, but Midge interrupted her. "Don't worry about that, hon. Reverend Helms can get the money. We'll find help for those boys."

Mrs. Englin said, "I suppose it's against the law."

There was silence, then Midge said, "Yeah, lots of stuff is against the law. Human decency's against the law a lot of times. But I'm not going to let that stop me. I didn't rob that bank. I'm just thinkin' about three miserable human beings."

"What will you and Reverend Helms tell the doctor?"

"I'll tell him something he'll want to believe. Reverend Helms knows him."

Mrs. Englin waited until Midge could call her back. It took about two hours, then the telephone rang.

"We're all set," Midge Tellet said. "Reverend Helms and I talked to a Doctor Vayne. Henry gave me his number. He'll make the trip."

"When did he say he would go?" Mrs. Englin asked.

"He'll go tonight, along with me and a nurse, Mrs. Blue. I told you I'd tell him something." Midge Tellet was plainly pleased with the manipulations.

Mrs. Englin told her as best she could how to get to the Englin house and what the signal was in case the house was being watched. Midge said she understood the directions, that she was real good on directions. She was excited, and Doris Englin was glad someone else was going to do something for those poor boys.

The doctor was excited, too. In fact, the idea of the trip stirred the adventurer in them. Midge had carefully cloaked her meaning, discussing it with the doctor on the telephone, but he sensed the unusual nature of the trip. He didn't ask many questions. If something went wrong unexpectedly he wanted to be able to say he didn't know much about it— although he doubted they would actually hold a doctor accountable who was just doing his duty. Dr. Vayne had known Henry Helms and had liked him even though he knew Helms was an ex-convict. Besides, the trip would be interesting if for no other reason than this woman Midge being along. He had only met her over the phone but he already liked her immensely.

The three left Wichita Falls late that night and drove the road to Seymour and Albany. The doctor kept laughing and telling the women that he absolutely did not know anything about the men he was supposed to be looking for, and that there hadn't been a hint of their being fugitives, and that the two women, even the nurse, were along merely to keep him company and awake on the drive.

They got to Albany with no trouble. There had been a bottle handy, and things were nice and easy. They circled the Albany courthouse square but couldn't decide which of the roads they should take from there. Midge Tellet, who had said she was good on directions, found herself confused. Mrs. Englin had said something about either going to Moran or *not* going to Moran—she was inclined to remember it as *not* to go to Moran, to go straight out from Albany . . .

Finally, down a dark side street, and lost, they decided to ask for help. They weren't depressed, despite the grimness of their mission. None of them had known Louis Davis, so their concern was for the living.

They found themselves south of the courthouse a couple of blocks, and they parked by a wooden bridge. The doctor had an automobile Blue Book which had road directions in it, but none of the book's trips were detailed enough to include little places like Moran.

Just as they were the most undecided, they saw a car coming from the north. The doctor stepped out and flagged the automobile down. There was one man in it.

"What do you folks need?" the driver asked the doctor.

"We're lost," the doctor said. "We're looking for a place out of here somewhere, called the Englin lease or the Lash lease. Which is it, Midge?"

From inside the car she answered, "The people's names are Englin. It's an oil lease house. It's between Moran and Putnam, or something like that."

The driver of the other car said, "Yeah, I know where that is. The Englins. They live on the old Lash lease. It's pretty far—they expecting you this time of night?"

"Well, yes and no," the doctor said. "It's a sort of emergency. I'm a doctor."

"Oh," the man said, "then you just follow me and I'll take you right to it. You might have trouble finding it at night, otherwise."

They drove off following the other car. By now it was early morning and very cold, but the interior of the doctor's car was snug, and they laughed and sang some. They had no trouble keeping the other car in sight. They turned and twisted around section corners and down dirt roads, throwing up a cloud of dust in the headlights.

"That man's a Good Samaritan," Mrs. Blue said, "and we'd never have found this without him."

"That's the way with these West Texas people," the doctor said. "They're the best people on earth at helping you in a tight."

"This must be miles out of his way, wherever he was going," Midge said.

The car ahead slowed and bumped cautiously over a cattleguard. It went about a hundred yards and stopped. They could see the house, no lights inside, darkly outlined against the sky. They all got out, and the driver of the car waited beside his vehicle for them.

"Well, this is the Englin place, but it don't look to me like anybody's home. You sure you're expected?"

"No question about it," the doctor said. "If this is the Englin place, we are expected."

The other man said, "Maybe we better see if there's anybody here before I leave. You might get lost again trying to get back into town."

The doctor went and knocked on the front door. After several raps a voice from inside said, "Yeah? Who is it?"

"I'm Doctor Vayne, from Wichita Falls. We're here."

The door opened and Robbie Englin said, "Oh. You got ladies with you. Wait a minute and I'll light the lamp."

There was a scratch and the yellow light glowed.

"Come on in. There's nobody here but George and me." Then he saw the other man. "Oh. How are you . . . I'm Robbie Englin."

The other man turned to the group and said, "Well, I'm Orien Biggs, the sheriff of Shackelford County. I'm goin' to have to place all of you under arrest as accessories after the fact for the armed robbery of the First National Bank of Cisco, Texas, and the murder of Chief of Police Bit Bedford."

Midge turned to the doctor with a helpless look and said, "Oh my Lord."

DESPITE THE FACT THAT the place where he arrested them was in Callahan County, Sheriff Biggs took all the people to the Shackelford County jail in Albany. When a deputy asked him about it privately, Sheriff Biggs said it was a case of "hot pursuit" which, under Texas law, allowed officers of one county to chase and catch someone else in another county.

"But you leading them there—ain't that entrapment?" the deputy asked.

"Mutrey, you've got more law than you've got sense," the sheriff said. "Did I purposely entrap those people? They flagged me down on a public highway and asked me to lead them. That's just a technicality, according to how you look at it. If they was entrapped, they entrapped themself."

Mutrey said, "Hell, I ain't about to inspect a gift horse that close."

"Why hell no," the sheriff said, "me seein' 'em in the first place was just a damn fool piece of luck. Wouldn't ordinarily be up anywhere near that late. I never had the least idea who they were until he said 'Englin.' Then when he said he's a doctor, I knew in reason they were sent down here to try and help out that bunch of fugitives. I couldn't hardly believe my luck."

The people seemed to accept their arrest with resignation. Doctor Vayne was considerably upset that Sheriff Biggs would take him to be some sort of criminal, too. He kept assuring the sheriff that he was a respected physician.

"Well, doctor," the sheriff said, "you should have thought about that when you started down here to help out a bunch of fugitives from justice. The men are criminals, you know. The worst kind of murderers. You could just as easy have got your throat cut in the bargain."

"But I didn't know who it was," the doctor protested, "I just knew the Helms family is all. I didn't know he was wanted by the police."

"I ain't going to argue with you. But you knew he was an ex-con, didn't you?"

"I knew Henry had a record . . ."

"That's what an ex-con is, doctor: a man with a criminal record."

"But I have never known him to be vicious."

"Me neither," Midge Tellet said, "and I know him real well, too."

"Well, my friend Chief Bit Bedford didn't know him that well, I guess," Sheriff Biggs said. "Your friend Helms, or one of his gang, give Bit five slugs in the belly with a .44 and whether it was done to be vicious or not, Bit's dead."

The sheriff had made Robbie drive the doctor's car ahead of him from the lease back into Albany. He had warned him that one false turn and he would shoot out the tires and Robbie along with them. Robbie was annoyed and hurt at the idea that he was guilty of something, or that he would try to escape.

Mrs. Tellet at first was bewildered and silent at her arrest. It wasn't as much fun as she had thought, this wild goose chase with the doctor. But by the time they all got back to Albany the excitement had about overcome the fear, and she was beginning to be herself again. She had on her man-tailored khaki shirt and britches and her little, cute mid-calf boots—her bootees, she called them—and despite the long drive, and the dust, her reddish hair looked good in its mannish bob. She liked this sheriff. Felt safe with him. He was straightforward but tough, and he laughed at her wit, even when it was nervous wit and he knew it. He had style, like a sheriff was supposed to, and her dark eyes flashed that he was the kind of man she admired, even if he wasn't out to do her any favors.

Dr. Vayne kept asking if their arrest couldn't be kept out of the papers, that it would ruin his reputation otherwise. And Mrs. Blue, he insisted, hadn't any notion of what they were supposedly going to do—just came along to attend to an injured man or two. She ought to be left out of it altogether, he said. But the sheriff said there was no way he could help either situation. In the first place, the robbery was big news. Papers as far off as Chicago and St. Louis were calling down twice a day to find out any new developments. These arrests were the biggest break since the capture of Louis Davis while he was still alive. And, the sheriff said, even though he couldn't prove as much, he felt sure Mrs. Blue had gotten some inkling of their mission on the trip down.

"You don't come driving across three or four counties at midnight just to lance a boil," he said.

Robbie Englin, once in Albany, seemed resigned to what had happened.

"I knew that sooner or later I'd just be in jail over Henry Helms," he said to George, but without as much bitterness as might be expected. George Barns, the cowboy, protested more than anyone else at being under arrest.

"Sheriff, I don't even know these here men you're talking about. Ask Rob here, or Mrs. Englin. I just come down to drive Mrs. Simpson to spend Christmas. We walked into this thing without no warning of no kind."

Sheriff Biggs told him that if he wasn't part of a conspiracy to aid fleeing criminals, then he had nothing to worry about. "But I ain't leaving anybody out there on that lease to give them fellers help or spread the alarm. Arresting you is the only way I have of holding you."

As soon as he had returned to Albany the sheriff had called in a description of his catch to Cisco and to Wichita Falls. Mrs. Tellet, Dr. Vayne, and Mrs. Blue hadn't tried to give aliases. The Wichita Falls police went out immediately and arrested Freeman Tellet, although he told them he was relieved to see them, that he was only too glad to go to jail, for his own protection.

"Listen," he told the officers, "I know that Henry Helms and his whole gang. They're after me. As long as any of them are alive and loose my life isn't worth a plug nickel."

Tellet made a good interview for the newspapers. He described how Helms "dominated his confederates by gun power" (as one reporter wrote) and told of the shooting incident in his home.

"You gentlemen can go out there and count the marks in the floor," he was quoted as saying. "There was ten or eleven shots fired at me when I refused to go get my daughter and bring her back. 'You better get her back here or you're a dead man,' that big Ratliff fellow said to me. I was in no position to argue."

Midge, reading what her husband said, was right proud of Freeman for telling the truth and all and not trying to get revenge on her and the boys.

Midge herself made a good impression on the newspaper men who interviewed her. She admitted making the Santa Claus costume that Ratliff wore, but she said she never did know what the boys wanted with it. She also said she had known for some time that Helms and Ratliff had criminal records, but not Hill.

"He was such a strange boy," she told the reporters. "A nervous kind, always talking about going away and never coming back. I don't think he ever wanted to be a criminal, myself."

She admitted Helms had earlier asked her to get in touch with Dr. Vayne in case there was medical trouble. She said she thought nothing of it at the time, knowing how funny Helms was about trusting strangers and people like that. He knew Dr. Vayne and didn't have to explain everything to him every time he called on him for services. Somebody from the press asked her about her husband and how he took all this confidence in her from a bunch of ex-convicts.

"I never told my husband any of this because he's so open with his talk," she said. The Wichita Falls reporters, fresh from interviewing Freeman in the safety of his jail cell, had to agree.

. . .

AFTER THE FUNERAL for Louis Davis, the police picked up Mrs. Englin, Wilburn and his wife, and a brother, and held them all in custody. Mrs. Englin, who had driven back to the lease, was not put in jail but was kept under guard—her daughter-in-law staying with her—at the Opera House Hotel in Cisco. She was visited by Mayor Williamson and, relieved of the decisions of the past three days, told her story freely. She said she wanted to take all the blame for anything wrong that was done where it involved her or her family. She especially didn't want Rob to get in trouble, because he had been opposed to her helping the men in the first place, even before there had been a robbery.

She related everything, starting with that first visit Friday morning (that seemed such a lifetime gone, although it was less than four days), and how Rob refused to let Helms in his house and just barely allowed him on the lease. She told of the second visit early Christmas morning, and that she fed the fugitives, and she admitted she had denied it later in the day when the Cisco police questioned her. She took the trip to Wichita Falls to go to Louis's funeral and to talk to Nettie Helms and try and comfort her, she said, and to be with her surviving brother. The arrangements for Dr. Vayne were made by the Helmses.

Mayor Williamson later told some of the people in Cisco that he thought Mrs. Englin had been very dignified and that he thought she had told them everything she knew. Whatever she had done, she had done what she felt like she had to, under the circumstances.

8 / SATURDAY MORNING, following the robbery, the Texas Rangers joined the hunt for the Santa Claus bank robbers. Captain Tom Hickman, whose exploits were the constant fodder of detective and "true crime" magazines, brought in a pack of bloodhounds for trailing the fugitives, and set up a command post with his associate, Sergeant Manuel T. (Lone Wolf) Gonzaullas, who was to become as legendary a Ranger as Hickman.

Right off the two Rangers found out the hunt was going to be unusually troublesome. The trampling of the posse the night before made it impossible for the hounds to trace the subjects. The dogs were given the Santa Claus suit to sniff, and they set up a great belling and bawling, but they got nowhere with the scent on the terrain.

About mid-morning that Saturday, someone from the east side of Cisco reported he had had his car stolen: a Ford touring. The owner hadn't tied in the theft of his car with the bank robbery because he hadn't known the fugitives were still at large. Almost everyone in Cisco had gone to bed that first night feeling sure the capture had either taken place or was only a matter of a few more hours.

A description of the Ford was sent out all over West Texas and roadblocks were set up on all the main roads and highways. With the organization taking place, it was forming the biggest net that had ever been spread in that part of Texas to catch fugitives. Late Saturday a suitcase and some bloody rags were found on the Irving Finley farm, seven miles south of Cisco. This only served to take the officers off the real trail for a while. They probed southward, while the three fugitives had turned in the opposite direction and were now holed up in the Brooks pasture, many miles to the northwest.

The rumor of the blonde-headed woman kept coming and going the first two days. Despite the official announcement by Mayor Williamson that there had been no woman with the bandits in the hold-up of the bank, false reports persisted: two men and a woman, three men and a blonde, all the men answering the description of the Cisco fugitives, had been seen at Fort Worth, at Abilene, at Santa Anna in Coleman County. Some of the officers seemed more interested in proving there really was a woman with the fugitives (perhaps in hopes of supporting the chief's dying words) than they were in finding the real robbers.

Discovering that Doris Englin, Davis's sister, lived in the area was the best break so far, Cisco police felt. They had accepted her denial that the fugitives had been around, the first time she was questioned, but they felt certain that sooner or later something would involve her because she was the only person the robbers could get in touch with. Then, the arrest of the doctor and the two women cleared up one thing: who the fugitives were. Although police had been fairly sure of their identity, they now knew what they looked like, who they were, and what their associations had been.

The cold wave of the first Friday night held. By Monday it was intensified by rain and sleet. Mayor Williamson felt that Cisco's honor was at stake and he badly wanted the fugitives to be found and brought to justice by someone from Cisco and not an outside agency. His son Chapman, and his son-in-law Walter Sikes, an insurance man from Amarillo, were spending full-time out with the various posses and law officers. There were estimated to be fifty cars patrolling the roads and 150 men manning roadblocks. The fugitives had nowhere to go, despite the fact that their actual location was not known. Unless the hunt was called off, sooner or later the three men would have to come out and would be spotted. And nobody involved in the network of searchers and check points was of a mind to withdraw. Their area was huge—as big as many eastern states—but they were determined and, rather unusual for that part of Texas, the entire group displayed enough patience to ensure the success of their long-range planning. They would search, and they would wait, and they would bet that the robbers had to make a drastic move.

ON CHRISTMAS DAY they ate, at least. There was the food Doris served them—although they didn't take time to eat as much as their hunger would have liked—and later on they had the cold chicken and dressing and cake. Compared to the day before, they had done well, although it didn't take long for the food to wear off. The cold was as annoying as their hunger. Henry Helms said he'd personally give a flat hundred dollar bill for a pot of good, hot Arbuckle's coffee like Nettie fixed. They needed sleep, but were too keyed up to get much. They cat-napped and dozed now and then, but never again slept several hours in a row as they had Saturday after their wild and fearful escape from the posse Friday night. The visit to the Englin home had given them a grimmer picture of what they had done and what they faced. Individually and collectively, they were in a sober, even depressed, mood.

Bob Hill was for trying to go east. For one thing, the searchers probably didn't expect it. There was nothing toward the west but wide open spaces. Back a few years before, when a man could get on a horse and escape cross-country, simply disappear into the wilds of West Texas, the Big Bend, or Mexico, it might have been the safest place. But now, with a car having to have a road, and everything fenced—well, east was best. East was people, the safety of numbers. Nowadays, people gave more safety than space. If they could make Fort Worth, or Dallas, their trail might be covered by the presence of so many others. And after that—well, Bob Hill didn't know. He couldn't plan that far. Neither could anyone else.

Ratliff and Helms felt the group's only hope was to get to Wichita Falls. There were contacts there; the only contacts they had. Hill pointed out that the law was bound to have all their families and even their friends picked up by the time they escaped—if they managed that feat.

Later Christmas Day they came out of their hiding place again at dusk, and with Ratliff and Helms overruling Hill, decided to go back to the Englin place.

When they arrived the "safe" signal was on, so far as they could tell. But they parked the car nearly a mile from the house and crept up to it on foot. Helms went to the door and knocked. Robbie Englin, inside, asked, "Henry? Is it you?"

Helms said, "Yeah. We're back."

Robbie opened the door quickly and the three went in the house. Henry told him, "Listen, Robbie, you shouldn't use my name when you answer the door. What if I'd been a deputy or somebody from the police? Don't ever do that again."

"All right," Englin said, "I guess that was a pretty stupid thing. But I don't want you getting the idea you're going to be able to be coming here all the time, either."

Helms said, "This is the only—" but Englin stopped him.

"Now listen. I don't mean it personal. But they came out here this morning, just a few hours after you all left. Two policemen from Cisco. So they're suspicious of this place. Doris told 'em she was going to Wichita Falls for the funeral, so they might not be back today, but it'd be best if you didn't show up here again."

Helms said, "Robbie, we had to take our chances. Until we can get clear to Wichita, this is the only place we can find out anything."

Englin gave them a little food. He showed them that there was very little to give. They left after being there but a few minutes. With Doris gone, on top of everything else, the Englin place was not very enticing. They didn't say anything to Robbie but they planned to return in hopes Doris was able to get the doctor to come. Doris hadn't told Robbie of their request.

They decided they might try to make a wide circle around Cisco to the south—the direction they felt was least likely to be alerted to them. Helms was driving. Ratliff's wounded leg was worse, and he could scarcely hobble. Hill's arm was paining him sharply, and he had a continual fever which led him in and out of a chill. The rain and sleet, springing up and blowing hard from time to time, were particularly discomforting. Hill looked all over the Ford, under the seats, but could find no side curtains to put up.

"What in hell are we going to do even if we make it to Wichita?" he asked. "They know who we are. We don't have any money."

Ratliff, in the back seat, warned: "Listen, Bobby. Don't start talking surrender. We know for certain now—that's out. This has just got to make a man out of you."

"What if we did surrender? Do you think we'd all get the chair?"

Helms grunted, "Hell yes, we would. If we were alive to go to trial in the first place. I don't think we *could* surrender right now. Maybe in a couple or three weeks they'd be toned down enough not to shoot us on sight. But I doubt even that."

"They ain't going to shoot me when I surrender," Ratliff said, "because they ain't going to get first chance at it." He pulled down his hat and slumped as low in the seat as he could, to stay out of sight and to stay out of the cold as much as possible.

It was midnight as they neared the little town of Putnam, on their way toward making the southward circle. "I wish to God we could all go soak in that mineral water bath there," Ratliff said. The hotel at Putnam was a minor health spa for West Texas, with hot mineral baths from a private well in the basement. They were approaching the intersection of the highway to Cisco when Helms slammed on the brakes and swung the light car around, off the road and into the ditch. Hill fell hard against him with his wounded arm, and Ratliff rolled onto the floorboards.

"It's the posse," Helms yelled. "That big car. I can tell it's the posse."

Sure enough, a big sedan was moving slowly along the road, a spotlight sweeping the fields on either side.

"Have they spotted us?" Ratliff asked.

"We've got to run anyway," Helms said.

"Maybe they won't see us," Hill said.

"They can't miss us," Helms said. "They see this car with nothing but men in it and they'll be all over us, shooting first and asking questions later."

Helms backed out of the ditch they were in and turned the Ford around in the direction from which they had just come. "Duck down. Make it look like there's just a driver," he said.

The Ford, running without lights, picked up speed and for a mile or so they thought they had gotten away without being seen by the other car, but the instant Helms turned on the headlights, the other car seemed at once to speed up.

"That's a Hupmobile or something big like that," Ratliff said, peeking out the back of the car. "The way the headlights are placed, it looks like a big, fast one. They'll catch us sure as shit stinks if we don't get off this straight road."

"This road'll take us to Moran, won't it?" Hill asked.

"Eventually it will. We don't want to go to Moran, anytime. Take one of the right-hand roads along here when you come to one. We might throw 'em off if we can find a ranch road."

"Well I'm for getting off this one," Helms said.

"Hey, here's a road that looks like . . ." Hill said.

Helms looked up too late to slow down, but he swung the car into the right-hand road. He saw the cattleguard too late. The left front fender and wheel of the Ford crashed into an iron pipe and the heavy gate post; the automobile swung around and bounced through a ditch, taking out a couple of fence posts as it did, then came to a halt headed in the opposite direction. The violent impact tumbled them around, especially Ratliff, who was halfway thrown from the car by the time it stopped. Helms turned off the lights and without a word, except for a groaning curse from Ratliff, they left the car, heading for the brush. Ratliff only made it to the ditch.

The lights of the other car were coming up fast and as the three men were readying their guns to shoot it out, if needed, the big sedan went by. It didn't slacken its speed but drove on north, leaving a cloud of dust swirling up in the red of its taillight. After the lights disappeared from view the three men got up from where they had thrown themselves on the ground.

"Godamighty, that was close," Helms said.

"We must have made that right turn so quick they never seen us do it," Hill said.

"Come on, let's get the hell out of here," Ratliff said.

"They may be back in another minute and we'll be standing here congratulating ourselves. Let's get moving, back toward Putnam."

But when they looked at the Ford they had to change their plan. The front fender was crushed against the wheel and water was pouring from the radiator.

"That's the first damn wreck I ever had driving a car," Helms said, "the very first goddam time. I never seen that cattleguard until I was right on it."

Ratliff said, "We can't worry about that, Henry. We've got to get out of here. Try and see if we can nurse her along for a couple of miles. If we can just get out of this vicinity."

Helms tried cranking the Ford but the motor wouldn't start. "She's dead as a dodo." He needn't have announced it. "We can't even push, the way that front wheel's crushed in by the fender."

"Then we'll hoof it," Ratliff said, "but I don't know what the hell I'm going to do. I don't think I could walk a hundred yards if you was to offer me a half-interest in Mama Turley's big Breckenridge whorehouse."

Helms spoke: "Look, ain't that a house, on down this road? It's some kind of building."

He and Hill bent down so as to silhouettte the horizon against the night sky. "Yeah, that's a house or a barn," Hill said.

"Let's go see if it's a house," Helms said. "If they've got a car we'll tell 'em my wife was going to the hospital and we had a wreck."

"What if they find out there ain't no woman with us?" Hill asked.

"What the hell do you think? If that's a house with a car we won't give a damn, once we get our hands on it."

"I'll take anything," Ratliff said, "a car, a buggy, or a spring wagon. Just so we ain't walking."

. . .

R. C. WYLIE WAS AWAKENED by someone outside, calling. He looked at the Big Ben alarm clock by his bed and saw it was after midnight.

"It must be Carl, having trouble," he told himself, as he got out of bed.

He opened the front door a ways and from the darkened front room asked, "Carl? Is that you?"

"No, sir," a voice answered back. "We've had a wreck. We're in trouble."

The Wylie farm was gifted with several oil wells, so it was better equipped than most of the surrounding farms. It had a Delco lighting plant, for one thing, although there was no telephone because Mr. Wylie didn't see how he would ever need it except to gossip over, and he didn't do much of that. He had bought a new Dodge automobile, however, and this was the car his son, Carl, was out in.

Wylie turned on the porch light and saw three men. Two of them kept out to the edge of the light and one stood by the door.

"We're taking my wife to the hospital and we've had a wreck," the one by the door said. "Down on the road past the cattleguard. Our car won't move and we'd sure like to get you to take us into Cisco, if you've got a car."

Wylie said, "I've got a car but my son Carl is away in it. He should be home pretty soon."

The spokesman turned to the others. One of them said, "We'd better wait. We sure need a car." Another one called to Wylie, "You got a telephone, maybe we could use?" Wylie said no.

"Is there any place around here close that might help us?" the man on the porch asked Wylie.

"Nothing on either end of this road. It goes to the Moran

highway to the east and to Putnam road to the west. There's the Heatley place, but it's a good three miles. Carl'll be getting here pretty quick. He don't usually stay out past midnight."

Wylie started to ask the men into the house to wait, if they wanted to, it being pretty raw outside, but something about them made him uneasy. He wished the woman was with them, for one thing. But on the other hand, he felt sorry for anybody being broke down out here, so far from town with a sick woman.

"You men want to step inside . . . maybe get your wife from the car?"

The spokesman said, "No, we'll just stay outside. She might want us. She's all right, in the car."

"She's not fixing to have a baby, is she?"

The man hesitated, "No . . . she's just sick with the jaundice. Got chills and fever. Vomity and all. She comes from East Texas, and you know how chills and fever and yellow jaundice is with people from there."

Wylie closed the door and turned off the light in his bedroom but left the porch light on. He was still suspicious of the men. He wished there was some way he could warn Carl to keep going and not come back here. For once he wished he had a telephone.

Shortly before 1 A.M. he saw the lights of the car coming from the Cisco end of the road, and then the Dodge drove up. His son, Carl, was twenty-two-years-old and a strapping two-hundred-pound man, but one of those gentle sorts. Carl had been working in the Moran oil field as a driller and was about ready to start thinking of marrying some girl, now that he had a little money coming in on his own. He sure didn't want to farm.

He and a younger cousin, a boy named Riley who was sixteen, had been to a Christmas party and had stayed later than they had expected. As they drove up to the farm house, coming back, Carl had seen the three men standing in the light from the porch. It was unusual for his father to be up this time of night, so Carl knew the men must have come asking for help of some kind. He drove up front and stopped. One of the men walked over to the car, and just as Carl was about to say, "Howdy," he saw the pistol the man was pointing at him.

"We're taking this car," the man said. Then young Riley, who was sitting on the dark side of the car away from the rays of the porch light and unseen by the gunman, slipped out his door, ran behind the car, and got around the house, into the back door.

The men scrambled to the car and the first one, the one with the pistol, said to Carl, "Okay. Haul ass. We're getting out of here!"

Carl was momentarily baffled as to whether they wanted the car or wanted him to drive: "What do you mean?" he asked.

"Haul ass, goddam it," the gunman said, "before that son-ofabitch starts something in the house." One of the men had run around behind the car and now got in beside Carl. The gunman and the other one crawled into the back seat. "Get moving! Make this baby roll out of here!" the gunman said again. Just as the Dodge was pulling away, the front door burst open and Carl's father came running out onto the porch with a shotgun. Carl didn't see him but one of the men in the back seat yelled, "Duck down!" and Carl heard the blast. The shots peppered the car and hit Carl in the left arm.

"Keep driving—and fast," someone ordered him.

"I'm hurt," Carl said.

"You're not hurt as bad as the rest of us," the man in the front seat said.

They came to where the Ford was blocking the road and

Helms, with the gun, said to Carl, "Okay, big boy, put her in low and let's push that sonofabitch out of the way."

Carl thought for an instant how mad his dad would be if he ruined the new Dodge. "What if the bumpers don't meet?" he asked.

"You just push the sonofabitch and let me worry about the bumpers," Helms said.

Carl eased the Dodge up to the Ford and put the Dodge in low gear. Gently, he let out on the clutch, and the vehicles touched. The Dodge nudged the Ford forward. The Ford's wheels had cut at such an angle, from its collision with the cattleguard, that within a few yards it had cleared the road and was sitting half in the ditch.

"Now where?" Carl asked.

"Go north until I tell you different," Helms said.

They drove through the fateful cattleguard and turned toward the Moran road. Helms finally said, "You yelled awhile ago that you were hurt. Did your old man hit you?"

"Yes sir. It felt kinda hot, but it isn't hurting much now."

Ratliff said, "Your old man's lucky, standing out there blasting away with that shotgun and us with a couple of dozen guns ourself. Standing there in that porch light . . ."

"Yeah, if we weren't so crazy about his car we might have gone back and killed him," Helms said.

"Shut up that kind of talk," Hill said. Then he said to Carl, "You've got nothing to worry about if you just do what we tell you and don't try any tricks."

Ratliff asked Carl, "Do you know who we are?"

Carl kept his eyes on the road when he answered, "I think I do."

"Ain't you kind of scared to be with us?"

"Yes sir, I am. But I hope I can get this car back to my daddy in one piece. It ain't six months old."

Helms said to him, "Well remember this: if there's any shooting, the people shooting at us won't know the difference. It'll be your car, and it'll be you the same as us."

"I hope we don't meet anybody, then," Carl said.

"If we meet the right bunch, I guarantee you, we're going to do some shooting."

Hill spoke up, "Henry, do you reckon the message got through?"

Helms didn't answer.

"I mean, about that certain person you mentioned might be willing to come . . ."

Helms realized Hill meant the doctor. "Oh, yeah. I'd forgotten about that. It's been enough time, hasn't it?" He said to Carl, "Pull off here. I'm taking the wheel."

Carl didn't want to turn the car over to one of the men. He asked Helms why he wanted to drive.

"You're going too slow. I'll take the wheel," Helms answered.

Carl stopped the Dodge and Helms said, "Don't try anything cute, like trying to run off into the dark and get away."

"Not much place to run to, out here. Besides, I want to be sure and get this car back to Dad." Helms took the wheel, and Hill got in the rear seat. Carl Wylie moved over to the right-hand front seat. Helms laughed after he got the Dodge rolling, "I got to say one thing, buster. You got your nerve, the way you keep trying to hang on to this car. You're more scared of your daddy than you are of us."

"Well, I know how he is," Carl said. Nobody spoke any more.

They approached the Englin place and again they pulled far off the road and hid the car. Henry said, "All right, you all stay here and I'll be back." He didn't want Carl to know he was going to a house.

The house was dark when Henry tapped. Once again Robbie asked, "Who is it?" and Henry whispered, "It's me."

Henry told him not to light a lamp, that he didn't want any light seen in the house. He didn't tell Englin there was a hostage in the car, but he did say that if there was any extra food at all they had to have it. "We're going to make a break for it," Helms said. Englin gave him two oranges left from the Christmas stockings and said that was absolutely all.

"Rob," Helms asked, "did Doris say anything to you before she left about somebody coming down here from Wichita Falls?"

"No, but I suspicioned she had something up her sleeve when her and the kids took off."

Helms said, "Well, it wasn't nothing she knew anything about, neither. But I asked her to get in touch with Nettie and another friend of mine there and see if they might be able to get a doctor down here. We've got to get some kind of medicine for Marshall and Bob or they're going to pass out on their feet."

"You think a doctor's coming here?"

"This is the only place one could come if he does."

"What makes you think he would come tonight?"

"If Doris got to Wichita without any trouble there'd be plenty of time for him to get back down here. He'd likely travel at night."

George, who had stayed in the other room, came into the kitchen where Robbie was talking to Henry. George had never seen any of the fugitives, but he knew this was one of them.

"Robbie," he said hurriedly, "there's a couple of cars looks like they're fixing to come up here."

Helms said, "Goddam, that may be the doctor. I'll be hid until we can find out." He ran out the back door and slipped as far away from the house as he could. There were two cars coming up the road. He looked back and saw them stop and he thought he saw Midge in the headlights, but he couldn't be sure. His heart was beating fast and he felt the biggest surge of good feeling he had felt in a week. It was friends. He almost broke out and ran to them, he was so glad to think it was someone coming to help. But he knew he had to wait. It wouldn't take long for Robbie to signal, as soon as the coast was clear.

But no signal was given, and he saw all the people standing near the house, then saw them go inside and come back out shortly afterward and get into the two cars. When the cars drove away Helms ran to the hidden Dodge and told them what had happened. All they had been able to see was the arrival, then the departure of the two vehicles. Helms was undecided but thought maybe they ought to go back up to the house, but Hill and Ratliff were in favor of them getting the hell out while they could and coming back later. Helms warned Ratliff not to say too much in front of Carl. He particularly didn't want the Englin name mentioned, or Midge's. The episode baffled them all, particularly since they knew that Robbie knew they were nearby. It was ominous. Either the cars were people who weren't connected with the manhunt in any way, and Robbie had to go with them on business or something of that nature, or the cars were officers, and Robbie had been picked up. At this time of night nothing else would explain it. And, of course, if the cars had been friends then Robbie should have signaled for them to come in —Henry, at least.

Ratliff said, "I think we'd better get back to where we can be hid for a while and think things over." Hill and Helms agreed. They asked Carl if he would get down on the floor and not look at the direction they were going in, and he agreed. Helms at first wanted to blindfold him but Carl assured them he would not look.

"Besides," he said, "if you only knew how bad I am about directions anyway. Especially at night. I'm easily lost in a car."

They got back to the pasture and drove almost a mile into it, trying to find some bushes that were thick enough to hide the car and cut off some of the cold wind, but it didn't work. The north wind bit right through their clothing.

Helms produced the two oranges and they split them up.

"You don't mind me not offering you none, do you?" he asked Carl.

"No, you go right ahead. I had a good supper."

"It's sort of growing off by now, ain't it, big boy?" Ratliff asked.

"Yeah, but I'm not as hungry as you fellers. I know for sure."

Hill sensed the difference in the four lives—Carl wasn't hungry because he knew that unless they had to shoot him, he would get to some food. They, on the other hand, had no such certainty waiting for them.

Before they bedded down in the car, they talked about what they should do about going back to the Englin place. The mystery of the two cars, and their subsequent actions, made their decision hard, and also depressed them. They talked so as not to let Carl hear a name he might remember or figure out what situation they were discussing. But all three were cast down by the events, particularly Helms, who (although he did not tell them the extent to which he was inspired) had known the first upsurge of spirit and hope that any of them had felt since the robbery. Now even this limited happiness was cut off by the unknown acts of the persons involved.

"Look, talking and wondering about it is just making it worse," Ratliff said. "I suggest we quit wondering what happened and get some sleep." They finally decided to do that.

. . .

THEY WERE PLANNING ON spending all day in the pasture, making another attempt to break out of the net that night, but not long after daybreak they heard the sound of a motor. It was an airplane, flying low to the south.

"I've got an Irish gold belt buckle says they're looking for us," Ratliff said, watching the slow-moving machine in the sky.

"If they're looking for us they'll be doing it by sections." Hill said. "That means they'll be making a sweep back over this way pretty quick. We better pull out."

They waited until the airplane was gone from the sky, then eased their way out of the pasture, onto the ranch road that ran by it. They headed south before circling back north toward the Englin lease. They decided there was nothing to be gained by trying to be too secretive with Carl. Although they used no one's name, they simply drove to the house without making any bones about it being the home of friends that might give them aid. Henry slipped up to the back door again, but there was no one home. He decided against breaking into the house, knowing that the police would know who had done it. He went back to the hidden Dodge and told them the house was empty of people.

"Of course," Helms said, "something could have happened to somebody in Wichita Falls. They could have come down and taken everybody back with them."

But that didn't make much sense. Robbie knew that Henry had been waiting out there somewhere, near the house. If it had been friends he could as easily have yelled and brought him in. It had to be something unexpected— something dangerous, like the law. Their spirits were crushed almost as much by the mystery as the possibility of the event.

Later Monday they decided this was the time to try and break out of the net of lawmen surrounding the area. They even found a filling station in a little village in Callahan County and got gasoline. The man that sold it to them looked half asleep, even in the daytime, the only person who hadn't heard of the manhunt, Hill suggested. Carl Wylie just barely had enough money to pay for the gasoline. The little place, a feed store, had nothing to eat, not even a candy bar. The men were afraid to hold the man up. This could be their only source of gasoline, in case they had to try again at breaking out.

With a tank full of gas they could get pretty far, but every time they started to go around Cisco, from any direction, they saw evidence of the hunt. Once they almost blundered into a roadblock, out north of Cisco's big dam.

They made one more pass at the Englin place, at dusk, but there were no signs of life and their signal shade was standing at "safe" just as it had been, so the signal was meaningless. They went to a pasture—a different one from where they had been when the biplane passed over them— and decided to spend the night there. It was cold and they had nothing to eat, and they could not dare make a fire now, with the possibility of an airplane sweeping up on them of a sudden. For a while they debated the possibility of the airplane flying at night, but convinced themselves that the pursuers were so determined in their pursuit that they would make the effort.

They suffered terribly, and even Carl felt sorry for the wounded men, Hill and Ratliff. Hill was without an overcoat, and Carl let him take his and wrap up in it.

Monday night they decided to go back and try to get some more gas at the same little store in Callahan County, but after dark they couldn't find it. Two cars came toward them on one road and they took a quick left and spent hours winding through the low hills of the Callahan Divide before coming out near the spot where they had originally made their turn off the road, which represented a total waste of time and gasoline.

Just before dawn Carl ventured to say what had been on his mind for several hours.

"Fellows, I just don't see how you're going to make it. Every time you get on the highway you hit a roadblock, and when you get off on those back roads, you're sooner or later going to run into the patrols. I think that come daylight that airplane will be back up, looking for you a section at a time. They'll surround you tight, by the hour."

"We'll die fighting if we're surrounded," Helms said.

Carl shook his head, "Well, maybe you will, but I don't want to die with you."

Hill suggested, then, "I think maybe we ought to let Carl go."

Helms was driving the car, and he slowed down. "Now wouldn't that be smart of us. Just like sending a Western Union telegram to the police asking them to come get us, 'we're through.'"

"Well," Hill said, "we sure can't keep on carrying Carl around with us very much longer."

"Okay, so we'll turn Carl loose," Ratliff said, "but I think we better keep hold of this car."

"I do too," Helms said. "It's better than a Ford."

"And every law in seven counties is looking for it," Hill said. "It's the most popular car in Texas by now."

Carl protested then, "Now, I think I've been fair with you. I've done everything just the way you wanted me to. I've co-operated when I could. So I think you ought to leave my car. I asked you that at first and it's the only thing I've ever asked, that you give me back my dad's car."

Hill said, "Oh hell, Carl. We weren't really planning on

keeping it. Besides, you've got a right to have it back, I say. You've done just like you said. You've cooperated when you could have given us a hell of a lot of trouble."

"And he could have got his ass shot off, too," Helms said, "don't forget. He wasn't doing it out of the goodness of his heart."

Carl Wylie interrupted, "I don't want to get into an argument over whether or not I did it scared or did it voluntary. I took you to be fair and I've been the same way as best I could."

Helms shrugged, "Oh, what the hell. We'll give you back your car. But we've got to get another one first."

Driving through the dark of early morning, they sensed they were near some city which, for that area, was larger than the scattered villages and communities that they usually passed. Ratliff said that if they were going to get another car it would probably be easier to do it in a big town. They agreed, and Hill and Helms tried to figure out where they were, after circling and stopping intermittently most of the night.

"I think we're pretty close to Breckenridge," Helms said. "Somewhere on the south side." The houses they saw were mostly small, but there were no automobiles visible. Within a short time they were in a residential district of more substantial homes and Helms said he thought they ought to park the Dodge and go looking on foot. "If nothing else, the headlights attract attention."

Helms and Hill got out to look for another car, leaving Ratliff, armed, and Carl in the Dodge. The first car they found, an Overland, couldn't be started, but they did take a quilt that was lying on the front seat of the open car. A block away from the Overland they saw a big, closed coupe.

"That's the baby I want," Helms said, "out of this goddam weather." But the coupe was locked, with the windows rolled up tightly. Helms thought he knew how to start it without a key, but he didn't know how to get inside without breaking the glass. "There's not much point to stealing a closed car if you have to break the glass out," he said. "Besides, it might make enough noise to bring out the neighbors."

"Marshall knows some trick to getting into cars," Hill said. "Maybe we ought to go back and find out."

They went back to the parked Dodge, and Ratliff described how he had seen a car window jammed open using a blanket one time before, but as he recalled, the car window had been rolled down just a fraction. "Why don't you just break out the glass. Use that quilt to muffle the sound," he said. "Hell no," Helms said, "I either want an open car we can take easy, or a closed car that's closed, if we're going to have to work hard to get it."

They finally settled on another Ford, an older car that didn't look any too well kept. But it did have plenty of gas in it, they found when they measured.

With the new car they told Carl they would turn him loose, along with his dad's Dodge.

"How's your arm? Does it still hurt?" Ratliff asked.

"Yeah, it's pretty sore. I expect the first thing I'll do is get a doctor to look at it."

"You be sure and tell him it was your own daddy shot you and not one of us," Ratliff said.

"No, I'll tell the truth, that none of you mistreated me a speck."

Helms grunted, "We could plug you yet"—but he grinned.

They shook hands with him, beginning with Ratliff and Helms last. Ratliff said, "Carl, when you get back to Cisco, don't tell 'em where we are. Just that one thing."

"I don't know it, in the first place," Carl said. "I don't know where that pasture is we stayed in and I don't know where you're heading."

"Heading for hell, I'm afraid," Hill said, "I wish I was going with you."

"Well," Carl said, "I wish you boys whatever luck you've got left."

They drove off in the Ford after asking him not to watch what direction they were driving in, although it was a half-hearted command. At five o'clock that morning Carl Wylie walked into the Cisco police station, the town they were in having been Cisco and not Breckenridge. Carl's first request was for a doctor to treat the arm his dad had fleshed. He told the police the bandits had stolen another car and were probably heading for Wichita Falls. He said they had been laying-up in a pasture somewhere toward the northwest part of the county but he didn't know just where. As for the men, Ratliff and Hill were badly wounded, Ratliff almost immobile from his injuries. Helms alone was still in one piece.

"They said they'd die shooting, and they have a twenty-five pound sugar sack full of ammunition," Carl said. He also said he had seen Marshall Ratliff before, around Baird and Cisco, but hadn't said anything to Ratliff about it.

"You should have shot 'em while they were asleep," one policeman said.

"I couldn't do that," Carl said. "In the first place, they played fair with me. In the second place, they're careful with their guns and not going to sleep all at once. They're keeping a watch out."

Besides, he added, he didn't think anybody would have to shoot them. Carl said he didn't see how any of them could last another twelve hours. Which was a fairly poor guess.

"THIS SURE AIN'T the car the Dodge was," Helms said.

It was still dark and cold. They were going north, cautiously, over the oilfield roads between Cisco and Breckenridge. They had been encouraged, earlier, when they thought they had made it into Breckenridge unseen. Then they had discovered they were only on the unfamiliar north side of Cisco, far to the south of Breckenridge.

The Brazos River would be their biggest problem, if they made it around Breckenridge.

"I wonder how come they took up the roadblocks around Cisco?" Ratliff asked. "You know, we ran into that one there by the dam, right near where we come this morning, and now there's not a sign of it."

"I reckon they think we're moving out, so they're setting up roadblocks further away," Hill said.

There were only two crossings of the Brazos they could hope to make: South Bend and Bunger. Both were almost certain to be guarded, but the Brazos was too big a river for them to get a car across without a bridge, so they had to risk it.

"Do you think old Carl will tell them where we're headed?" Helms asked.

"I don't see that it matters much. They pretty well have things choked off anyway."

Ratliff, after changing into the Ford from the Dodge, had become silent. Hill looked back where he was lying and saw his eyes were open but Ratliff seemed to be asleep.

"Marshall's in pretty bad shape," Hill said.

"We're all starving to death," Helms said.

They wound their way north, through the communities of Ray Lee and Harpersville, seeing the lights of the farm houses along the way where families were already up, eating breakfast. Hunger was now a worse enemy than the cold. They had been without food for twenty-four hours.

They got to Breckenridge as the sun was coming up but were afraid to try and get any food. They all agreed it was the best break they had had in two days to have been able to get this far north without being spotted. Holding up a store would ruin their possibilities of escape. By skirting to the east they managed to avoid Breckenridge itself. They were looking for a little crossroads station or store where they could get some food with their last few cents. They found nothing of the kind, however, and by daylight they found themselves to the north of Breckenridge. Helms stopped the car.

"We're taking quite a risk traveling in daylight like this," he said. "We've got to decide whether or not we keep traveling or we hole up in some pasture."

Helms reached back and shook Ratliff, "What about it, big boy?"

Ratliff looked around confusedly and didn't comprehend. "What's what . . . ?"

"Shall we hole up or run for it?"

"Ask Lee . . ." Ratliff said, his chin rolling back on his chest. "Ask . . . Lee . . ."

Helms looked at Hill. "He's babbling," Hill said, "and I'll be doing the same thing in a couple of hours."

"My goddam guts are babbling," Helms said. "I tell you, if I find me a little grocery store out here somewhere, I'm sure as hell going to knock it over. I'd as soon be shot to death as to starve."

The countryside was flat and brushy, but to their right, a few miles distant, was a wild stretch of the Brazos River where it plunged into a line of hills, carving gorges among the cedar brakes and leaving steep-sided banks that couldn't be climbed. It was as rough a stretch of country as could be found along the entire river, called Possum Kingdom, and there were few farms or dwellings of any kind amid the wilderness stretch.

"We might try for the Brazos bottoms," Hill said. Helms shook off the suggestion. "Once they found out we were in there they'd have us trapped, sure. They might have one hell of a time twisting us out, but we'd sure have one hell of a time ever getting out, either."

"Well it looks to me like we've got just one chance, then," Hill said. "We go on to South Bend, and try making it across. You've got to cross the Brazos River to get to Wichita Falls and there's no way, short of Mexico, to prevent it."

"We'll never die any younger," Helms said. He started up the car, and looked at Hill. "Bobby, if we're ever going to make it, we've got to make it now. But this car won't do more'n forty, so don't you go attractin' anybody to chase us."

SHERIFF JIM FOSTER, of Young County, hurriedly mobilized his posse when he got word from Cisco that the three bandits were believed to be coming his way. He set up his main barricade at South Bend because that was where the road crossed the Brazos on its way to Graham and, ultimately, Wichita Falls.

"Keep out of sight, that's the most important thing," he told his men. "Let 'em get right up to it before you do any shooting." There were several volunteers from Eliasville and Graham along with his deputies and special deputies.

By daylight the ambush was in place. Two official cars were parked across the highway and some sawhorse type barricades were set up at either end of the autos. The men in the posse were scattered along the road, hiding behind houses or in the fence rows.

By eight o'clock some of the men had begun to grow impatient. Sheriff Foster took a couple of thermos jugs of hot coffee out to them. It was cold work, and a gray day.

"Just stick to it," he said. "This is the first time we've known for sure where they were. This is our big break."

Initially the word had come up to Young County that the three would be traveling in a Dodge. Only after eight o'clock were they informed, down at the South Bend barricade, that the car they sought was a Ford roadster which had been stolen from in front of Cecil Hibbert's house in Cisco.

But even with this additional news, by nine o'clock several of the men were convinced the fugitives were not going to try the South Bend crossing.

"I bet they got word," one of the special deputies said. "They've probably got spies all over the country. I'll bet they know what we're going to do, even before we start."

"Hell, they're plenty of other places you can cross the river. You can cross it up toward Seymour and in through there. We're here freezing our butts off on the forty-sixty chance they're going to try and make it through here."

It was a few minutes after nine when, "Look!"

The hoarse whisper rang out like a shot. Sudden, complete silence fell on the group, but like the ripple of power through a muscle, the men braced at the word.

"Keep down," a whisper of authority ran over them, "if it's them they'll likely . . ."

The Ford roadster had pulled up at a filling station at the south end of South Bend's single street. Sheriff Foster was holding back the men with him, steadying them: "Wait a minute . . . wait a minute . . . let's be sure it's them. Can you see how many's in there?"

"Two is all I can see," one of the men said.

"Give 'em a little time."

They waited as the Ford paused at the station. But then, across the road and almost opposite from the filling station, someone walked from behind a building and appeared at the roadside. Then another man joined him and the two started across the highway toward the Ford.

"Oh, goddam . . . goddam . . . get back . . . keep back . . ."

"Somebody's after that reward money," another man whispered.

Before either of the two figures was near it, the Ford suddenly moved, making a U-turn, skidding on the pavement, and going back south from where it had first appeared.

"Let's go—it's them!" Sheriff Foster came out yelling. Shooting at the car began immediately, while the two official vehicles roared into life and came around the barricades in pursuit of the Ford.

"It's them! It's them!" A dozen men were running down the highway, jumping onto the running boards of the cars that now began streaming out in chase.

"We got 'em now! We got 'em now!" Foster told his men, and the pack picked up in a yelling, shooting lunge.

THEY DIDN'T REALIZE they were so close to the place until the road made a sharp left curve into South Bend and Helms was looking down the village's main street. He saw the barricade immediately. So did Hill.

"Goddam, it's the roadblock," Hill yelled, simultaneously with an exclamation from Helms. Helms swerved the Ford off the road and pulled into the driveway of a small filling station, the car's motor still running. They could see no sign of men except the two vehicles across the road ahead.

"Where are they?" Helms asked.

"Shit, they're bound to be here somewhere," Hill said.

"We've stepped off into it for sure."

Helms looked around, "Maybe we can fight 'em off from this place." The station was closed. Everything in South Bend had closed for the ambush.

"Maybe they're off somewhere," Hill said. "Maybe they're not looking for us."

Helms shook off the suggestion, "Hell yes, they're ready. They're around here, watching us."

"It sort of looks like they're hoping we'll turn around and go back," Hill said.

The seconds were drawn out as the men in the Ford tried desperately to come to a decision.

"Christ, if we only had—" Helms interrupted his own sentence, "There! There's one coming at us! Shoot him, Bobby! Shoot him!"

The man appeared from behind a house, coming toward them. Helms shoved the Ford out of the deserted station, whirled it around on the highway, and hit the accelerator full. "We've got to get out of here," he shouted.

"Get off this goddam road quick as you can—it's an ambush," Hill was yelling.

The force of the violently swerving car shook Ratliff in the rear seat and he was sitting up, dazedly, looking around but saying nothing. Hill looked back and shouted to him, "They've spotted us. Roadblock."

Ratliff looked back out of the car and saw the pursuit forming up. Already one of the cars from the roadblock was gearing up the highway after them.

"Oh Jesus, I wish we had that Dodge and not this drag-ass Ford," Helms said.

"Get off this highway quick as you can," Hill said. "They'll catch us sure on a straight run. We can't outrun 'em."

The Ford stayed on the highway to the end of the pavement, less than a mile from the filling station where the chase began.

"That black car is coming like hell," Hill said to him. "It can hold the road a damn sight better than this one."

Helms put the Ford into a severe left turn and they bounced onto a sand road. Ratliff had drawn a pistol and was trying to fire it out the rear of the Ford at the other vehicle but the distance between them was too great for pistol fire, although the bigger, black car was closing in on them rapidly.

"This sonofabitch don't go any further," Helms shouted, seeing that the road seemed to come to a dead end a short distance ahead. "It don't go any further. We've got to shoot it out."

He aimed the Ford for a fence at the north side of the road. There was an open pasture, then a line of thicket a few hundred feet across the pasture.

"We'll run for that cover. We've got to beat them out of here," Helms yelled.

"We don't have time," Hill said. "They're right on us now. There's two carloads of 'em coming right on us. We've got to keep 'em off."

Ratliff had come fully conscious now and had dragged out a shotgun instead of the pistol. He fired the shotgun back at the lead car. The posse, its members firing as they came, was only a hundred yards away. When the two pursuing cars jolted to a rough stop, the men were piling off the running boards and out of the cars, fanning out in a line and running toward the trio. Hill watched almost as if he had lost the connection between the advancing men and his own part in the drama. It seemed to him everyone was moving in slow motion, not making a sound except for the bullets, which crisscrossed around them, whining at full speed.

Helms kept yelling for them to get to the fence. Ratliff leaped out of the back seat and hit the dirt road running. He turned toward the posse with the shotgun leveled waist high, but before he could pull the trigger, Cy Bradford let his own shotgun roar, and Ratliff fell to the sandy earth and did not move.

Helms started toward Ratliff but a spray of bullets backed him around the Ford, and he and Hill cut for the fence, turning to fire at the posse every six or seven steps. Hill had two automatics and was laying down a sweeping pattern of gunfire. Helms emptied one revolver and was turning to make a run for the fence when Hill heard another loud *ker-whump* and saw him stagger. It was Cy Bradford's shotgun again. Helms almost fell, but he caught himself, swayed semi-erect, and got off a return blast at the posse with a second pistol.

"Get over there," Hill yelled and gestured toward the line of thicket beyond the pasture. "Over there . . ."

"You got the sack?" Helms yelled back. "You got the ammo sack?"

Hill shook his head violently, "I got it—you make the woods."

Cy's shotgun went *ker-whump* again and Hill suddenly felt a new, fiery pain somewhere in his body without his mental mechanism registering the exact place. He was not consciously controlling anything—his legs, his eyesight, the fingers pulling the triggers—and certainly not his mind. As he climbed through the four-strand barb-wire fence, he found himself thinking disjointed thoughts, comparing this battle to the one at the bank and, wildly, recalling a vicious clod fight he had been in as a boy, when he was caught between two sides and got badly bashed by the rock-hard clods of clay.

Out of the corner of one eye he saw Helms moving through the fence, into the field. Firing, running, stooping low, firing again, the two of them got to the edge of the woods. When the posse members stopped where Ratliff had fallen, Hill and Helms pulled further back in the brush, given that few seconds head start. Not knowing or caring, now, in what direction they ran, they fled blindly toward survival.

SHERIFF FOSTER CAME UP, as soon as it was safe, and pushed the men back from where Ratliff's body was lying.

"I don't want none of you thinking it's your right to give this fellow the coup de grace," he said.

"Hell, Sheriff, he's done couped all the grace he can," a special deputy grinned, nudging the motionless body with his foot. "This rascal is ker-poot."

Foster knelt down and took one of Ratliff's wrists, groping for a pulse.

"He's dead, ain't he?" somebody asked from the crowd that circled the bandit.

"I think he's still alive," the sheriff said. "Don't know for how long, but I feel a pulse now."

"Then let's give him a few minutes before we shoot him and maybe he'll die of his own accord."

"He'll die of his own accord, regardless," Sheriff Foster said. "We're taking this fellow to the hospital."

"But hell, Sheriff," one of the men complained, "just a second ago we was all tryin' our best to kill him, and now all he needs is just a little help to save the state the cost of burning him."

"We're going to let the state do it, if God don't do it first," the sheriff said. "We're takin' him to the hospital."

He turned to Jim Davis, the city marshal of Graham, and Roy McCarren, a special deputy from down the road at Eliasville.

"Jim, why don't you and Roy take him in my car to the sanitorium? I better stay here and flush those other two fellows out of the brakes while we've got 'em cornered."

He looked around the posse, "Cy, you're from Eastland County; you know which one this is?"

Bradford, his deadly twenty-gauge shotgun cradled in the left arm, shook his head, "I'm 'fraid you'll have to wait till the Cisco people get here. I don't know this bunch."

"What about the reward, Sheriff?" another man asked.

"Why? You didn't get him," the sheriff said.

"Well, I figure Bradford wouldn't take it, him being a peace officer and it being in his line of duty."

"Hell," someone else said, "I thought sure it was my load brought him down." The posse laughed.

"I wouldn't count on any reward," Sheriff Foster said. "I've heard lots of talk about that five thousand dollars the bankers are offering, but I ain't seen none of their money."

"If it's like the bankers in Breckenridge, you'll have to put up ten before you can collect five, anyway," a Stephens County man said. Everybody laughed again.

Sheriff Foster looked across the pasture. "I sure's hell hope somebody's going after them others, or was you boys lettin' them get away on purpose so you'd have a little something to do the rest of the day?"

"Shorty Lawson's going south with a couple of men and Billy Porterfield's taken three or four others across over to them woods. They're pinned in 'tween here'n the river. They ought to be in our hands by noon."

Ratliff was still unconscious. Four men worked their arms under him to pick him up, the sheriff warning them not to let his head hang loose. "Might kill him from shock. We need to find out everything we can from him before he dies, if he does. Might as well be useful to somebody as long as he's alive." They put him in a car.

The sheriff warned the Eliasville deputy, "Keep an eye on him, Roy. Make sure he ain't playin' 'possum." Roy McCarren grinned and held up a sawed-off shotgun. Jim Davis backed the car around carefully and drove off toward South Bend. Graham, where the hospital was, was ten miles north, beyond South Bend.

At the Graham Sanitorium they found three old wounds and a new one on Ratliff, on the left leg between the hip and the knee. But this wound wasn't bad enough to have brought him down. The doctors said the man had simply fainted. He was in bad shape, not so much from the shotgun peppering of Cy Bradford as from his old wounds.

Shortly after noon Tub Wilson of the Cisco police arrived and was taken to the hospital room where the wounded man was under guard.

"That is Marshall Ratliff," Tub announced. "You got the big one. He is old Santa Claus. I have known him for years."

Tub pointed out that Ratliff, who was blond, had dyed his hair black in an attempt to disguise himself, but some of the hospital personnel said it might be that it was just dirty. Tub said no, that was the kind of a thing Ratliff would do. He knew him well. Knew both the Ratliff boys, Lee and Marshall. And that was the way they did things. They worked harder at playing than at working.

"If it hadn't been for Ma Ferguson, the woman governor, he'd still be in Huntsville," Tub said. "Him and Lee got eighteen years in 1926, but she pardoned them the first of the year. I expect money changed hands."

Ratliff, always slender, was greatly emaciated and hadn't shaved since the night they left Wichita Falls. The hospital attendants at Graham said they doubted he would survive the day. At first he was thought to have lockjaw because he could not open his jaws to talk. Later it was found that the shot that wounded his chin had hit the hinge of his jaw and had gradually paralyzed it.

But Marshall Ratliff's dirty, unshaven, unfed condition may have caused the medical people to overestimate his nearness to death. By Wednesday, with sleep, food, protection from the elements and treatment, his health was held to be good enough for him to travel, although he still wasn't talking, and he was taking food with great difficulty. Cy Bradford and another deputy from Eastland County went up to Graham by car and brought Ratliff back to the Eastland jail. He had six wounds, doctors found, and three bullets were still in his body.

On Tuesday, December 28, a group of Cisco businessmen and civic leaders took it upon themselves to announce that the five thousand dollars reward for the death of Louis Davis should be given to the family of the late Chief Bit Bedford and to George Carmichael, the Cisco policeman wounded at the bank. The sixty-year-old Carmichael lingered in the shadows in a coma. He was the recipient of a civic blood donation drive. High School football coach W. B. Chapman was one of the first Cisco citizens to volunteer, and he urged his boys, the Big Dam Loboes, to follow suit.

But Mrs. Blasengame quickly moved in on the announced idea of an automatic distribution of the reward money to the two fallen officers.

"I'm not taking any of the credit away from what they did," she said, "but who do you think broke the news of that hold-up in the first place? If me and Frances hadn't have run out of there and broke the news, they'd have never been there to shoot that Davis fellow in the first place."

Someone pointed out to her that the reward was for killing a bank robber, not just for reporting him.

"Well my Lord, did you expect me to grab up a gun and go over there and shoot him? I'm a lady, not a policeman. How do they expect a lady to collect one of their rewards if they're just going to give it to somebody that's carrying a gun?"

Nobody knew what to do about it. She had a point, but she didn't, it seemed to the people of Cisco. Most of the women thought her argument made sense, although none of them exactly looked forward to ever collecting a dead bank robber reward. Several men, even some who thought the reward money should go to the officers, accepted the importance of Mrs. Blasengame's role but pointed out that the purpose of the reward was definitely to instill the fear of death in would-be bank robbers, not just the apprehension of criminals. In other words, the reward was a deterrent to the idea most of all. Others said the whole question merely pointed up the sordid effect such a reward had on humanity.

As a matter of history, no reward was ever paid by the bankers association in the Santa Claus bank robbery. The decision made by the association officers was that it was impossible to tell who actually had gunned down Louis Davis since there were so many persons firing at the time. And not everyone, even aside from Mrs. Blasengame, was willing to concede that Bit Bedford and George Carmichael were the most likely ones to have hit him. There had been lots of shooters, and before long nearly every one of them thought he remembered how it could have been his bullet that laid Davis low.

Mrs. Blasengame said if that was the way they were going to handle things it was certainly the last time she'd risk hers and Frances's hides to turn in a bunch of bank robbers.

9 / THE BRAZOS RIVER, eastward from South Bend, makes a series of turns which loop back and forth so acutely that often, by land, you are less than a mile from some other part of the river which is five or six times that distance by water. South Bend, Brier Bend, Gooseneck Bend, Salem Bend, Herron Bend—the names and the features interlock like the fingers of your two hands clasped together.

It was (and is) rough country. Some of the isolated valleys are historic as the site of the earliest settlement or of Indian massacres and battles. All of it is remote, the loops of the river cutting off communication with even close neighbors. Along the river itself the landscape is thick, brushy, leveling out now and then for a pasture. The river also shallows out every couple of bends to make a natural crossing, and it was at these natural fording places that the early settlers stopped, or in some instances, set up tiny communities, few of which survived the nineteenth century. Bridges were scarcer than fording places, because the Brazos is a wide river, no matter how shallow, and subject to inundations which spread it a mile or more. Bridge engineering, even under modern technical impetus, is difficult and extremely costly. The main bridge was at South Bend, in 1927, and there was another bridged crossing at Gooseneck Bend, with a third bridge, a toll way, over on Herron Bend. Those were the only ways an automobile could cross along a lengthy stretch of river. So two men on foot had a slight advantage over a more numerous posse on wheels. They could walk into a country that couldn't be driven into.

If they could walk.

Helms had been hit in the right arm and right hip by rifle and pistol bullets and had buckshot in his back and a painful graze wound on the collarbone. Hill, already suffering from his bad wound in the left arm and a graze wound in the back, had been pelleted in the head by buckshot at South Bend.

They ran by instinct, stumbling over rocks and bushes, looking back more often than forward, gasping for breath. They went on and on, unconscious of time or distance.

They reached the Brazos before they stopped this blind flight. They had been traveling several hundred feet apart, but always within shouting distance of one another. At the river itself they pulled up. Helms swayed toward Hill, who was squatting at the foot of a giant pecan tree.

"How long has it been . . . ," he gulped for air, ". . . since they shot at us?"

Hill swallowed and shook his head, "I don't have any idea . . ."

They listened, above the panting of their breath and the lunging of their hearts, but could hear no sounds of men coming after them. Hill looked down and was somewhat amazed to discover he still carried the sugar sack containing their extra ammunition.

"We better parcel this out," he told Helms.

They had three pistols apiece, and they stuffed their pockets with bullets. Helms was shaking from the cold and from the effect of the wounds he had received. Hill gave him the overcoat they had gotten from Carl Wylie.

Helms hugged himself inside the coat. "I guess they got Marshall," he said, "I seen him go down, and it looked to me like he was dead."

Hill didn't say anything. He could almost feel his wounds getting stiff, binding both his body and his mind, as he sat at the foot of the tree.

"We got to keep moving. This is worse than that first time," he said to Helms.

"I don't know a goddam thing about this country," Helms said.

"I don't neither," Hill said. "But if we keep to the river I expect we'll have cover all the time."

They walked southward down the river for a mile or so, then cut back west to keep from having to cross a public road they had come to.

"I reckon we'd better travel along the roads at night only," Helms said.

After they were sure the posse was not right on their tails, they decided to lay up in the brush until nightfall. Walking was painful and they didn't know where they were. They burrowed into a clump of high grass and cedar and oak brush and slept for several hours. They talked very little; there was very little to talk about.

The fact that they holed up probably saved them from capture that first day. The posse initially was so certain the pair would be captured that pursuit was maintained in a careless way, even when contact with the men was lost, shortly after the gunfight on the road. In fact, a number of the posse members quit the chase and went back to Graham or Eastland County, announcing the hunt was over. News of the capture of Helms and Hill was awaited with assurance.

But by nightfall, as no word came of a capture, the law officers began the uneasy job of checking out their deputies and civilian volunteers. You guys actually seen them two since they escaped us? Where exactly was it they went into the brush? Are you sure you still have 'em surrounded? The answers were hesitant and uncertain, and assurance melted.

A new call went out for help, and the posse increased in size until more than one-hundred-fifty men were surrounding the Big Bend of the Brazos, a sizable loop where Helms and Hill were believed trapped.

It began raining during the early part of the night. Not hard; no downpour, but uncomfortable.

"Shit," Helms said, pulling his hat down so that the rain wouldn't run off the brim and down the collar of his overcoat, "this ain't enough water to kill our scent, in case they bring in bloodhounds, but it's plenty cold enough to freeze our ass."

"Next time I suggest we hit a bank in the summertime," Hill said.

"Don't kid about it," Helms said, "I ain't in no kiddin' mood. I'd give my left nut and two more like it for a car."

"We wouldn't get five miles," Hill said, "as few roads and bridges as there are around this part of the country—anything you can get a Ford coupe down will have a dozen deputy sheriffs patrolling it. And I imagine they've got a regular army guarding every bridge over the Brazos within a hundred miles."

"You suggest, then, that we just die out here in the woods from frozen-ass? Is that it, buddy?" Helms asked.

"The only way we can cross that river is on foot. We find us a shallow place and we can wade it. It won't be too hard if we can find a fording place."

"You mind if I let you do the finding?" Helms asked. "I'm flat scared of water in the dark, especially with quicksand the way I've always heard it was in the Brazos."

Hill wiped a streak of rain that was running down the creases around his mouth. "Don't ask me, Henry. We'll have to luck out on it. I don't know this part of the country any better than you do."

As the rain increased in intensity Hill began changing his mind about a car. A car would be dry, he told himself, and if nothing else, you could at least make the attempt to crash the blockade at some point. On foot you just waited while the net was pulled in tight.

"I tell you, Henry," he said to Helms as they made their way, mostly in the dark because the moon was shielded by the cloudy sky, "if we can spot a car, maybe we better take it. Might as well die dry trying to run our way out as die freezing wet."

They found a farm house near Bunger, a tiny community up in the Gooseneck Bend area, and saw a Ford parked in a shed back of the house. Helms said he was afraid he couldn't run, in case somebody spotted them trying to take the car, so Hill said he would make the attempt. A flash of lightning and a tremendous clap of thunder broke just as he stepped out of the sheltering shadow of the woods below the house. He couldn't tell if it was the thunder or the sight of him that caused it, but suddenly several dogs began roaring away. Hill slipped down along a fence toward the shed where the car was parked, but the barking continued. The back door of the house opened and someone bawled, "Bell, Blue, Tickey—what are you hounds barkin' at? You got somebody cornered out there?"

Hill held his breath and waited by the fence, afraid the next flash of lightning might expose him completely to dogs and man.

The dogs started up their yelling and barking again, but Hill still had not seen them.

"I'm gonna get my gun," the unseen voice from the back door yelled out at the night. "You hounds, I'm a-fixin' to come out there and shoot whoever it is sneaking around."

Hill didn't think the farmer knew anyone was really out there; he suspected this was a bluff the farmer was making in case someone was listening. The sonofabitch might not even have a gun. But he couldn't take a chance. Too goddam many things that shouldn't have happened had happened already. Besides, he had noticed something more important than the dogs or the car either: the farm house had a telephone line. If that old farmer really got suspicious he could call the laws and get a dozen officers this way in five minutes. They weren't all that far off from South Bend, or even from Graham.

Hill got down and crouched his way back into the woods and found Helms.

"Henry, that Ford might as well be locked in the Bank of England. There's three or four hounds baying their goddam heads off every time you move a toe, and the farmer is suspicious as hell about what's going on around his house. Did you hear anything that went on just now?"

"I heard the dogs barking."

"Well, the farmer came out and yelled about how he was going to blow somebody's ass off. I figure he was bluffing, but he has a telephone, and God knows, if he got too upset he'd probably call the sheriff."

"We could always shoot the sonofabitch before he got a chance to call anybody. Cut the telephone line and shoot him and take that car," Helms said.

"I'm not shootin' ever again at anybody who ain't shootin' at me," Hill said. "I don't like the shape things are in."

They had drawn back into the woods. Helms said, "Hell, do you think I like what we're doin'? You think this is my idea of fun? But I'd like to know how the hell you think we could have stopped, once it got started?"

Hill sighed, "I'm too tired to think. I ain't thought straight in a week, it seems like. Or a year."

"It's been longer than that since I done anything but run," Helms said. "Seems to me we've been doing this all our lives. Running and cold. I can't remember sleepin' in bed with my wife or havin' a hot cup of coffee for breakfast—and it's been less than a week since I was doin' both."

Neither said anything for a long period, while the wind moved through the empty branches, and the mist of rain clung like a cold breath to the skin of their faces.

"Let's get out of here," Hill said. "We can follow the road in front of that house. It'll take us somewhere."

They went along the road through the dark, passing no lighted houses and not being found by any more hounds. After a while they discovered they were closer to the river than they had known, and sometime before midnight they crossed the Brazos at what was called the Old Caseyville Crossing, wading the shallows. In the rugged, low hills on that north shore they found shelter under a huge, flat rock and decided to spend the rest of the night. They were wet past the knees from fording the river and were so miserable they decided to risk trying to build a fire, not caring what the consequences might be.

They collected small pieces of wood and tried to break up some branches to get dry kindling, but it was all rain-soaked. One at a time the matches flared, then died after futilely burning against the damp sticks.

"If we had some paper," Hill said, "we might get it started. Or if it was daylight and we could reach some dry grass . . ."

"I'm not sure we could find any if it was daylight," Helms said. "About the only thing we're going to come up with in the dark is a cottonmouth moccasin."

"I'd even burn a piece of my shirt if it wasn't wet too," Hill said.

They stopped trying to light a fire when they got down to their last four matches. They stacked their small supply of sticks under the rock in hopes it would dry out for later use, and laid themselves out on the dry dirt to sleep. But they got little rest. The fever rose in both men, and Helms began a meaningless muttering and arguing almost as soon as his eyes closed. It was nearly dawn before they were unconscious. When something woke them, they discovered it was daylight.

What woke them was a sound—a sound that gradually became the sound of a motor overhead. They crept from under their rock and watched the sky. An airplane came skimming over the treetops, moving back and forth in a careful search pattern. This time there could be no confusion as to its actions: this airplane was looking for them.

Texas Ranger Tom Hickman was disgusted with the way things had gone at South Bend. Here a big, armed posse had let two crippled criminals get away from right under their noses, just because everybody in the posse was so interested in collecting the reward for the one they thought they had killed. And they had only wounded him in the first place.

Hickman and Sergeant Gonzaullas got to the hunt area the night of the shoot-out and set up headquarters in Graham. Hickman had already wired Fort Worth for a biplane to come out and join the hunt as soon as the sky cleared enough, and he hoped it would be the next morning. If, by Wednesday, the rain had stopped, the plane could take up Gonzaullas and reconnoiter the whole area of the bends of the Brazos.

Rumors had started coming in as soon as Helms and Hill had disappeared into the brush. They were given astounding powers of distance. They were reported surrounded at Ivan, several miles south, and at the same time a bunch of men at Oil City had armed themselves to rush a farmer's barn near there before they discovered the noise they heard inside was a cow giving birth to a calf.

Another report out of Pickwick, far to the southeast, was more creditable and got official attention for several hours. Two men reportedly lost an automobile in a mudhole, then fled when someone showed up leading a pair of mules to pull them out (at a good fee, as was the custom of farmers who lived near convenient mudholes—mud-farmers, they were called). Hickman, who knew human nature, was not surprised when this turned out not to be the fugitives but a man and woman who had been out doing what they had no business doing and getting caught at. The newspapers either took up each as a joke or in great headline seriousness, according to how close to deadline time such stories came in.

Wednesday morning Hickman put the dogs on the trail, but they got nowhere. The rains of the night before had aided the bandits and hindered the posse, and the fugitives' track was blotted out. So far as the pursuers could determine, the two men had crossed the river four times, but the last time it couldn't be distinguished whether they had come this way or gone that.

One sheriff in the hunt (there were as many as eight at certain periods) stated publicly: "Time will probably catch them quicker than the posse." They were believed to have no food, and they weren't getting much sleep, moving around the way they were, and their wounds were bound to be getting worse—enough blood had been found at the South Bend battle site to make it reasonably sure that they were badly wounded. Each of the hunters, working with his coat up around his neck and his hat or cap pulled down as far as possible against the wind and the rain, imagined what it must be like to be fleeing from everything in this, tramping through the roughest brakes the Brazos had, getting stiff and aching—"they won't last long" was the general opinion.

Ranger Hickman also brought along two machineguns to

use in case it came down to the men trying to fortify themselves in a cave or something. The whole chase had been an
embarrassment to him, and though he didn't think it had
been his fault, he couldn't very well speak out and put the
blame on his fellow law enforcement officers because he had
to work with most of them on an everyday basis. He told
Martin Koonsman, an ex-Ranger who was now with the
recently organized Texas Highway Patrol, that next time he,
Hickman, found out the citizens were organizing a posse to
chase lawbreakers, damned if he wasn't going to join the
fugitives, for it would be safer.

The sky had cleared during the early morning hours of
Wednesday and the airplane carrying Sergeant Gonzaullas
flew all that day, circling, criss-crossing, and dipping low
over the area where the men were believed trapped. Nothing
was seen, but on the ground Hill and Helms were constantly
being startled and changing their plans by the sudden appearance of the plane, low on the horizon, roaring in on
them. This meant they were seldom able to walk in cleared
areas or along even the loneliest roads where they might
otherwise have made good time.

Wednesday night their hunger drove them to desperate
measures. Although there were two cars parked near a large
house, and at least three men had been observed by them
going in and out, they slipped up to a nearby barn and hid
inside. No dogs barked at them this time and there were no
animals in the barn for them to disturb. They found some
feed corn in a bin and filled their pockets with ears. They
were afraid to stay in the shelter of the barn for too long a
time, because the men in the house seemed to be preparing
for some kind of work or movement which might bring them
to the barn; so with the corn, Helms and Hill worked their
way back into the brakes and this time were able to start a
small fire and they parched the corn on the ear. It was not a

very successful way to prepare the hard, dry corn as food, but it was the first thing to eat they had had in three days.

Wednesday night was warmer, at least, and the two fugitives managed to move about rather freely, but their movements got them nowhere. Each time they tried to go some distance in a certain direction, they encountered search parties or spotted roadblocks. They were within a wide area but they were firmly trapped, notwithstanding. They could only move safely by night, and by day they were afraid to stay in one spot for fear they would be found by search parties or spotted by the airplane.

Thursday, bright and early, the airplane was up again, and if the pilot hadn't become so excited it might have meant their capture right then. They were walking across a fairly open space when they heard the drone of the airplane engine, coming at them from their rear. Both Helms and Hill dived for cover, but not quick enough. When the pilot spotted them he banked and came back as low as he could, sweeping over where they lay and giving them notice they had been seen. Helms lay back cursing with a pistol ready to fire on the plane if it returned.

"Might as well try and bring that sonofabitch down. He's seen us for sure now," Helms told Hill after the pilot had made his first, low pass.

"If you can do it with a pistol," Hill said, "do it."

But the plane did not come back over them, heading back to Graham instead to alert Hickman of the whereabouts of the bandits.

The posse was now down to fewer men, but Hickman had planned it that way. Most of the members were law officers, except for some like Walter Sikes, the son-in-law of the Cisco mayor, and the mayor's son. On hearing that Helms and Hill had been seen, a party of fifteen or twenty searchers was sent out to the specified area in cars, probing as deep into the thicket as possible, and began beating the woods along the south shore of the river. But Hill and Helms had fled across the river as soon as the airplane had disappeared, and they thought maybe they were safer now than they had been because their location would be erroneously reported.

"The trouble with your airplane," Hickman told Koonsman, "is that it can't hover over your fugitive and keep him in sight. Your airplane has to fly back to the airfield before it can land and give you the word, and by then your criminal has escaped."

Hickman, Gonzaullas and Koonsman all said they looked forward to the time when radios, either between car and airplane or airplane and headquarters, would be standard equipment for law enforcement agencies.

As for the two fugitives, the move across the river away from the airplane was not the blessing in disguise they thought it to be. On the other side of the river, congratulating themselves on outwitting the machine, they suddenly heard the unmistakable sound of a large party of men coming toward them. They could not turn around and go back across the river because that was the very area the airplane would report them in, and now, to their surprise, came this group, cutting them off from the north. The group sounded so large, and was seemingly so spread out, that Helms and Hill could do nothing but scurry to the river's edge and try to hide among the rocks. They found a flat, projecting slab of a boulder near the water line and got under it, squeezing themselves beneath the stone so as to be invisible except from the water itself.

The posse members were talking and laughing, not trying to be quiet, so Helms and Hill knew the chase for them was centered elsewhere. Two of the posse climbed up on the very rock under which they crouched. Fortunately for the fugitives, the members of the posse were not really looking for them in this particular place but were headed down the river for another area which Sheriff Foster thought might furnish a good hiding place. After a few minutes the posse went on its way, but Helms and Hill didn't dare stir for an hour or more.

Helms was getting worse, physically. Much of the time now he talked incoherently. But during one period on Thursday when he did make sense, he told Hill they had only one chance: if they could get to the town of Graham, there was someone Helms knew who lived there—Rutter was his name —and ran some kind of hotel or boarding house. He would help, Helms said. If they could get to him and get food, aspirin, warm blankets—even some sleep—then they might kick their way out; take a car and make it. Not back to Wichita Falls but in the other direction, to Mexico, to Central America. Wichita Falls was dangerous. Maybe for one night, to see people. But not even that long if . . . the talk rambled in and out of circumstances and Hill, who was comprehending reality only a little better himself, dismissed everything but the name Rutter and the connection with some kind of public place. Graham was a city of six thousand population or more with quite a bit of oil activity surrounding it and Hill felt that even as battered as they were, they might not be taken for fugitives but for oil field workers.

On the basis of Helms's ramblings about this supposed resident and his hotel, Hill spent a great part of Thursday half dragging, half carrying Helms north from the river toward the town. It was a miracle that they made it to the city limits, but they did. Graham had been an armed camp for the previous sixty hours, with law officers from a dozen surrounding places operating out of there, and the fact that the fugitives were thought pinned down on the Brazos, several miles from Graham, probably accounted for their success. At any rate, Helms and Hill got to Graham.

They walked the alleys of the town, not daring to ask anyone where Rutter's hotel or boarding house might be. They simply looked at as many places as they could safely view, trying to see a sign. When night fell, Helms was delirious and Hill saw the earth rolling in waves around him, he was so sick, tired, and hungry. He dragged Helms into a barn and they both collapsed on the board floor. At dawn Hill felt no better and Helms was, if anything, worse. Hill managed to get his companion on his feet although Helms was still out of his head. All Hill could think of was getting back to the safety of the brakes around the Brazos River. The notion of safety in a boarding house, or safety in fleeing to Wichita Falls, was all gone. Only the survival offered by the wilderness urged Hill and the burden that was Helms toward it.

At 7:45 A.M. a boy came to the Graham police station and reported: "These two guys came up and asked me where they could find a rooming house. I thought at first they were hobos off the Wichita Falls and Southern, they were down there by the tracks. I thought they were drunks, maybe. But this one guy looked familiar. It was that Helms one, I feel pretty sure. They both looked really beat out."

Jim Davis grabbed up his guns and called the three men who were in the station waiting to go out on the hunt along the Brazos.

"Come on, that's bound to be them. Let's go."

He grabbed the boy, "Come on, son. You're going with us. You take us."

The boy turned pale: "Officer, I don't want to go. I told them the Eagle Hotel just so I could get away from them. That's where they'll be—over on the west side. You don't need me to get you there."

Davis hesitated, then said, "Okay, son. Stay here. They'll be easy to find, I suppose."

Davis, Deputy E. H. Little of Comanche, Walter Sikes, the civilian, and Deputy Sheriff E. G. Williamson of Young County, got in a car and drove the short distance to where the boy had said the men should be. The officers spotted the pair, moving heavily on their feet, heading out of town.

Davis jumped from the car and yelled, "All right—halt where you are!"

Helms turned around, saw the armed men and swayed but did not move otherwise. Hill started running and Davis fired three shots rapidly at him, then took off after him on foot.

"He can't make it. He's too wore out," he yelled at the others. "Don't shoot. Don't kill him."

The chase was a short one. Just as Davis approached him from the rear, Hill stumbled to his knees with his hands in his overcoat pocket, his guns undrawn.

"You damn fool," Davis said to him as he lifted Hill to his feet, "how come you run like that with all of us armed like we are?"

Hill shook his head wearily, "I figured we'd be killed because of the bank reward. I'd just as soon be killed running as with my hands up."

"THE TWO MEN were literally riddled with bullets," Hickman told the reporters. "Helms is semiconscious, but won't even admit to being in Cisco. Hill is cooperative."

The chase ended, dozens of law enforcement officers began returning to their regular duties all over West Texas. It had been the biggest manhunt in Texas history, involving the largest area and the most men. It had also been the first such widely spread net to utilize some modern modes of equipment, things that would become standard for police within a few years. Only the reporters stayed with the story, having ended another chapter but not the whole volume.

Helms and Hill were put in the Graham jail the day of their capture. Two doctors who looked them over said privately they didn't expect Helms to survive. He had a temperature of 103 degrees, and his wounds were badly infected. Hill would most likely lose his left arm.

The captured men found out Marshall Ratliff had not been killed at the South Bend gunfight as they had supposed, but the other prisoners in the jail assured them all three would burn before the month was out.

"They'll try you one day and burn you the next," a big roughneck, held on a murder charge, told Hill. "They're going to make an example of you boys. I wouldn't be surprised if the state bought two extra electric chairs and lined up all three of you to ride Old Sparky at once." But Hill was too dazed to connect himself with this talk of death very much. He drifted back and forth in his life, before the hold-up one minute, then into the long chase. He could not readily grasp all the commotion around him that had been stirred with the capture of Helms and himself. He found himself detached, thinking the discussions must involve two other men—men who must have been powerfully important to create this much interest and be known by so many different kinds of people. Each time Hill closed his eyes he found himself believing he was at another place: in an open car with a sharp wind burning his face with cold; wading the night waters of the Brazos, fearfully clutched-up in the gut from the unseen dangers of a deep hole or quicksand he could never pull his weak body from. Food was strange and overpoweringly pungent when offered. His ears rang continually with a thin, metallic hum that persisted throughout his talking and his listening.

Saturday Helms and Hill were moved down to the Eastland County jail, recovered enough (as one deputy said) so that they had a fifty-fifty chance not to crap-out on the way. Gonzaullas and Deputy C. D. Paine were in one car with Helms; Hill was in another with Deputy Parks and Cy Bradford.

The drive down to Eastland was quiet, for Hill was so confused and weary, still, that he didn't care what happened next, and Helms was beyond much conversation. Nothing mattered now except the running was over, and so was everything they had done for all their lives.

10 / THE SANTA CLAUS BANK ROBBERS were
dead or captured, but the casualty list
from the affair continued to grow. Saturday morning after
Helms and Hill were captured, County Judge W. F. Persley of
Graham was unloading a shotgun used in the manhunt when
it accidentally discharged. His leg was shattered and had to
be amputated.

The "dead robber" reward of the Texas State Bankers
Association was creating bizarre mischief. Out at Andrews, in
the Permian Basin oil fields, a petroleum company scout,
whose job it was to secure new leases for drilling wells, was
pursued by a zealous mob of citizens who, because he was a
stranger in the territory, said they were convinced he was a
bank robber. He survived a high-speed auto chase over miles
of unpaved roads, but caught thirty-seven shotgun pellets in
his legs, not to mention the damage done to his vehicle.

But the worst episode had taken place at Stanton, nearly
two hundred miles west of Cisco, along the T & P Railway.
To this small town had come a deputy sheriff of a neighboring
county, and a friend from Wink. They had picked up four
Mexican laborers who spoke little English, and by offering
them high-paying jobs had persuaded the Mexicans to get
in their truck and go to Stanton with them. The two Anglos
let the four out with instructions to wait "over there by that
building" until they ran a short errand. "That building"
was the Home State Bank. While a church house across town
mysteriously flamed up, drawing most of Stanton's twelve
hundred or so inhabitants, the two Anglos rushed up to the

four bewildered Mexicans and fired on them with pistols, killing Hilario Nunez and Norberto Flores, and seriously wounding Victor Ramoz.

The deputy and his friend proclaimed they had found the four men loitering about the front door of the bank preparatory to robbing it. They failed to mention their role in depositing the men there. But it was a little too raw even for Texas, where Mexicans were often held to be a dispensable commodity. Instead of being well-rewarded heroes, the two Anglos found themselves in jail—although the deputy repeatedly protested that he himself was an officer of the law and should have his word accepted about such things as Mexicans with felonious intent. At this point Governor Dan Moody (despite the fact his father-in-law owned a bank in Abilene) announced that he thought the "dead robber" reward was morally wrong. But the president of the bankers association announced right back that he thought it was good and useful. Bankers having considerable more power than governors, the reward stayed for the time.

In Cisco, little Frances Blasengame was still being interviewed and was still making cute remarks, which were picked up by newspapers all over the nation. A Fort Worth reporter, talking to her and her mother, mentioned Santa Claus, and Frances put in, "But really, that was not Old Santa. I saw his pants and they were just like Papa's."

Newspapers were full of first-person accounts of incidents during the robbery, the chase, and the capture. Deputy Sheriff Frank Whaley of Abilene aroused the ire of the three jailed robbers when he told, via print, how he had threatened the dying Louis Davis.

"After I found out Bit Bedford had died I told Davis, 'Unless you tell the names of your pals you will be left in the open cell and they'll string you up.'" But it hadn't worked, and the press reported solemnly that Louis Davis had died "true to the criminal's code of never revealing the names of his confederates."

An Eastland County grand jury hastily returned armed robbery and murder charges against Ratliff, Helms, and Hill, and called for quick trials. Governor Moody went through the formality of revoking the parole of Helms, and newspapers throughout Texas commented editorially that these three, all of them previously released from Huntsville, should serve as examples of the folly of light sentences and early paroles.

And at least two more Cisco men who had been participants in the gunfight at the bank came forward to say they were the ones who killed Davis. There were whispers that the bankers association was encouraging everyone it could to step out and claim the reward so as to muddle the true situation and allow it not to pay any reward at all.

On Saturday, January 7, a week after his capture, Robert M. Hill alone of the three bandits pleaded guilty to the armed robbery charge. Helms and Ratliff—Ratliff at least, Helms being still almost comatose and not expected to live—wondered if Bobby Hill was trying to pull something with this fast plea. The three men were not allowed to see one another, of course.

That night policeman George Carmichael died of the head wound he received in the bank fight.

Ratliff, in his cell, scratched a red *X* across the date and took his first solid food in ten days.

THE HEARINGS BEGAN January 16. Judge G. L. Davenport refused to move the trials from Eastland and ordered Ratliff to face the armed robbery charge first. District Attorney J. Frank Sparks would conduct the prosecution, assisted by his fire-eating deputy, Sterling Holloway. Governor Moody had made a move often practiced in Texas law. To avoid letting the defense hire some noted defense attorney—in this case Will W. Hair of Abilene—he had appointed him to the case as a special prosecutor.

But the notoriety of the Santa Claus bank robbery case was enough to attract some other noted defense lawyers, regardless. When Ratliff went to court he was represented by former judge J. K. Baker and J. Lee Cearley, of Cisco, both of whom had formidable legal reputations.

Rumor was passing around that the state was going to try and pin the deaths of both Bit Bedford and George Carmichael on Henry Helms. Most of the witnesses, the rumor reported, had said Helms was the one who stood at the back door of the bank and fired a pair of .44s, which was supposed to be the type of weapon that killed the policemen.

Ratliff's trial began January 23 in the old Eastland County courthouse. The old redstone structure was being torn down and a new, modernistic white brick one would be erected immediately, so Ratliff's trial was the last ever held in "Old Red." As a matter of fact, only the courtroom was in use, the rest of the building having already been evacuated.

Someone told Ratliff there had never been a legal execution of a man from Eastland County—that three men had been sentenced to die but none of them had actually been put to death.

"That's a record I don't plan to break," Ratliff told his lawyers.

The courtroom was mainly crowded with Cisco people who came over from ten miles west. Several of them expressed sympathy with Ratliff's mother, Mrs. Rilla Carter, who was well known and liked in Cisco from running a cafe there for three years.

Ratliff was brought to court opening day by Cy Bradford, who told him, "I'm sure getting tired of having to herd you around, big boy."

Alex Spears was the first person to testify in Ratliff's trial. He told how Santa Claus walked into the bank about 12:15 P.M. and refused to speak until Spears asked him twice how he was. "Then he just grunted," Spears said. The banker pointed out that Santa had gotten a pistol from Jewell Poe's teller's cage and stuck it in his suit, but none of the other witnesses could make a positive declaration that they had seen Ratliff use a gun during the hold-up.

Carl Wylie took the stand to describe his twenty-seven hours with the bandits, and told of Ratliff's wounds and how he acted during the manhunt. Rheba Tellet, who didn't look at him while she was on the witness stand, testified that she had fitted the Santa Claus suit to Ratliff that Thursday night before the hold-up.

The whole story was told, gradually. The state was not attempting to prove that Ratliff had killed anyone, just that he was part of the robber group—indeed, that he was the Santa Claus, and had worn a disguise because he was so well known in Cisco. The last witness was Mrs. Englin's daughter, Mrs. Simpson. She described the first visit of the fugitives to the Lash oil lease, and then the jury went out to ponder.

On January 27, at 2:40 P.M., the jury brought in its verdict. Ratliff seemed to have regained some of his old self-confidence, joking with the deputies and lawyers who spoke to him. The newspapers described him as being nattily attired in a brown suit with shirt, tie, and hat to match. It was evident that the nature of the testimony—staying away from his involvement in the deaths of the two officers—had given him some kind of assurance that he wouldn't face the electric chair after all.

He was found guilty of armed robbery and was given ninety-nine years—mainly because none of the witnesses actually testified having seen him fire a gun.

Marshall was overjoyed, and didn't try to conceal how he

felt. He turned to the ever-present Cy Bradford and ex-claimed:

"That's no hill for a high-stepper like me."

The people in the courtroom, and later the newspaper readers and the people on the streets around the territory, were reported to be disgusted at the sentence. A lot of the Cisco people, remembering how Marshall and Lee had eased off their first bank hold-up prison term, grumbled that Marshall would be out in five years if ninety-nine was all he drew down. They had expected blood for blood and they thought this trifling penalty would be the end of punishment.

They were rather remarkably off the mark.

HENRY HELMS's TRIAL was set for February 20, 1928. Ratliff's ninety-nine years for robbery seemed like a good omen to Helms. For the first time since the chase and capture, he thought he might not have to die, he told one member of his family. Helms had said little to anyone, and the press found him hard to interview. He was becoming the least publicly attractive of the men.

The trial was conducted in the Eastland City Hall because the old courthouse was being demolished. In fact, the Saturday before the Helms trial began, the celebrated incident of "Old Rip" the horned toad took place when the cornerstone of the old building was opened. "Old Rip" (for Rip Van Winkle and "Rest In Peace") had supposedly been placed alive in the cornerstone when it was laid in 1897. When the symbolic stone was opened in 1928, out crawled the lizard (despite the names "horned toad" and "horned frog," they are lizards), still living after thirty-one years. Whether it was a gentle fraud or not, Eastland suddenly found itself the center of international attention, and the double attraction of an immortal reptile and a death penalty trial brought crowds of people.

From the first, the state went for the throat, trying Helms. It said this man must die. His wife and their five children were present, but that didn't slow the prosecution from making Henry Helms bear the burden of the fatal shootings. He had recovered from his wounds but still came into the courtroom pale and drawn, well down from his accustomed 185-pound weight. His dark hair had turned very gray, and he looked much older than his thirty-two years. His oldest girl was twelve, just the age of Laverne Comer.

Alex Spears testified again, telling how Helms held two guns on Poe, and how he had stood at the side door of the bank, shooting up and down the alley. Freda Stroebel described how she was pushed in front of the bandits as a shield, then how she ran away but stumbled and fell, having to lie in the alley, seeing George Carmichael crumpled there mortally wounded, while shots flew over them "from all directions." One after another the witnesses put Helms in that back door, firing two pistols up and down the alley; they made him the one who handled the firearms most expertly and savagely, who gave the orders as to how to battle the ambushers outside.

Ellis Oder, a radio repairman, told of seeing Bit Bedford die, cut down by the gunman in the rear door of the bank. Even Carl Wylie's testimony sounded menacing as he told of Helms saying to him, when Carl was a hostage, "If we meet the right bunch we're going to do some shooting." Helms, the prosecutor pounded in, was a cold, bloodthirsty man who ached for a gunfight, and who relished the chance to shoot when the chance came.

It went to the jury at 4 P.M. Saturday and they reported back Sunday morning at 10:20. Their verdict was guilty—the sentence was death.

Helms, hearing the verdict, sat looking at his feet. His wife, Nettie, cried softly. Finally Helms asked one of his lawyers for a cigarette. He lighted it and began smoking. Nobody spoke to him as they waited for him to finish. When he stubbed out the cigarette a deputy reached out and tapped Helms, making a motion for him to stand. Then he hand-cuffed himself to the condemned man and led him back to the Eastland jail. As they were leaving the makeshift court-room Helms paused, looked back at the bench, and said to the deputy, "Well, they poured it on me."

They got back to the jail and a hush fell over the cell block where Helms was being kept when he and the deputy walked in. As the jailer was locking Helms back in a cell another inmate yelled over, "Well, Henry, what did they do?"

Helms, still standing, gripped the bars.

"They did it," he said.

ROBERT HILL'S TRIAL started March 19 in Eastland. By then Helms had been moved to the Dallas County jail and Ratliff was jailed in Abilene. The police didn't want to keep all three of the men in the same jail. It was still rather generally believed that the three bandits were part of a larger gang of bank robbers that might attempt to rescue them, or that a mob might try and grab them if all three were known to be available in the same jail.

Hill's attorney, appointed by the court, was L. H. Flewellen. He told the court that Hill was ready to confess all his sins, that he was willing to take the consequences. After three days of routine testimony concerning Hill's presence in the bank during the robbery, attorney Flewellen made a dramatic announcement: next day Robert Hill him-self would take the stand and give the whole story.

The courtroom was packed when Hill was sworn in the

following morning. He told the quiet room that Ratliff planned the robbery and that he had told them no one would resist the hold-up but Poe.

Hill told the story of his life. It had been a mess. His attorney called him, over and over, "the boy who never had a chance." His father had died while Bob was a baby and his mother remarried, but she died while he was still a little boy. He was taken to live in the State Training School at Gatesville, at age eleven, then returned for two more years at about age fifteen. The courtroom gasped when Superintendent C. E. King testified that there was no record of any offense having been committed by young Hill to have caused him to have been admitted or returned to the reformatory school. Apparently he had been sent there just because nobody could figure out what to do with him.

He said he had met the Ratliff boys while he was serving time at Huntsville for what Hill insisted was "the railroad job" in Eastland County early in 1926. When he got out of prison he found Mrs. Carter—the Ratliff boys' mother—who was like a mother to him, the boy who never had one.

Hill told all. From the shooting in the bank to the escape that first afternoon, through the long and weary drudgery of trying to evade the net thrown over the area by the lawmen, to his capture—he unburdened himself. He repeatedly told the jury that he never deliberately shot at anyone, but always fired over their heads; that he resisted the use of firearms on other occasions. He said he was the last man to leave the bank, and that when he got to the alley all the men who were fatally wounded were already down.

He told the courtroom audience that the bandits' plans were working all right at first, but that then they had heard shots coming from the east end of the alley—and they knew they were discovered.

"I then fired a number of shots over the heads of those

in the bank to stop anyone from coming in, but I never at any time tried to hurt any of them," Hill said from the stand.

Hill told how he drove the bandit car out of the alley. One remark of his drew a chuckle from the audience, which knew the details from having read the many newspaper stories.

"As I was starting the car, some old fellow stuck a shotgun in my face and attempted to shoot it. But for some reason he never did fire it." Cafe owner Day, in the courtroom, let out a big laugh.

Hill said he never did see Bedford, but he heard Marshall Ratliff say that Bit was kneeling at the east end of the alley and that they would have to go out by him. Hill said he believed he was making thirty or thirty-five miles-an-hour by the time the Buick had emerged and had started up Avenue D. Some of the spectators whistled; that was pretty fancy driving, under the circumstances.

Hill said that he and Alex Spears had been struck by the same burst, which came from outside the bank. Hill said he thought it was buckshot or small-caliber pistol fire.

Young Woody Harris testified that he had watched Hill closely when the bandits had stopped him and his family in their Oldsmobile. Every shot Hill had made, the boy said, was deliberately aimed over the heads of the posse. Another bank employe admitted that Hill fired only into the ceiling while they were inside the bank.

But there was some testimony to the contrary of the picture Hill attempted to paint of himself at the hold-up. Vance Littleton said Hill wasn't very gentle when he was herding him out that back door toward the Buick.

"Don't you run, big boy, or I'll shoot you in the back," Hill said to Littleton—who ran anyway, and escaped.

Hill came off the stand dripping wet with sweat. He had formed a friendship with one of the newspaper reporters covering the trial and he relied on that man's impressions as much as he did on his attorney's. When the jury retired, Hill said to the reporter, "This tells the story, doesn't it?"

The reporter said, "Yes, Bob, this is what it all boils down to."

Hill looked toward the door the jury had gone out through.

"You covered many murder trials?" he asked.

"Half a dozen or more," the reporter said.

"How many of them got the chair?" Hill asked.

"Well, in the first place, you've got to remember that a reporter wouldn't be covering just any case," the reporter said. "It would just automatically be pretty sensational. So naturally, the state was asking for the chair in every one of them I've covered."

"How many of them got the chair?" Hill asked again.

The reporter frowned, "Some did, some didn't. I don't remember."

Hill shook his head, "You remember. They all got the chair. These Texas juries . . ."

The reporter protested, "No, Bob, they didn't all get death. I guarantee you they didn't."

"I'll get death," Hill said.

"But there's no reason to think that," the reporter said. "You gave a good witness. They believed what you said. I think you convinced them."

"They weren't listening," Hill said. "They weren't interested. They had their minds made up before I ever opened my mouth."

"I don't see how in the world you can say that. I've seen too many juries," the newspaperman said.

"You wait," Hill said, and fell silent.

The jury sent word to the judge that a verdict was reached on the first ballot. The news created a stir in the courtroom.

Just before the verdict was read, and as the jurors were filing back to the box, Hill asked the reporter how long they had been out.

"Forty minutes, just about, by my watch," the reporter told him.

Hill winced. "That means death then."

"Not necessarily," the reporter replied.

"They told me . . . my own lawyers told me . . . that a quick verdict would mean death, in this case," Hill said dully, "and forty minutes is awful damn quick."

The reporter could only be silent.

A few seconds later, U. F. Casey, foreman of the jury, stood and addressed the judge. He did not look at Hill:

"Your honor . . . we find the defendant, Robert M. Hill, guilty as charged," he turned toward the table where Hill was seated, "and assess his punishment at ninety-nine years in the penitentiary."

Hill turned unbelievingly to his lawyer and the reporter:

"I got my two nines!"

It was announced by the state, a few days later, that Robert Hill would not be tried for murder. The state admitted its case was weak with so many witnesses willing to testify to Hill's reluctance to shoot at people. Besides, Hill's own appearance on the stand had been most effective, and a new trial, even for murder, would be little more than a retrying of the robbery charge. He went directly to Huntsville and began serving his sentence without lodging an appeal.

But his escape from the electric chair after he had accepted the inevitability of death seemed to have intensified rather than diluted Hill's moroseness. It was as if, having come so close to disaster, the discovery that he possibly need never have been life's outcast outraged him. He had chosen to die for his sins, and sudden forgiveness was as bitter as the former inevitability. He didn't deserve either.

So Hill, first a victim of fate, became a victim of rising expectation, and felt doubly cheated by life.

MARSHALL RATLIFF WENT on trial at Abilene on March 26 for the murder of Chief G. E. (Bit) Bedford. It was Ratliff's twenty-fifth birthday.

"You'll never see twenty-six," a bailiff told him, joking, on their way from the jail to the courtroom.

"I'll outlive you," Ratliff said back. "I'll be one of those model prisoners they talk about and I'll be out of the walls by the time I've got gray hair. You can't keep a good man like me down."

Judge W. R. Chapman, who was from another district, was supposed to have presided, but he got sick and once again Judge Davenport was on the bench. Ratliff's attorneys privately felt it to be a bad sign. They hoped to capitalize on their client's rather good-natured way of looking at things— he was beginning to look as strong and as handsome as before the manhunt—but the atmosphere of the courtroom, the minute they stepped into it, seemed ominous. The entire central West Texas region was angered that already in two of the three trials the culprits had escaped death. The crime seemed too huge for the blood of Helms alone to pay it off. The whole crime and manhunt business had been in the papers too long and too big to come to this sort of anti-climax.

Ratliff, now described by the press as "scar-faced" because of the bullet wound in his jaw, made the mistake of appearing to be jaunty and unrepentant. Under the rule of the court, his mother was forbidden to sit by him during the trial because she was being called as a witness; she could not, in fact, remain in the courtroom. So Rilla Carter paced up and down the halls of the Taylor County courthouse, having to catch the trial by snatches, seeing her son only at recess.

Rilla Carter told the court, when she was called to the stand, that she had been unfortunate in her marriages, not from her choice of mates, but by force of fate. Her first husband had died while the boys were young. She married again, but her second husband lived less than a year. The mother pointed to her three married daughters as being exemplary wives, and she said she knew the Cisco people would agree she had been a good fellow citizen. If she could just have controlled her boys.

Most persons thought Ratliff's mother had made a good impression with her testimony.

People around West Texas began remembering the family in letters and stories—especially Marshall. Some told that he had been married young and had children, but it didn't take. One person recalled, "He was a boy with lots of life and mischief, always wanting to do everything but keep order in the school room."

A woman said, "I remember one time in school I sat at a desk in front of him. He caused me so much disturbance until I had to move into another place to study my lessons."

There were darker hints: "When he was about fourteen or fifteen he was always passing dirty notes to the girls. In fact, I was always afraid of him."

One teacher, a Miss George, had tamed young Marshall, her former pupils said. "We just had a one-teacher school, with twenty-five or thirty students—just a country school. One day Marshall was causing trouble and disorder, and Miss George asked him several times to be quiet. He would not obey her. So she finally came back to where he was sitting, got him by the collar of his shirt, and pulled him out into the aisle and got him on the floor. She got on him and she really gave him a working over. One of his sisters, who was also in the class, got frightened and asked our teacher not to strike him again. The teacher let him get up off the floor, and he got into his seat, and didn't cause any more trouble at that time. They finally expelled him from school."

Mrs. Carter, talking to the press, said she was trying to get Marshall interested in religion again while he was in jail in Abilene during his trial. She said she had made him go to church when he was a boy, like you generally had to do with boys. For a while he had taken a real interest in church. They went to a strict fundamentalist church, too. He was especially interested in singing. Had a good voice, she considered it. He'd had trouble in school, Mrs. Carter admitted, fighting and getting in trouble with the teachers. She blamed them for a lot of the way he got to be, the ones that always seemed to have it in for him.

Every day his mother would hand Ratliff a new packet of materials which exhorted the fallen one to look to a Higher Power for his hope:

> *Where is thy hope, poor sinner?*
> *What are you going to do?*
> *Hope is a God-given anchor*
> *Lavished so freely on you.*

A feature writer for the Abilene *Reporter* carefully documented the poems and the words to the hymns she gave her son, quoting from those stirring spiritual ballads:

> *Hear the Gentle Spirit's call:*
> *Jesus is pleading for thee.*
> *There is pardon free for all:*
> *Jesus is pleading for thee.*

"He never had a chance," she said from the witness stand, refusing to cry as she testified. "He never had a chance. When he came back from prison they wouldn't give him a job . . . they wouldn't forget, or let him forget . . ."

Jesus is passing this way today;
Call him, weary one.
Ask the Savior to help you
Ere sinks life's setting sun.

Rilla Carter said she was fifty years old and that she hadn't seen her son for three months prior to the hold-up. She thought she might have been able to change things if she had been able to get him to come to her, or if she had been able to go to him. She never knew where he was. She felt there had been a time when things might have been different, when he might have been talked into straightening up and making something of himself.

"Almost persuaded," harvest is past!
"Almost persuaded," doom comes at last!
"Almost" cannot avail; "Almost" is but to fail;
Sad, sad, that bitter wail—
Almost—but lost!

Marshall wore a black bowtie to his murder trial. It looked good on him, the girls said. There were lots of them in the crowd that lined the way from the jail to the courthouse, and filled the courtroom itself. He had a rough kind of charm. He smiled a lot, even now, especially when he was not before the judge. There were plenty of girls would . . . but it was too bad, wasn't it? Too bad.

But if in sin you still linger,
Sad, sad your end.
Lost forever, lost forever;
O, how sad.

Most of the state's witnesses told their stories again, but this time the stories had peril in them for the man who had worn a smiling Santa Claus mask. It was established now that this was the man who was there, behind that mask, within that red suit. What he was being tried for went beyond that, and the atmosphere of the trial and the courtroom was tighter, tenser, than the judgment in Eastland had been.

Friday, March 30, the members of the jury went out to decide the fate of Marshall Ratliff, the Santa Claus bandit charged with the murder of Police Chief Bit Bedford and his associate policeman George Carmichael.

They were out two hours. There was never much question what their verdict would be. Their decision was death in the electric chair.

The high-stepper knew this hill was too steep. Marshall shrugged, the press reported, and gave a smile "of vast contempt."

His mother wailed out, "God . . . my boy. God! My boy!"

The bailiff came over to him and attached the handcuffs and shackles, then said to him, "Let's go, big boy."

Ratliff left the courtroom, then the crowd filed out and left the place deserted except for Rilla Carter, her head buried in her arms at the attorney's table, weeping over her lost child.

THE SANTA CLAUS BANK ROBBERY case was closed. Or as good as closed, they said. Hill wouldn't appeal, being only too happy to go down to Huntsville with ninety-nine years riding him instead of him riding that infernal black chair, Old Sparky. Helms had appealed his death sentence, but his appeal was denied.

Ratliff, too, appealed. But his ninety-nine years for robbery was affirmed in April 1928, and his motion for retrial on the murder charge was overruled later in the same month. He and Helms went to Huntsville to live on Death Row until their final motions for rehearing could be considered by the

Court of Criminal Appeals. "Then the date can be set to kill 'em," police and lawyers said, making a joke of the presumption that nothing was going to stop the state from having the lives of these two. The death verdicts would stand, everyone predicted: two lives for two laws. The case, you might as well say, was over; just a matter of very little time and a few hundred volts.

But the story wasn't half finished.

"I'LL NEVER RIDE Old Sparky," Ratliff told them from his cell on Death Row. "I never have believed I will."

"You crazy sonofabitch," another Death Row inmate warned him. "You're in here for killin' a law. They'll have your ass. There just ain't no way you can keep from dyin'."

Because the men on Death Row carried a kind of ghastly importance—they were considered already a part of the next world—they were given small privileges denied other inmates. His mother had brought Marshall a little wind-up phonograph and some records, mostly hymns, which he played at all hours as the mood moved him.

Going down Death Row to the green door that opened to the execution chamber was almost a common occasion in the Texas state penitentiary in those days. The death sentence was passed freely by Texas juries and was inflicted steadily. Not all governors were heartless, however. Most of them were in the habit of giving at least one stay of execution to every man who faced death. But a stay was only for thirty days, and meanwhile there was always another to "walk the last mile."

Death Row was a community. Their cells were the homesteads of those citizens who faced a common fate. The fate itself made their reasons for facing it unimportant. They were roughly affectionate toward each other and it was the impression they wanted to leave with their fellow inmates that dictated the manner in which most of them faced the green door. The outside world, even families, had ceased to exist as a determining force by that final night.

Some of the inmates were dour and silent. Some were mad from the time of their crimes, or had gone mad in the afterwards. These mad ones alone might not conduct themselves according to the code of the doomed. It was a code gotten from—what? Tradition? Legend? Or from some reservoir of common values created in humans by the uniqueness of that awesome experience? The mad ones might be forgiven if they did not share, or if they raved and nattered. But unforgivable was the citizen who held himself to be above the others, somehow better than his condemned fellows. Somehow, innocent, not of the crime as convicted (all considering themselves that), but innocent as an Adamic right; using this innocence as the explanation of why he was there, as a means of extrication not from the penalties of crime but from the undeviating wages of life. For these men were almost wholly from the mud ruts and alleys of living. To assert that man had had a chance at any time, that any agency but malignant fate had ever controlled him— not even some blind operation of chance, although this was the sole extenuating circumstance that might be allowed, that fate was as blind as it was malign—was to create an outrageous proposition, an infuriating upheaval of values; and these closely held, basic values were, no matter how illogical, all that kept most of the inmates from rattling insanity.

These doomed did not use any of the beliefs and assurances that sustain and sweeten the end of ordinary neighbors, although sometimes, for some gain, an inmate might become perfervid in religious conviction during his last days. The bright promises of the Unknown for these men could have no strength to compare to the Known already handed them by chance and a jury of their peers. "It has always been this way," they told themselves, "and the Hereafter can't be much different from the heretofore." It was a belief in devils, and only by questioning their devils could a fellow citizen of death's community make of himself an outcast.

THE BIG WOODEN, old-fashioned chair which used 1,200 volts to kill those who sat in it, was behind that green door, only a few feet from the death cells. In all prisons that used the electric chair as a means of execution, a tradition had risen that when the switch was thrown the load on the prison electrical system was so great the lights dimmed, and thus all the inmates throughout the prison knew another soul had been sent aloft, or somewhere, in release. But this was a myth which, if it ever was true, applied only to those earliest years when electrocution was new and the lighting systems were as crude as the death chamber. No, the truth was, it wasn't that much of an effort for an electric current to bring death to a man. The human body, at its mature extremes, was easily dysfunctioned of vital indexes. And by 1928 the electric chair had been the standard form of execution in Texas for decades. The execution chamber at Huntsville had its own set of electrical circuits and was not wired in to the rest of the prison; thus, if the lights suddenly dimmed, the death chair had nothing to do with it.

But the men on Death Row didn't need suddenly dimming lights to know what was going on behind the green door. They could count the minutes from the time one of their fellow citizens walked, or was dragged, through it and they could know almost to the second what was taking place those few yards away.

Marshall Ratliff had one phonograph record that he was

fond of playing on those drab nights when someone came by his cell, headed for human oblivion. It was a scratchy, nasal-voiced recording of *When the Roll Is Called Up Yonder* in which a tinny-sounding male quartet avowed:

When the trumpet of the Lord shall sound,
And time shall be no more,
And the morning breaks eternal, bright and fair;
When the saved of earth shall gather,
Over on the other shore,
And the roll is called up yonder—I'll be there!

Played on a portable phonograph at midnight to accompany the pace of the doomed and their guards, it should have been both frightening and infuriating. But no one ever asked that Ratliff be restrained from playing his dirge. The music and the man who played it, and his reasons for playing it, whatever they were, were all part of the community of death, and as such were not only pardoned but accepted as the right and proper procedure.

Perhaps the others had an understanding of Ratliff's need to play it which was as obscure as his own motivation for the act. Certainly no one felt Ratliff was making fun of them—or if he was they felt his joke's real point came directly at him even more than at his listeners. It was another kind of reassurance, a recognition, another kind of individuality to fit those solitary slivers of society.

THE MONTHS PASSED with Helms and Ratliff waiting to hear from the appeals court. On the first anniversary of the hold-up neither man had had the date set for his execution. Then it became 1929.

Robert Hill, meanwhile, was making a bad prisoner, although he had been sent to work on a prison farm and was not kept behind the walls. After a year in prison, he took an opportunity for flight, although he knew it would add to his time and might even bring him back to face a murder indictment. Orders went out to shoot Hill on sight, but his luck stayed with him; he was pulled off a freight train less than forty-eight hours after he had escaped, and returned to prison unharmed.

During the past year, the "dead bank robber" reward had been quietly withdrawn. The bankers association had defended it as necessary to combat the rash of hold-ups, but soon even judges and district attorneys came out against it. The infamous Stanton case was only one of many, several said.

Frank Hamer, a tough old Texas Ranger, first spoke out in March 1928: "I can't keep silent any more," he told the Associated Press, "I have seen too much. I know too many of the so-called 'bank robbers' who have died over this state who were nothing but pigeons, sent to their doom by grasping, dishonest men who are much worse than any of the bank robbers they profess to want to see die." Hamer asked that the bankers association, if it must give a reward, make it applicable only at night so the likelihood of a frame-up would be lessened and innocent bystanders would not be endangered.

"Hundreds of persons may die in the frantic attempts of some to claim the reward over what may well amount (by robbery) to a few hundred dollars." The Cisco robbery was an example of what he meant. Without the reward, he implied, few if any of the dead and wounded would have been struck down. He said some officers made up what he called "a murder ring" and nothing more.

The bankers association protested that live robbers, when captured, "seldom are identified, more rarely convicted, and most rarely kept in the penitentiary when they are sent there." But within a few weeks the "dead robber" reward was cancelled.

Frank Hamer, who was to receive greater notoriety a few years later in connection with the criminal career and deaths of Clyde Barrow and Bonnie Parker, was too ruggedly honest for the public to doubt him. When he said he couldn't stomach something, even the bankers of Texas had to revise their thinking.

HELMS WAS THE FIRST to hear the judgment of the Court of Criminal Appeals. He was taken to Eastland to hear the verdict, and there he was told that his conviction was affirmed. Judge Davenport set September 6, 1929, as the date for his execution. Helms was driven back to Huntsville by Eastland County Sheriff Virgil Foster, who had been elected to the office in 1928.

"Henry, you might as well prepare to meet thy God," Virgil said he told him on the way back to the penitentiary.

"You'll be seeing me again, I promise," Helms told him.

"I'd like to know how you think it, except if I come down to witness your electrocution."

Henry Helms shook his head, "I don't know, right now, but something will turn up; something will change things. I don't deserve to die for what I did. It's not right."

"The judge and jury said you did," the sheriff told the prisoner.

"But it's not right, anyhow. They had it in for me. I was the one they went after."

"Hell, looks to me like they went after old Ratliff, too. He got the same thing you did, big boy."

"He'll not burn neither. We didn't none of us fire the shots that killed those policemen. It was their own goddam people did it. You know it and I know it, too. Everbody knows it. It was those crazy sonsofbitches shooting every which way."

"I don't know nothing of the kind, Henry. All I know is what the judge and jury says. They said it was you. You and Ratliff. You brought it on yourself, whoever it was. There wouldn't have been no shootin' if you and your bunch hadn't done what you did to begin with."

Helms rode in silence most of the rest of the way, but Virgil Foster admitted he mumbled to himself from time to time, and wasn't nearly as friendly as he had been, not that it made much difference to the sheriff. Men heading back to Huntsville after having an appeal denied weren't ordinarily given to being overjoyed at the prospect.

Helms, his last hope of appeal and reversal of the death penalty being lost, began letting go. September was just a few weeks away, and the man who had shown the least emotion, the least of either fear or hope, began to show the most dismay. Despite his boast that the sheriff would be seeing him again, there was really nothing in sight to cause even that faint whiff of optimism.

Then a man named Harry Leahy, whom neither Helms nor Ratliff had known outside the walls, changed their outlook for them, giving both the condemned men a new idea and a new inspiration. And continued the story of the Santa Claus bank robbery for several chapters.

HARRY LEAHY HAD BEEN convicted of murder, and because there were no acceptable circumstances to change the verdict—such as finding his wife with another man, or having his victim reach for a handkerchief which might conceivably have been a dangerous weapon (reasonable alternatives under Texas law)—he got the death sentence. It really is not of great importance as to why he got the death sentence or from whence it came; the important fact is that he drew the ultimate penalty and was sent to the state penitentiary to have it delivered on his head. Thus he joined Helms and Ratliff on Death Row in Huntsville.

But Harry Leahy didn't stay in that tiny community for the ultimate release planned for him on that first visit. His lawyer discovered a little known statute in Texas law, a sanity escape clause. It provided that even if a man had been sane at the time of a crime and at the time of his sentence, if he were found to have become insane later, then the death penalty must be postponed until such time, if ever, as he regained his sanity. It was a last resort, which offered no freedom but did have hope in it. Postponement was better than execution.

Friends thus filed an affidavit that Leahy had become insane as a result of being confined. Their petition alleged that he was now insane and should not be executed in that state of mind. The lower courts refused to accept the suit and eventually it took a ruling in the affirmative from the Supreme Court of Texas to get Leahy off Death Row and back to where he was sentenced in order to undergo a sanity hearing.

He had become incoherent, had thrown away his food, and resisted all efforts to feed him, and acted in what was considered to be a generally deranged manner. At the trial, those who knew him before his conviction testified that Leahy had always shown signs of mental weakness and had acted peculiarly any time he was under stress. And what could be more distressful, they pointed out, than going through a murder trial, the subsequent conviction, and then confinement on Death Row? The petition and the sanity trial immediately made headlines all over the state, and the newspapers, and other guardians of public morality, were outraged. The very idea that a criminal could become insane was repugnant to the Texas public. Of course a criminal was insane, letter writers to the editor pointed out; ordinary sane people didn't go around committing crimes in the first place. But to escape punishment by making a virtue of their insanity—absurd!

But once Leahy filed his suit and it was accepted by the Supreme Court, the idea became popular throughout Texas. Almost every inhabitant of Death Row—except a few of the colored who as a rule had no lawyers—got excited. (Some on Death Row, also, were too insane to understand the possibilities inherent in such a ruling.) The inmates began getting in touch with their families, or their lawyers, and several appeals were filed under the sanity clause for hearings. At least one man won his case without much trouble.

But as is so often the story with pioneers, Leahy's own efforts failed. His sanity hearing resulted in his being certified sane, therefore worthy of execution because he would thus grasp the import of his punishment and presumably learn a lesson from it. When he was brought back to Death Row everyone there already knew about the trial result. What they wanted to know was what went wrong, and why, and how could such things be made not to go wrong?

"I just couldn't act the part," Leahy is supposed to have confessed to Henry Helms. "They finally got to me. I couldn't keep going."

"Well, watch me put it over," Helms is supposed to have said back.

HELMS HAD TO MAKE his point quickly; his execution date was only a month away. So, by whatever motivation, he apparently did. He grew lank and didn't shave or get his hair cut. He began to hum and to sing disjointed melodies all day in his cell, turning a strange eye on the jailer and his guards. One tune, a kind of chant, became dominant, as Helms sang in a broken voice, "I ain't a-gonna sing no more, no more . . ." He would go through the familiar melody a few times, then pause and shout, "Aye, aye, captain!" or merely bellow out, "Hey!" One day the guards found his cell littered with minute shreds of newspaper. From then on Henry Helms carefully stripped, then particled, any piece of paper, no matter how large or small, he could get his hands on. Even his Bible, given to him by Nettie when he had first gone on trial, was torn into confetti, a page at a time.

Prison authorities, of course, smelled a rat. They laid traps for him, hiding to observe his actions when he thought none of them was in sight. At first the guards reported that his singing stopped once they were out of earshot, but the truth was, the singing never stopped and the guards finally admitted it didn't.

"I'm determined the sonofabitch ain't going to do it," one guard told the superintendent. "He can get as crazy as a bedbug, but it ain't going to be *me* that has to admit it to some goddam judge that'll turn him loose."

"There isn't any judge going to turn Henry Helms loose," he was assured, "crazy or not. That boy's gotten too much attention."

But as for Helms, "Well, watch me put it over," he was supposed to have said, and if he said it he meant it. Perhaps he really did go mad, a self-induced madness or just the natural results of living as he had for the past two years—or all his life. There is something to the idea that any criminal mind is unstable—as we define things socially—to begin with. Helms had certainly undergone the kinds of tensions and pressures physically and mentally that few persons ever have to face: the months out of prison with insufficient income for his large family and the pressure of needing a job and not being able to keep one; the days before the robbery; the emotional explosion of the event itself; the lengthy, harassing manhunt and chase; the trial for murder with its too-pre-dictable finish. The stay on Death Row was possibly the least of his ordeals.

By late August Helms's family had filed an appeal under the sanity statute and it had been accepted. Helms was to appear once more before Judge Davenport, this time for examination of his mental processes.

Sheriff Foster and two other officers went to Huntsville and picked him up for the trial in Eastland. They claimed that not once, on the trip back to West Texas, did he sing. But they were all devout police officers, so we will never know whether they heard him sing or not. Something would have kept the sound from their memories, present or no. The important fact to them, of course, was that Helms was at-tempting to thwart justice and the efforts to give him the end he deserved.

His first appearance in court was shocking, even for those people, including the press, who were prepared, or thought they were prepared, for the sight of Helms feigning insanity. Even Judge Davenport was taken aback. A gaunt, bushy-headed man, wild-eyed and swaying, was propped up in front of the bench to be asked the routine questions that begin any kind of legal hearing. Helms's answers were sounds without meanings.

He continued to sing his song, "I ain't a-gonna sing no more, no more," in a low but penetrating monotone. He shouted, in varying degrees of loudness, "Aye, aye, captain!" at those inopportune intervals. Sometimes the shout rang out just as some official was making a point, sometimes it chimed in as if to answer a query by the judge, or to comment on someone else's remarks. The spectators, who had come to scoff, went out confused and annoyed.

"That sonofabitch has dodged the chair for too long. It just don't seem right, him killing Bit Bedford and now claiming to be crazy and not burning: I don't care how looney he is."

That was the consensus: insane or not, Helms ought to pay the penalty—the Supreme Penalty. It was almost a Christian obligation on the part of the court and the jury to make the decision quickly and firmly; there were others who needed to be taught the lesson, yea, even unto the second and the third generations.

While the witnesses went to the stand and left it, giving contradictory testimony, as in all sanity hearings, Helms chanted or tore paper or did both. He reached over and snatched a legal document from the hands of his own lawyer and reduced it to shreds, shouting, "Hey! Captain!" in triumph as he threw the bits toward the ceiling.

Hammering him down from the bench did no good—was impossible. Judge Davenport maintained his dignity with difficulty, remarking privately that he thought a good clout behind the ear might bring Helms back to his senses, but that he, the judge, was too old a man to give it.

Helms's sing-song was so incessant, so uneven and unpredictable and thus so upsetting to those around him, that it became fashionable for spectators to leave the courtroom and vomit. Especially the women, who made up a big part of the crowd.

"I'll tell you, if I'd had to stay in there one more minute they'd be taking me out of there cuckoo, too."

"You think, then, that Henry Helms *is* crazy?"

"For heavens sake, no. I don't think he's any more crazy than you are. I mean, he'd drive *me* crazy, listening to him and that weird, silly singing he's doing."

"You mean then," the reporter asked, "that you could be made insane watching him and listening to him, but that there is no way Helms himself could have been driven insane by what he has undergone?"

The ex-spectator became cool, we are told, her eyes and

mouth tightening: "Now listen, Mr. Reporter, you trying to put words in my mouth? I mean I know good and well that Henry Helms is trying to escape the electric chair, and so do you. Now if that's crazy well it's crazy like a fox, as they say —whatever that means."

Eventually the judge ordered Helms cleaned up, if he couldn't be shut up. His lawyers had done everything they could to keep this from happening, but when the bench finally ordered it there was no way to avoid the action. Back in the jail, where it took place, Helms fought, singing and shouting, laughing and screaming for the captain, but despite his struggle, four deputies gave him a haircut and a shave. A newspaper account of the day before, after that haggard and harrowing court appearance, read: "It is difficult to believe that this weird, pathetic creature had been a deadly killer just a few months before." Sentiments like this, the lawmen felt, could lead to difficulties.

So Helms was returned to the courtroom looking cleaner, neater, and a bit meeker, but his chant was unchanged. So long as he wasn't touched or disturbed he did nothing but repeat his musical routine. When a bailiff tried to take his arm, however, he twisted and fought until subdued—which was often as not a fairly simple matter, but highly disconcerting to the hearing.

From the first the family had gotten nowhere with their son and husband. His mother seeing him initially on his return from Huntsville, had said, "Henry, don't you know me?" He ignored her, shouting only, "Aye, aye, captain!" after she turned away crying. Nettie brought their eighteen-month-old baby for Henry to see, but he gave both wife and child a blank stare.

The Reverend Helms testified his son had run away from home at age eleven, then just as suddenly returned, with no explanation of why he left or where he went. Two years later the boy had left home again with the same abruptness and remained away for quite a spell.

"Could it have been, Reverend Helms, that you were too strict in his upbringing?" the Helms lawyer asked.

The minister shook his head. "We just done what the Bible said do. Henry never had good cause to go bad. He was just queer, that's all. From the first."

His mother said the same thing of the man on trial. He had been not so much a discipline problem as peculiar. "We believe in 'spare the rod, spoil the child,' but that wasn't what was wrong with Henry. It was deeper than that, like he didn't know what was real and what was not. It was in his head."

After his marriage, the court heard, Henry left the house one morning, climbed into the hayloft of a barn, and refused to rejoin the human race.

"He couldn't be coaxed nor cajoled to come down. He just stayed up there till he'd made up his mind to come down. It was the better part of three days."

"What seemed to be the cause for this behavior?"

"Wasn't ne'er cause at all that we could tell. He'd been happy enough, him and Nettie. He just got tired of people and climbed up in the loft where none of us could get to him. We thought he was mad at somebody, at first, but he wasn't. He come down of his own accord finally."

The state, countering Helms's claim of insanity, relied on a group of five superintendents of insane asylums—all state employes, of course—who testified that they had examined the man and considered him sane. Dr. T. B. Bass, of the Abilene State Hospital, gave a measured, telling medical testimony concerning the nature of mania. Henry Helms, he said, had supposedly been mad for seventeen days. Dr. Bass then refuted the possibility from the stand:

"There is not the foul odor about the mouth which comes with swift and acute mania."

An alienist, hired by the defense, protested that Helms was obviously of unsound mind, no matter how long or why it had been acute. But as one juryman noted, this fellow had been hired by the lawyers "to say precisely that."

It didn't take long. Twenty minutes after the jurors had filed out of the courtroom to consider what had been seen and heard, they returned with their verdict. Henry Helms was of sound mind and should be executed in the electric chair by the state of Texas.

The silence in the courtroom was broken by the chant, "I ain't a-gonna sing no more, no more . . ."

The execution would take place as set previously: September 6, 1929. It was now August 31.

Henry's mother, carried from the courtroom by her husband and children, became hysterical. Nettie began the task of scraping together everything she could lay hands on so as to be able to stay in Huntsville near her husband during his last week. Just about everything the family had, including the money of Henry's father and mother, had gone for legal aid in this last attempt to beat the shadow of death. All Nettie wanted now was just this last week; not allowed at his side, but as near as she could be.

ALL THE WAY BACK to Huntsville, with Sheriff Foster and his deputies, he had sung.

> *Oh, I ain't a-gonna sing no more, no more,*
> *I ain't a-gonna sing no more . . .*

"You can turn it off now, Henry," the sheriff said. But Helms looked at him uncomprehendingly. "Aye, aye, captain!"

"Henry, there's no point in you wastin' your breath on us. We know you're crazy." The deputies laughed.

"I hope to God we don't have to make this trip over again," one of them said.

"Don't worry. We won't," Sheriff Foster assured him. Henry stopped singing, looked at Foster, and remarked, "You said that before—remember?"

"But this time . . ." the sheriff started talking, then frowned, but Henry was singing again and didn't pay the slightest attention to another word of the conversation in the automobile.

Back at the state penitentiary in Huntsville, Helms was placed in the Death Row cell nearest the green door. He talked to Ratliff from time to time, and he wrote out a kind of letter and will to his family. He was allowed to see Nettie but not his children. He seemed to be more upset about this than anything else. The oldest girl was getting to be quite a lady now and he kept insisting she should have the final advice of a father as she approached womanhood. But the prison officials were adamant.

His family pleaded with Dan Moody to give Henry a stay of execution, to prolong his life for at least the customary thirty days. The governor waited until the final day to make public his decision. He announced that he felt that Helms had had every chance to prove he should not die and that the condemned man had failed to do so.

Late on the afternoon of September 5, just before Henry Helms was to die at midnight, the assistant warden came down Death Row and stopped in front of his cell.

"Henry . . . Henry," he said, "Listen to me."

The humming and chanting continued, going on like a rope hawser being pulled endlessly out of a hole: "I ain't a-gonna sing no more, no more . . . ain't a-gonna sing no more . . ."

"Henry . . . can you hear me? We just got the word. You hear me?"

His eyes did not move. Only his mouth opened and closed, mumbling quietly, "Ain't a-gonna sing no more, no more . . ."

"The governor is going to let you die, Henry."

Suddenly the chant stopped. Henry Helms looked up through the cell bars at the warden.

"The governor—he's going to let you die."

There was no sound, no movement.

"What do you want for your last supper, Henry? We'll give you anything you want."

Helms continued to stare at the warden without speaking or moving his head.

"How about some fried chicken? You want some good old fried chicken for your last supper?"

Helms shook his head from side to side. "Bring me cabbage and sausage," he said softly. "Nettie knows how I like it. She can fix a pot."

The warden looked uneasy. "What else you want, Henry? That's not all, is it?"

"Tomatoes," he said. "You got any tomatoes?"

"We got canned ones, I reckon," the warden said. "May still be some fresh ones coming in from the farm. If there isn't, you want some canned ones?"

Helms shook his head in acceptance, "And coffee. How about coffee?"

"Sure, Henry. We got gallons of coffee. Good coffee, too. Roast it right here on the place."

"And I want some pie," Helms said, dropping his head for the first time. "Any kind of pie they've got."

"We'll fix you up, Henry," the warden said. "We'll have you the best meal you've ever had in your whole life." He went down to the prison kitchen to have Helms's wishes made up.

Later, when the food was brought to his cell, Henry didn't eat but a bite or two of any of it. "Nettie fix this?" he asked the guard who had brought the food and stayed outside the cell to watch him eat. The guard shrugged, but Helms didn't even listen for an answer. When he was finished with the food he asked the guard to give Ratliff his pie, but the guard didn't.

A short time later Henry Helms was taken from the cell, bathed and shaved. While he was out of the cell, it was carefully searched, and a crude weapon was found—a big nail wrapped in strips of torn blanket to form a handle and make a kind of dagger. Prison officials were of the opinion he had intended using it on himself if he had had the nerve.

The Reverend Helms had asked to be allowed to pray with his son, but the warden refused. He said he had found such cases to be harder on the survivors than it was worth. A Baptist chaplain did come and kneel in the cell and pray for Henry's forgiveness in the sight of God, but Helms merely watched him. When a Catholic priest came to his cell, Helms showed a slight bit more interest. The priest had established a meager sort of relationship with him during the long tenure on Death Row. But this night the priest got only silence, despite the fact that Helms bowed his head when he prayed.

The assistant warden returned to the cell to go through the formality of reading the death warrant. A number of newspaper reporters had asked permission to attend the execution—viewing the death from a glass enclosure provided by the state for the official witnesses.

The warden told them, "The only way you boys can make it is either to be official state witnesses, or to be there at the request of the condemned man. If you can get Henry to say okay to it, we can let five of you watch."

The assistant warden went back to Helms's cell and explained the situation to him. He asked if Helms wouldn't designate the reporters as his witnesses. Helms just looked at him, then shook his head in refusal. "They can wait," he said softly.

He had been very quiet after returning from his death bath and shave, standing without moving or making a sound or sitting almost motionless in his cell. Then, a short time before midnight, two guards entered the cell to take him for his walk to the green door.

"On your feet, Henry. We're going in," one of the guards said.

Helms swung around and began battling furiously. The two guards, not expecting a fight, were knocked aside at first, and help had to be called. Even after Helms was subdued, he pushed his heels into the floor and had to be dragged, kicking and fighting from time to time, the entire thirty feet to the execution chamber. The four sweating guards finally slammed him into the electric chair and popped down the restraints. Just as quickly, Helms became calm.

The inside of the death chamber was white, the overhead lights dazzling. Only Henry's labored breathing could be heard after he had been strapped in the chair and the electrodes clamped in place.

The execution already delayed by Helms's furious resistance, now had to be rushed back on schedule. The warden (talking to reporters afterward) said he asked Helms for any last words. "The man had nothing to say." Another official pulled a black cap over Helms's head. The warden moved away and lifted his hand.

The executioner, standing behind a curtain in back of the death chair, could not be seen and was not known except to a few high prison officials. At the sign of the warden's hand, the executioner's own hand closed the big, copper knife switch and 1,200 volts were fed through the body of the man in the chair. Hit by this load of energy, the body twisted and jerked against the restraints for perhaps a minute, then it remained at a rigid attention. For ten minutes the volts continued battering away at the animal resistance strapped there in the seat. Then the current stopped, the dynamo stopped humming.

A doctor in attendance stepped forward, pulled away the blue denim prison shirt and put a stethoscope to the body's chest. There was no vital response. The doctor stepped back and made the ritual announcement:

"I pronounce Henry Helms dead."

The officials opened the little green door from the inside, stepped out, and walked silently down the dimly lighted hallway that is called Death Row. The men in the cells pretended sleep or lay without turning their heads as the procession passed. The body in the execution chamber would be taken out another way.

Then it was quiet. None of the others seemed to have noticed that for the first time since the Santa Claus bank robber had been there, the death march down "the row" had not been accompanied by the playing, on Ratliff's phonograph, of *When the Roll Is Called Up Yonder* (*I'll Be There*).

11 / MARSHALL RATLIFF HAD a little more time. The date for his execution had not been set. In Cisco, some of the citizens were worried that he, too, might try for a sanity hearing. His death sentence had been held up too many months already, they felt, by legal foolishness and manuevering.

Then from Huntsville came the word—Ratliff, too, was trying the sanity dodge. From the night of Henry Helms's execution, the Santa Claus bandit began changing: glum, mumbling, jerking his head constantly, refusing to eat. He also seemed to be losing the use of his hands and feet, and he talked deliriously when he talked at all.

The other inmates of Death Row, who might be expected to take a cynical view of any efforts their fellow convicts might make to escape the hot ride, were genuinely puzzled by Ratliff. At first they all assumed his was an act. But his response to Helms's death was too genuine to be assumed. Fear had walked almost visibly into Ratliff's cell that night, and for the first time in his life he had faced a reality.

Not long after Helms's execution, Bob Hill escaped for the second time, this trip with seventeen others. Most of them were recaptured within a few hours, but not Hill. Ratliff, told of Hill's escape, gave no sign of recognition.

"That might have been you, big boy. If you'd have played ball," a guard said. Ratliff replied, "I have sinned against the Holy Ghost and have fallen short of the grace by which we are saved."

"Oh, come on now. Don't start that scripture crap," the

guard said. "We know you're just as sane as anybody here."

"Many shall come in my name, saying 'I am Christ' and shall deceive many," Ratliff said.

In October, Rilla Carter filed a petition in the Walker County court at Huntsville for a sanity hearing for her son. The Eastland County officials were furious when they heard about it. They looked upon the filing for a sanity hearing as a sneaky stunt, an attempt to keep Ratliff's fate from being decided by his fellow citizens of Eastland County who knew him so well. Judge Davenport hurriedly issued a bench warrant to get Ratliff out of the penitentiary and bring him back to Eastland, not for a sanity hearing but to stand charges of having robbed, with firearms, Ellis Harris, the owner of the Oldsmobile, back there that first day of the hold-up.

At this the Walker County judge became enraged—too late to stop the Eastland officials, however.

"This is nothing but kidnapping," the Walker County judge told members of the East Texas press. "Those people are bound and determined this man shall not be tried for insanity. They have overreached the machinery of the courts."

Davenport replied calmly that Walker County had no jurisdiction in the case and had had no business accepting Rilla Carter's petition in the first place.

The legal harangue notwithstanding, Marshall Ratliff was back in the Eastland County jail by late October, suspended between heaven and earth: no date set for the new trial, no date set for his execution under the old death sentence, and no sanity hearing set, although a new petition was being drawn up for presentation in Eastland County court.

There were rumors that Ratliff, like Helms, had conferred with others in Huntsville, had talked with the men who failed in their last-minute efforts to prove they had gone insane; had studied their methods and decided where they had gone wrong. He was reported to have said, "I'll make it. I'll stick to it." That was to be his game: never to flinch, never to budge, never to give up. He was going to be crazy come hell or high water, the reports whispered; be crazy by sheer force of his determination. Just to BE crazy—not to have to act it or pretend. Be. Be   be   be.

All along, in Cisco, there had been more personal animosity toward Marshall Ratliff than toward the rest of the hold-up men. Henry Helms had gotten no sympathy and was heartily disliked, even despised, but Ratliff drew the active fury of the man on the street. The town considered him a smart-aleck and a know-it-all ne'er-do-well. On top of that, they were outraged that he had used a sacred symbol like Santa Claus to cloak his participation in a heinous crime— and that crime deliberately perpetrated against a man like Alex Spears, who had befriended the scoundrel in Ratliff's hour of need by going bail on his Valera bank robbery case.

Everything Ratliff had done had inflamed civic passion against him: his was the mastermind that planned the deed; his was the gun that fired a fatal shot—or all the fatal shots, and he had used two helpless little girls as shields against the rain of bullets he knew very well could cut them down.

For almost two years they had asked themselves, "Well, when is he going to die?" One after another their efforts to kill him had gone a-glimmering: when he was a fugitive, and fair game for any rifle; then his two trials, and his condemnation; the refusal of the appeals court to hear his case—but still he was alive. Now, this sanity thing was the goad that roused the most fury. He was cheating the public out of something it felt it had earned.

But when the Eastland County officers delivered Ratliff to the jail from Huntsville and reported to the sheriff, they were not so all-fired sure his time *had* come.

"Sheriff, it's hard to explain about Ratliff. He's nuts."

"What do you mean? You mean he's got so good at it he's fooled even you?"

"Naw, it's not just that. There's something wrong with him. I mean really. You just can't keep that kind of control over yourself. Like, you can stick pins in him," looking around the sheriff's office quickly to see if there was anyone who could hear, "and you can stick a lighted cigarette to his skin, see? He don't move or even notice."

"Maybe if he's that dead then he can ride out Old Sparky."

"I wouldn't be a damn bit surprised. He's spooky, I'll tell you."

The sheriff called Pack Kilborn, the jailer, and asked him to pay close attention to Ratliff.

"You keep an eye on that boy all day," the sheriff said. "Sometimes you might put a watch on him so he won't know it. See how he acts when nobody's looking."

Pack Kilborn could be depended on to analyze a prisoner's acts if he was trying to pull something. Pack, too, was one of the old-time lawmen who had to be tougher than the men they worked with to survive. For thirty years he had been a law enforcement officer, some of that time as sheriff of Eastland County. Now he and his family were living in the jailer's apartment in the jail house and Pack was running the jail well.

Ratliff was dumped into a cell bunk like a lifeless man when he arrived from Huntsville on October 24, 1929. He had to be carried from the car. Only his eyes were open and staring. He said nothing when asked a question, when goaded or poked. When he was raised from the bunk to a sitting position his head rolled from side to side. His feet and hands dangled useless, and if he was left erect on the side of the bunk, he would topple over on it but his feet would remain on the floor, and he would stay in that contorted position until someone placed him out straight.

"Ain't that a pitiful sight?" Pack asked Uncle Tom Jones, his assistant jailer. "You reckon that boy's really able to control himself that good?"

"I ain't seen its like," Uncle Tom said, "but then, these crazy people trying to escape the chair are a new sight to me anyways."

"But Uncle Tom, you've been a law for almost as long as I have. You've seen crazy folks in jail before, haven't you?"

"You know I have, Pack. I've handled many a one right here in this very jail house, waiting to take 'em to Wichita Falls or to Terrell to the asylum. Had 'em shit the beds and all over theirselves; tear their clothes off. You remember that Ranger woman we had, claimed Jesus Christ was coming in her cell sleeping with her ever' night?"

Pack laughed, "I always figured it might have been our trusty, Rex Myers, except I couldn't never figure out how even a crazy woman could get old Rex mixed up with Jesus Christ."

Uncle Tom shook his head, "Well, whether he's crazy or not, or just pretending, that Ratliff is going to be a chore to handle."

The prisoner was even more of a problem than the jailers had imagined. Most of the time to do anything with him took both men, because Ratliff was a relatively large person. Pack and Uncle Tom had to bathe and dress him, and take him to the commode and then wipe him. Feeding him was an even bigger problem. Pack Kilborn would put him in a sitting position and hold his head still while Uncle Tom put the food in his mouth with a spoon. Ratliff did eat; he would chew his food and swallow most things, choking only often enough to make both of them suspicious.

"Let's try something, Tom," Pack said, down in his office just before they were to go up and feed Ratliff. "Let's try something definite—something dangerous to him. See how he acts."

"All right, Pack. I think we've got every right to. I think we deserve a try, hard as we've had to work keeping that crazy bastard alive."

That night, as they were holding him in a standing position in his cell, the two jailers suddenly dropped their hands and let go of the limp prisoner. Ratliff swayed slightly, then toppled straight out, pitching full length to the concrete floor with no effort to catch himself or to break his fall. His face was skinned and a knot was raised on his head, but he didn't moan or move afterward.

The two jailers hurriedly pulled him up and swung him around, back onto his cell bunk.

"We better be careful what we try if we try anything again," Pack said, winking behind Ratliff's back.

Rilla Carter was the only one of the family who was allowed in to see Marshall. Her visits were fruitless. She got no more recognition than did Pack and Uncle Tom.

"Son," she said softly, stroking his face. "Can you hear me? Can you hear your mother?"

"I have sinned against the Holy Ghost, for which there is no forgiveness . . ." the mouth babbled but the eyes showed no comprehension.

"Don't feel bad, ma'am," Pack told her, watching Mrs. Carter's efforts to communicate with the prisoner. "He says that all the time. That and other things from the Bible about the Holy Ghost. He says a lot about the Holy Ghost."

He shook his head with a laugh, "Sometimes it gets sort of uncomfortable, I'll tell you. Like last night, while I was in here putting him to bed and talking through the bars to Uncle Tom, he just blurted out to me, 'Knowledge puffs you up like a stumbling block.'"

Uncle Tom said to her, "I've heard him talking something

like in tongues, too. One of the other boys in here says it's Latin and that your boy's a Catholic. That true?"

Mrs. Carter shook her head, "He's not a Catholic. We're Church of Christ. But I think he used to talk to a priest down at Huntsville. There's one down there the men get along with pretty well, they tell me."

Pack thought that maybe Ratliff, hearing them talk about Latin, would be tempted to try and use some again and that way they could know it was a put-on, but the prisoner never again repeated the foreign-sounding phrases he was reputed to have uttered. Mostly he merely babbled, and not even his scriptural-sounding utterances could be understood.

Food seemed to be the only thing that reached his senses. He still noticed when he was being fed, and he ate rather well. Pack, for this reason, remained doubtful of the veritability of his torpor.

"A man's got to be pretty smart to keep eating like Ratliff does," Pack told the sheriff. "Now, I've handled these crazy ones before who wouldn't eat a bite. They'd just flat starve to death before they'd take a bite. I'll be suspicious of Ratliff as long as he eats."

Feeding Ratliff, ten days or so after he had arrived, Kilborn suddenly jabbed at him with the fork, directly at his eyes. The tines barely stopped short of the pupil, but there was no twitch. Pack began to worry, then, and began feeding Ratliff with a spoon only. He was afraid he might put out an eye experimenting if he kept on using a fork.

"I guess you want to be fair," he told Uncle Tom, "but I just hate to think he's sitting there laughin' inside, putting one over on us."

Often the two jailers would cross Ratliff's feet a certain way when they lifted him onto his bunk at night. He would be in the same position the next morning. Myths began to build around his fantastic condition. Over in the new courthouse, Joe Jones, the county attorney, quoted his uncle, Uncle Tom, as telling the extraordinary trials Ratliff had passed.

"Uncle Tom vows he's taken pins and touched his eyeball with them, and Ratliff didn't move or blink," he said.

"You say the eyeball . . . how about squeezing another ball I can think of. Take a pair of pliers, like I heard they did to that old driller they caught cheating at dice that time at the Blue Mouse in Ranger. During the boom. You ever hear that story?"

Everyone laughed. "I think maybe you could do that to a corpse and bring him up to a sittin' position," someone said. The story of the contused testicle was well known around Eastland County—and a dozen other oil boom communities where it was also believed to have occurred. "Now he's growin' three balls," was the way the anecdote usually ended. The courthouse loungers agreed it wouldn't be a fair test of insanity, regardless.

"I guess you can say Ratliff is winning," they concluded.

The idea of a constant, secret watch had been tried. One of the jailers would creep up the stairs to the second floor, remaining hidden on the landing, then watch Ratliff's cell which was just to the right of the stairs. He never moved, or if he were babbling, he never stopped or said anything intelligent.

The babbling came and went. One day it went on for hours and didn't even stop when Tom beat on the steel sides of the cell with a big key.

"I had them two six-shooters . . . God have mercy . . . I've been executed. I am Death . . . I've been saved, but they've stolen my Bible . . . they've stole my pretties . . . why don't you give me back my Victrola? I've been saved from death. Praise God . . . I'd sure like a bite of that orange . . . emptied them first . . . hot coffee, Lord Jesus . . . I have sinned against the Holy Ghost . . ."

Pack listened, hidden, and shook his head in disbelief, "I'd just as soon he wouldn't go on like that. I liked it better when he was just a-layin' there dead."

By the middle of November, Pack Kilborn was ready to concede Ratliff was insane.

"He's laid there in that bunk for three weeks now, like he was blind, paralyzed, and crazy. You can gouge a finger in his eye and he won't flinch. I tell you, if he wasn't insane when he started it, he's turned hisself that way now."

A new problem had come up for Pack. Uncle Tom, who had a family of eight children and was fairly well off from oil having been struck on his farm, had only been hired as a special deputy to work in the jail while things were crowded and his temporary position was due to end on Saturday, November 16. But it would leave Pack with a houseful of desperate criminals: there were three other men under a death sentence besides Ratliff: Tommy Davis, a convicted murderer, was on the third floor, and Clyde Thompson, convicted of a double killing, was in the cell right across the aisle from Ratliff. Then a new prisoner, E. V. Allen, had been sent in under a death sentence for bank robbery.

"If we could keep Tom on the payroll until one or two of these fellows gets shipped on to Huntsville it might save us a whole lot of trouble," Pack told County Judge Clyde Garrett. "We've got our hands full. That Thompson, he's demented. There's no question about that one. We're liable to have him on our hands for quite a spell, until they hear his appeal. The load's just too heavy to lose Tom right now."

The problem with Ratliff, the judge said, was that they couldn't set a date for the additional armed robbery trial—it certainly not being done in the ordinary way since Ratliff already had a death sentence. The appeal for a rehearing on Ratliff's capital case wasn't set, either, but if he was sent back to Huntsville, that court over there would sure as hell find him insane, especially now, as Pack had already pointed out.

"That Walker County court is sympathetic to criminals," Judge Garrett said. "Why, half the town's made up of criminals' families living there, waiting for their kinfolks to break out of the penitentiary—at least, that's always been my own private opinion of the way things are around Huntsville."

Judge Garrett, listening to Pack's plea, finally said for him to ask Uncle Tom to stay on the job for one more week after he was supposed to leave.

"Oh, he wants to stay," Pack said, "but it's the money from the county he's worrying about. The treasurer says there isn't any more of the special funds they were paying Tom out of."

Garrett nodded, "Tell Tom Jones to go ahead if he wants to and I'll see to it the salary is taken care of." Although his title was county judge, Garrett's function was not that of jurisprudence. In Texas, the county judge is head of the county court, which is a governing body rather than a court of judgment.

Like so many other events in the story of the Santa Claus bank robbery, the decision to keep Uncle Tom on for an extra week as assistant jailer was one of those unimportant ones of the moment that turned out to have catastrophic significance.

12 / Cisco was having its problems. The town had gone into a huge civic expansion drive a few years back when the oil was bringing high prices and population was climbing faster than could be kept track of.

The big dam that created Lake Cisco had cost a good bit more than most cities of its size would have had the courage to bond, although at first it was altogether a thing of pride— the bluewater lake, the huge concrete dam, and at its feet, a swimming pool which was, Cisco said, the largest in the world.

But now, in November 1929, the rosy future had a gray presence. The oil fields around Ranger weren't holding up too well; production was dropping and competition had driven down the price of crude oil. The stock market panic of two weeks before had some of the financiers worried, but as yet the average Cisco citizen couldn't see how such a remote event would affect him. But nevertheless, the city faced a problem. Funds just weren't coming in. Even Randolph College, sitting on its hill just north of town, was fumbling and stumbling around for money. There had been so much optimism in 1922 when the Christian Church of Texas took over control—and now the campus was looking downright shabby.

Downtown, the new Laguna Hotel stood nine stories tall and three-fourths empty. The T & P Railway station, which stood a few hundred feet across a little city park from the Laguna, rattled around with a dozen or so passengers at train time, where the railroad used to have to send special trains that cut off at Cisco, the haul was so big.

Things came to a head when a firm of private auditors from Abilene had to be hired to look over the city's books. The report was not cheerful: the town was going broke. If there was some way you could send back the world's largest, hollow concrete dam, Cisco was ready to do it.

Some people, for lack of a better target, said that the Santa Claus bank robbery started it all. They marked December 23, 1927, as the exact beginning of the decline of Cisco's fortunes. Others, of course, saw this as ridiculous, and pointed out that booms—be they oil, gold, or diamonds— always collapsed, but that a real city, one like Cisco, which had built itself on a solid foundation of good citizenship, Christian morality, free competition, and decent taxes, could eventually come out of it not whole but a solider, wiser, and a better place to live for the experience. Now, Ranger, these people pointed out, might really suffer. Look what had happened in ten years. Ranger had gone from a peak of twenty thousand inhabitants to not much bigger than Cisco was, and not half as good a town. Already the biggest thing Ranger had to offer was empty buildings.

A few soreheads in Cisco blamed the whole thing on the city fathers who just had to have that big goddam dam out there—a whole ocean of water for a town of about the size to need a municipal horse trough. Trying to catch up with Abilene when she built her lake.

But regardless of who was to blame for the decline—the alarming condition—of municipal affairs in Cisco, the people there didn't like Marshall Ratliff, either. Whether that had a thing to do with it, things *had* started going down from the day he led his gang in the front door of the First National Bank. And they wished he would hurry up and die; just get the whole thing over with and stop this messing around with the so-called legal tactics. It would make things easier on everybody—and it might help get Cisco back to normal.

HE HAD LAIN in his bunk for twenty-five consecutive days now, insensitive and senseless. His mother had given up trying to arouse a spark of recognition in him, and the jailers treated him as one dead.

Ratliff and Thompson were the only two prisoners in the second-floor section of the jail. It was separated from the main cell block by a heavy steel door at the top of the stairs. There were some twenty other prisoners in the main section, but the actions of Ratliff and Thompson had caused Pack Kilborn to keep them separate. He didn't want the rest of them getting an idea this was the way to beat a rap; and besides that, Thompson, although given mainly to brooding, made fierce outbursts at unpredictable moments. Much of that insane noise, and the other prisoners might try to kill him just to shut him up.

On the night of Monday, November 18, Ratliff was fed as usual by Pack and Uncle Tom. The routine was the same, Pack holding Ratliff's head steady while Uncle Tom fed him a sandwich and a glass of milk. After the meal was finished, Uncle Tom usually sat for a while in a cane bottom chair in the corridor, leaving the door to Ratliff's cell open. He wanted to give Ratliff's body a chance to start assimilating the food, then he would shuffle him over to use the chamber pot, and then roll him onto his bunk and wrap him in for the night.

Pack finished up some little chores he had down below, then came up and unlocked the door to the main cell block where the other prisoners were on the third floor.

"Come on, Tom, let's see how our other two are doing," Pack said, referring to Tommy Davis and E. V. Allen, the other condemned men. Thompson, in his cell across from

Ratliff, had turned his face to the wall and was napping. Ratliff lay inert where they had left him after feeding him.

Uncle Tom joined Pack, stopping at the head of the short flight of stairs while Kilborn checked each of the other cells in the block. It was a matter of five minutes to secure the block. The two men descended the stairs, back to the landing from the smaller section, and stepped through the big steel door into the corridor between Ratliff's cell and Thompson's.

Uncle Tom went first, but just as Pack started through the door, out from behind it stepped a ghost: Marshall Ratliff. Eyes blazing, his face excited, holding a .38 Colt revolver, he was shouting: "The keys . . . throw me those keys and quick!"

HE FELT THE HANDS of Pack Kilborn release his head and it fell sagging to his chest. Tom Jones let him down gently to the bunk and said, "I'll wait and see if he needs to piss."

"Thirty-five, thirty-six, thirty-seven, thirty-eight . . ." He must count; counting to himself. Somehow it was vitally necessary to a plan. Yes, it was. Every night he counted. At the count of sixty he could look, but not one count sooner or later. Sixty. If there had been no noise of the big key turning in the lock it meant the cell door was not locked. "Fifty-eight, fifty-nine, sixty."

He opened his eyes. The door was standing open and no one was there. It was now.

Marshall Ratliff slid from the bunk. A pair of carpet slippers that his mother had brought him, which he had never worn, were there, and he put them on.

Out of the cell.

Thompson was asleep, or unmoving, with his head turned.

Into the corridor.

He could hear the sound of the bolts falling in the main

section. He could hear Pack Kilborn joshing one or two of the prisoners.

"You ain't goin' to like it outside, Coonie. Won't get the kind of food you get here in Pack Kilborn's Palace."

A rejoinder from the prisoner. A ripple of laughter from the rest.

Down the corridor to the steps that led below.

To the office. The door open.

They didn't carry arms in the cell blocks. Too dangerous. Too easy to overpower one of them when he was bringing food. When his back was turned. The guns were down here. In the office. Locked, so that none of the inmates could get in, even if they got out of their cells. But not now. Not now.

It seemed like another time. He seemed like another person. All his past life was past. He had been born only seconds ago. He had been born counting. Counting the steps, counting the seconds, counting something that meant something to him.

He was not sure where he was or why he was here, but he knew certain things. He knew that the cell door had been left unlocked one time, years, centuries ago. Left unlocked in the other life he seemed to have led. He sensed it one time, long ago. And he began counting. One . . . two . . . three . . . four . . . five . . . six . . . seven . . . eight . . . on and on. Too long ago to count. But that was when he had come to realize that the cell door was being left unlocked.

Then he knew that the unlocked cell door represented something. Something desirable. Something he had not hoped to achieve. He could not remember the first time he had seen it. Had opened his eyes and looked very hard at it and had seen it and the sense of something saying that it was desirable. Things passed and repassed in his mind, once this way, once that. It was difficult to remember which way they were passing when he tried to seize on them. Maybe it had been a week ago, maybe in another life, but the open cell door, the unlocked door, had waked him, had set off a buzzer and a light in his head which said, "Now . . . now . . . now . . ."

Once the buzzer sounded and the light lit up the inside of his darkened head, the next steps were illuminated. He could see them. He must go down the steps while they were still there to be seen. He must get through another door which was always closed but now was open. He must get a gun.

Get a gun . . . get a gun . . .

Then he must go out. Outside, into the night. Go . . . go . . . go.

He did not try to figure out who he was. He felt who he was rather than knowing who he was. He was not confused. Every movement was dictated to him by his being, his self, which watched to be sure of what the body proceeded to do. He did not have to think or to ask. He only had to be.

Down these steps, the being told the body. Softly. The slippers (still new and never before worn) feeling cold beneath his soles. The chill of the iron floor coming through them.

This was not a house, he knew that. No house had such ringing, chilling floors. Such cold, brown walls. But it was where he needed to go.

The bottom door was open. The office was lighted. The jailer's desk was there in front of him and the voice of his being said to him, "Open it."

He opened the desk, a shallow drawer, and there was the gun. It was a heavy revolver, a .38 Colt. The being, now standing above him and all around him, looking with eyes at every corner and listening with ears outside his own, told him, "Check it first." He thumbed open the gate of the pistol, put it up to his eye, and spun the cylinder. One bullet fell to the floor, but the voice of his being said, "Leave it. Get moving."

He saw two doors. Which one? You had but one chance.

He knew this. His hand left his side, the hand that did not hold the gun, and moved stealthily, certainly, to the knob. The door was locked.

The other door appeared. There was a light behind it. It did not offer the night and the darkness. It was to the living quarters of the jail. The hand again went to the knob, and the heavy, brass knob would not turn.

"They that are in shall not be out, and they that are without shall not enter," someone spoke to him. It was wisdom, and he heeded it.

Back up the stairs, the iron stairs. Back to the corridor, then another iron door. Someone was screaming to him to get right with God. First . . . get right with God. He tried to shut them up by putting one hand out behind him, motioning for whoever it was to stop, to quieten. "Cease your blasphemy," the scream said, "Repent of evil."

He looked at the revolver, looked down the round, deep barrel. It opened wide for his eyes to enter, and the scream said, "My yoke is easy . . . my yoke is easy . . .

He could take no more of it.

"All right," he screamed back. "Allrightallrightallright."

The corridor was silent. So silent he could hear the throaty rasp of Thompson's breathing. The scream had fled from him, down the iron stairs to the office below, and now it was bouncing around and rattling in that enclosure, for it, too, was in, and could not be out.

The voice of someone above him cried: "Behold, I stand at the door and wait!" He threw himself behind the thick, steel portal, his movement light and quick as a cat.

Tom Jones passed through, but the voice said, "No." Then Pack Kilborn, who turned around to shut and lock the door behind him, and the voice screamed, inside and wildly loud: "The keys . . . throw me those keys . . ."

Kilborn's face was frozen in amazement. Uncle Tom

Jones continued walking, going down the stairs to the office. Time had stopped.

Kilborn moved, in his sight, like a man swimming in oil. Gracefully the jailer moved backward, stepped behind the door through which he had just come, and with the same liquid flow of motion, Ratliff fired the gun at the unarmed man, but missed.

The sound of the shot shattered a million panes of thin, brittle glass in his head, unstopped ten thousand whistles and wiped away a deep coating of mist and water which overflowed everything before.

He was awake, he was alive, he knew what he wanted to do.

PACK KILBORN COULDN'T believe his eyes, and for an instant that was almost fatal, he stood trying to accept what they were telling him.

Marshall Ratliff. Not only on his feet, but holding Pack's own .38 Colt. He recognized the gun the way you recognize a pair of shoes or your eyeglasses; the familiar feel of it.

He only stayed amazed for that part of a second which allowed Ratliff to start speaking. Before his words were all out, Pack Kilborn was moving with the crisis, getting the door between him, with no gun, and Ratliff with his .38.

The shot which Ratliff fired gave off a thousand echoes, there in that steel walled corridor, but Pack knew he was not hit. He found himself running down the other side of the cellblock in a path that would shortly take him completely around it—there was no outlet on the other side—and back to where Ratliff was.

Apparently this was what Ratliff thought Pack would do, because he turned to cut him off at the other end of the U-shaped corridor around the cellblock. When he turned,

Ratliff saw Uncle Tom, who had whirled on the stairs at the sound of the gun and was coming toward him. Ratliff fired point-blank into Jones's body. The older man kept coming and managed to grapple with the prisoner before Ratliff fired two more shots into him, causing Uncle Tom to stagger back through the doorway, then crash down the stairs, landing at the foot of the stairs on the office floor.

Pack Kilborn turned and came back the way he had run, leaping on Ratliff from the side, trying to grab the gun from his hand. It was a desperate fight. Kilborn, older but heavier, against a man who had been so lifeless for nearly a month that they considered him dead, but now having the strength of frenzy.

Kilborn drove Ratliff with his shoulder against the door facing, but Ratliff kicked out with his knee, causing them both to slip, falling and tumbling, down the stairs and crashing on top of Uncle Tom, their fall breaking the deputy jailer's leg as he lay helpless on the floor, unable to move because of his bullet wounds.

Mrs. Kilborn, who was in the living quarters of the jail on the other side of the office, heard the shots and immediately called Sheriff Foster. She didn't know who it was making the furor, and with the doors locked from inside the jail, there was no way she could go to Pack's aid.

Ratliff ended up in a heap, and Kilborn leaped on top of him. Mrs. Malaquay Taylor, Kilborn's daughter who had been with her mother in the living quarters, had grabbed another of her father's guns and run to a side window through which she could see the struggle. Kilborn managed to twist the .38 around in Ratliff's hand just as he pulled the trigger. The bullet was fired into the ceiling. Kilborn fell to one side and his daughter, looking through the window, thought he had been wounded. She tried to get a shot at Ratliff, but her father was still on top of him, blocking the line of fire. She turned from the window and fired four times into the air. The sound of the shots immediately drew a crowd to the jail because the Connellee Theater, half a block up the street from the jail, was ending a movie and people were standing on the sidewalk, leaving or waiting to enter.

Inside the office Pack Kilborn now had possession of the pistol and he yelled to Uncle Tom, "Lock the doors. Be sure they're locked."

"I'm all stove in, Pack, I can't get up," Jones moaned.

The jailer put the pistol to Ratliff's head and pulled the trigger. But that sixth bullet, which he had let fall to the floor, was no longer in the cylinder, and the fact saved Ratliff's life. All that happened was a click.

Kilborn clubbed the pistol and began beating Ratliff over the head until the downed man was protecting himself with his arms and begging, "Don't kill me . . . don't kill me . . ."

Pack stood swaying over the prostrate Ratliff, then he took his keys and unlocked the office door to the outside. A crowd of people was there, with Police Chief Elmer Lawrence nearest the door. He leaped in as soon as Pack unlocked it, but saw that Ratliff, pistol-whipped, was no longer a threat. Just as he turned to Pack, Malaquay came running through the unlocked door holding her father's other pistol in front of her. She ran to Ratliff and holding the gun with both hands would have fired, while the prostrate prisoner yelled, "Don't shoot . . . don't shoot . . . I'm done . . . I'm done . . ."

"No, honey—don't," Kilborn cried to his daughter. Chief Lawrence, with a sweep of his arm, grabbed the pistol from the shaking woman and disarmed her.

"He needs to die. He killed Uncle Tom. He shot daddy," she screamed. Pack quieted her, taking his daughter into his arms.

"I'm not shot, honey. He didn't shoot me," he said.

"I thought I saw it," she said. "Through the window. I saw him shoot."

"I'm just banged around some, honey. Banged around a lot more than a man my age ought to be banged. But I'll make it."

Uncle Tom Jones was another matter. He was not dead, but he was in critical condition. He had bullet holes in his shoulder, in his chest near his heart, and in his abdomen. His leg was crushed and he was badly bruised from his fall down the iron stairs. But as they carried him out to an ambulance on a stretcher, he was apologizing to Pack for letting him down.

"I was the fool that caused it, Pack," the old jailer said. "If I hadn't have left that cell door open . . . but I guess I was so used to him just laying there like a corpse . . ."

"You saved my life, Tom," Pack told him. "That time when you grabbed him. You gave me just enough time to get back around the cell block and catch him from behind. If you hadn't had him there, we'd have both been dead, for he'd have lined me up with no trouble when I turned that corner toward him, if he'd been looking. But you stopped him."

"I may be a goner anyhow, the way I feel right now," Tom said.

"You ain't no goner any more than I am. You're too tough to let a damn punk like Ratliff get you."

The crowd waited outside the jail, trying to piece together the account of what happened inside as various witnesses appeared. All the doors of the jail were secured again, and the other prisoners were checked—in case there had been some kind of a conspiracy among them to take advantage of Ratliff's break—and found present. There was a good deal of muttering inside the jail as well as out at Ratliff, for Uncle Tom had been a popular figure in Eastland, not only with the public but with the prisoners.

Several of the men in the main section on the second floor

sent word to Pack to please leave Ratliff in the tank with them, just for a few minutes. "We'll see to it you won't get no blame. We'll take care of ever'thing," the spokesman for the prisoners said. Pack took the time to climb up and talk to the other prisoners when he heard.

"Boys," he told them, "this thing will have to be done right. He'll burn for sure, crazy or not, this time. He'll be taken care of. He hasn't got a chance."

Ratliff was patched up by a doctor, his head wrapped in bandages covering the cuts and bumps Kilborn's pistol-whipping had put there. But he had also reverted to his life-less state. His head sagged again, his eyes were closed, he would not answer questions or even give a sign he heard them. He was taken back to his cell, dumped on his bunk, and left inert as before. One of the deputies volunteered to sit guard on him, although he appeared to be dead and beaten down, so far as his potential for any more trouble was concerned. Pack felt a guard would be useful, in case there had been more to the attempted break-out than just Ratliff's miraculous recovery for that blazing time.

"Listen, Pack, that guy's no more crazy than I am," the deputy said. "My God. What do we have to have? Somebody sending a Western Union telegram saying 'Lookee here, fellers, I'm not crazy'?"

"You mean because he come alive like he did and tried to get out?"

"Why Godamighty, yes. What more do we want? I'd send the sonofabitch back to Huntsville tomorrow if I was a judge, and furthermore, I'd have him sittin' in that electric chair by the end of the week, and if all they're waitin' on is somebody to come throw the switch, then tell 'em ol' Johnny E. Weekes is headin' in on the next train an'll do it with no more hesita-tion than it would take for him to slap a mosquito. That's what I think about the whole goddam affair."

"I guess you're right," Pack said. "I wouldn't argue for a minute that Ratliff's not playin' his game, right along. But if you could have seen that face . . . those eyes . . ."

"Pack, that's what they all try to do. Give the impression they're crazy. Screwin' up their face. Makin' their eyes shine and all. Shit, they know what they're doing. Especially this here Ratliff. Goddam, I'd just like to take a pistol to him myself. Right there in his cell."

"Now Johnny, you know damn good and well you ain't goin' to shoot nobody in his cell, unarmed, even Marshall Ratliff."

"Well, I just hate to hear you soundin' like you was defending somebody like Ratliff. Like you was trying to figure out why he done it instead of just taking what he done and accepting the fact."

"Johnny, I expect you're right and I ought to have my head examined. I won't do it no more."

The crowd outside, once the jail was locked back up and the office was straightened out, dispersed. The fight had been a long one. Pack estimated it had taken at least twenty-three minutes, battling up there in the corridor, then tumbling down the stairs the way they had done, and wrestling around in the office, him trying to get to the gun and Marshall Ratliff trying to fire it. It wasn't the first time he had been in a jail break, Pack said, but it sure made an old man sore in his bones, going through this one.

The night passed without trouble and Tuesday, November 19, the word going around town was that Uncle Tom Jones, despite the number and the severity of his wounds, would live. It looked like Santa Claus had been lucky again.

Tom Jones was fifty-six years old. He was a former city policeman. Three years before, oil had been hit on his farm outside Eastland, and he found himself able to move to town so his five children could attend city schools.

A little after daybreak, Tuesday, a few people collected in front of the jail. They had only heard about the attempted break that morning when they got up and came into town. Pack asked a couple of them, whom he knew, what they wanted there at the jail, and they said, oh, they guessed this was the best place to keep track of how Uncle Tom was doing and to find out everything that was happening.

"Don't you work nowhere? Don't you need to be at work?" Pack asked a couple more, men in blue overalls that looked like maybe they farmed or did odd jobs around the warehouses and things.

Everybody assured him they were just down to satisfy their curiosity.

"I work for Zene Rowder," one man said, "but Zene told me I could stay down here as long as I wanted to if I would be sure and run up to the mill first time I heard anything exciting."

Throughout the day the hospital issued bulletins on Uncle Tom's condition. He remained conscious, although in some pain. He said he didn't want anything to kill the pain if it was going to knock him out because if he was going to die anyway, he wanted to spend as much time with his family as he could. Everyone assured him he needn't worry about that. He'd spend plenty more years with his family and his friends. They just wanted to make sure he knew he could always have something to ease the hurt.

About mid-morning Sheriff Foster and a deputy left with the prisoner Allen, taking him to Death Row in Huntsville. Allen, shaken by the events in jail the night before, told the sheriff that Bob Hill had borrowed a suit from him the time Hill was on trial, and now Allen didn't have any decent clothes to wear.

"Who are you going to impress, anyway?" the sheriff asked.

"Well, I'd like to get that suit back," the prisoner said. "I don't think Hill meant to keep it, but I don't figure he has much use for it either, even if he is still at large."

The sheriff said, "They'll catch up with Hill before long. That boy won't leave well enough alone. He's going to get himself shot by a guard, running away like he does. They'll get tired of that nonsense and shoot for spite." Hill had escaped from the Wynne Farm of the prison system for the second time.

Pack Kilborn had asked the sheriff if he just *had* to leave town that day. Sheriff Foster had said yes. Allen had been sentenced and he wanted to get him off his hands.

"That don't leave many people around here in case," Pack said.

"In case what?"

"In case Tom dies."

"You think they'll rush the jail if he does?"

"I know damn well they will. If he dies today. Maybe a day or two longer and they won't."

Sheriff Foster shook his head. "Well, Pack, in the first place, I don't think Uncle Tom will die, and in the second place, you can hold them off if they try anything. A few shots over their heads will break up a mob."

"Not of your friends."

The sheriff considered. "Yeah, I see what you mean. But I still got to go. I got to take this man to Huntsville, or we're liable to have two mobs on our hands at the same time, maybe."

So the pair of lawmen left for Huntsville. Then, later in the afternoon, another deputy appeared and said he had to take one of the other prisoners to an asylum for the insane.

"Now, this is getting serious," Pack told him. "That's

three of you going to be out of town tonight . . . and Tom in the hospital."

"There's more deputies."

"But I'm the man that's on the spot. Not them others."

"Aw hell, Pack, you ain't a-scared of a mob, are you?"

Pack shook his head. "You ever seen a mob? You know how they act? You wouldn't ask if you had."

The deputy said, "Maybe I ain't seen a mob, but I ain't seen nobody I was a-scared of if I had a gun."

"I have. I've seen both. I've seen a mob, and I've seen plenty of men I was scared of, gun or no," Pack told him. "You know, I got about twenty other men in this jail. Some of 'em is in here for stealing sheep, some is here for making homebrew, one of them is married to two women and he says it sure as hell weren't anything he planned—that it was a pure accident. Well, the long and short of it is that ever' damn one of those twenty men could get killed, once a mob got charge. It wouldn't make no difference to them whether a man was in here for killin' a law or for making homebrew. He get in their way and they'll burn him or they'll cut off his balls—and there's men in here that's just as good as you and me, except for something they can't control. You take ol' Rol Ely: He's in this jail for about the four-hundredth time. I even let him keep his bottle of jake in the cell with him. What do you reckon would happen to old Rol if that crowd come stomping into this jail arousin' him in the middle of one of his drunks? Why, he'd start preaching to them about the sins of the flesh and the error of their ways. And before you could snap a finger, he'd be lynched, too. He'd be lynched by men that ain't worth measuring to his belt, just because he's here."

"Well, goddam, Pack, let them fellers out that's just in here for being drunk and that sort of thing."

"Go on, son, you ain't dry behind the ears. You better turn

in your tin badge before you get yourself killed and ever'body you're doin' business with."

"Hell, Pack, you know I was just jokin'. I's just trying to make you feel better. You look all stove up."

"You don't worry about how I look. You want me to feel better, you get me plenty of men around this place in case Uncle Tom dies. That'll make me feel better than anything else."

Mrs. Carter had left Eastland the week before, after being unable to arouse her son's recognition. She heard about the attempted jail break and she wanted to go immediately back to Eastland, but a married daughter persuaded her out of the notion.

"How could it have been?" Mrs. Carter asked, discussing her son's sudden return to life, even for the few minutes during the break. "He laid there so lifeless, he was just like a rubber balloon full of water. He just lolled in all directions. I wish I could see him now. I know he could come back again if he come alive so suddenly."

But the daughter pointed out that the mood of the county was mean, and if the jailer died, and unless they got Marshall out of that place, it would not be wise for anybody connected with him to be known.

At the Eastland jail, throughout the day there had been a crowd. Sometimes it grew to as many as one hundred, sometimes it was down to a quarter of that size. Toward the end of the afternoon, Pack began to see faces he didn't know, men from over on the other side of Cisco, he supposed, or from around east of Ranger where he wasn't very well acquainted. He didn't like it.

He tried to keep an ear open to see if he could tell what the people around the jail were thinking. A lot of the talk was about everyday events—except that Ratliff's break was the biggest event there was to discuss. On the whole it was a quiet gathering. Nobody had raised his voice much, and so far there hadn't been any drunks or professional loudmouths among them. That was where your trouble could start, some rum-head blundering in and creating a scene, or worse still, one of those big, bully-mouthing bastards that showed up for mischief every time you got a dozen people together. A newspaper writer from Abilene had been mingling with the crowd most of the day. Pack edged him off one time, during the afternoon, and asked him what he was finding out.

"Oh, I'd say there's nothing to worry about," the reporter told the jailer. "They're here out of curiosity. They want to see what's happening. After all, this has been a long, drawn-out experience. It makes news all over the U.S.A. It's only natural the West Texas people would want to be here if something happens."

"Or to make it happen," Pack told him.

"Why are you so concerned about Ratliff's safety?" the reporter asked. "The sonofabitch sure wasn't very careful of yours."

Pack grinned, "I got black and blue marks all over me to prove that," he said, "not to mention these here two bad cuts on this hand."

He stuck his injured hand behind him, almost unconsciously, and said, "But at least it was man to man. What I hate is the way a mob gets. Greedy. It just wants to kill. Once it gets rolling, that's all in the world it can do."

He paused and glanced outside the office door. "You know, I've been a law a good long while. I've seen more than one mob, but I've seen one big one. A bad one that did what it set out to do. I won't go into the details, but I'll tell you this. It'll turn your stomach forever. Ain't nobody but a crazy man'll ever be part of a mob the second time, I don't care how enthused about it he got the first time. A mob gets rolling and it can't think, it can't fight—it can't even decide. It can just kill."

As dusk fell, and the crowd grew, Pack told his wife, and Malaquay, and his son, R. E., "Now if anything happens, and I mean anything, you lock yourself in those quarters, and you stay there and don't come out unless they set fire to the jail, like they done at Sherman."

"What about you, Papa? You think I'm going to stand by and let them shoot you?" his son asked.

"You stand by, irregardless. In the first place, I don't think anybody'll be shooting me, or anybody else, but in the second place, there's nothing you could do if they did. Just get yourself hurt. I can take care of myself, if I don't have to worry about any of you."

But by eight o'clock that night Pack knew something was bound to happen. The crowd had grown to hundreds, maybe even a thousand or more. Any spark would set them off: some piece of a rumor, or any bad news—even a dominating voice raised out would do it. He hoped nobody brought any bad news about Uncle Tom.

Then they started chanting. He looked through the office window and saw it was a bunch of kids—high school age kids—doing it:

"We want Santa Claus! We want Santa Claus! We want Santa Claus!"

The kids were laughing and clapping, just like at a football game, but the crowd was roaring it out. They didn't know what they were doing. None of 'em.

"We want Santa Claus. We want Santa Claus."

The line of chanters was swaying in time with the words. But the kids were being replaced by adults, men who were not familiar to Pack. He decided it was time to do something and do it fast. He threw open the front door of the jail and stepped out. He wished to God the Sheriff had left him a few deputies to back him up.

"Now listen folks," he shouted. The crowd stopped chanting and began shushing each other, whispering, "Be quiet . . . shhhhh . . . be quiet . . ."

"Listen," he shouted again. "You know me. I'm Pack Kilborn, the jailer here. I got more against this guy than any of you. He beat hell out of me last night and shot my old friend and deputy, Tom Jones. So I don't have to tell you I ain't got much love lost for Marshall Ratliff."

The crowd cheered when he mentioned the name.

Pack held up his hands for silence, "But listen . . . now listen to me . . ."

One or two men, whom he recognized, turned around to the crowd and held up their hands, too, requesting silence.

"Now you know the Court of Criminal Appeals hands down its decisions every Wednesday, don't you?"

Someone yelled out, suddenly, "Who gives a shit?" and there were several loud laughs, but others called out to protest that there were women listening.

Pack continued, "The Court of Criminal Appeals hands down its decisions on Wednesday, and that's tomorrow. I've got a hunch Marshall Ratliff's death sentence will be affirmed tomorrow and the state will be executing him in sixty days. So let the law take its course. Give it sixty days."

There was another yell from the dark, "They've had that case seven months and no date to burn him. Why're we waiting?"

Others shouted, "We're not!"

Some high-voiced man who sounded somewhat like a woman yelled, "Don't give him a chance to kill another good man!" It caused the crowd to laugh, the high voice of the speaker and the way "good man" sounded. The voice of a younger man mocked it, saying, "Who'd like another good man? Who'd like another good man?"

"We want action!" a woman suddenly cried out. The juncture of the two voices created a ripple of laughter over the crowd and they seemed to relax. Pack Kilborn thought, at that moment, he might have it whipped. If he could just get them to laugh again. Any kind of a laugh. "Nobody's going to do anything if I can stay here in this door," he thought. "It'll pass if I can stay right here."

But even as he was groping in his mind for something to shout to the crowd, something to keep them loose, a delegation pushed through and came to him.

"Come here a second, Kilborn," a big fellow motioned to Pack. "Over here just a second."

Pack turned. "Listen, Kilborn," the spokesman said to him, "you're going to get hurt, and there's no cause for it. You give us Ratliff and you can clear out. It'll make it a lot simpler than we have to rush the jail. Lot cleaner. Might be a lot of damage done. No tellin' who'll get hurt, otherwise."

Pack Kilborn shook his head frantically, "You know I can't, boys. Any of you that knows one thing about me knows I can't do it. It'll just have to be hurt. Innocent people getting hurt."

But even as he spoke and was shaking his head in denial of what they asked, almost as if on signal, the delegation faded into the mob, and then, from over to his left, Pack heard a booming male voice, one he didn't know, but the big bully-mouth bastard he had been waiting for all day. He heard the command, and he knew it was too late:

"Bring him over here!"

A dozen men grabbed him. Pack struggled, calling loudly for help, hoping someone in the mob could still be moved by friendship, might still turn the crazy tide he could feel sweeping across him. R. E. came from somewhere, fighting, crying, cursing, "Let him go, goddam you, let him go." But it was an easy matter for the mob to overpower both men, father and son. The hands were rough, ripping at Pack's pockets to get at the keys, searching for the gun he did not carry. He was pushed and pulled and faces flashed before his, in and out of his sight as in a nightmare, and he couldn't do a thing. He sensed that he, too, could die in the grasp of this unthinking machine, and all he could do was yell to R. E., "Don't do nothing, son—don't do nothing."

"Here's the keys," someone yelled. For a moment Pack was released, stood free, while a dozen or more men went into the office. He squirmed and shoved his way to the front of the mob, and found himself battling, fighting the leaders and trying to push them back, "No . . . no . . . not here . . ."

In that instant he was successful, but only because the leaders did not understand what he was trying to do. They thought, in that instant, he was telling them that Ratliff's cell was behind another door from the one they were attempting to unlock. They withdrew from the iron door to the cells, and Pack stood there alone, facing them in the office. Then the mob recognized its error, and the leaders rushed forward to him with a roar, and this time he was flung to the floor, and he heard, through a mountain of flesh that covered him, someone order:

"Here, Fats, you sit on the sonofabitch. Keep him down. If he tries to get up, strangle him. Crush his goddam ribs in."

Someone else yelled, the voice carrying through his body to Pack's ear, "Why don't we cold-cock him? Cold-cock him good?" He was under at least five men; one of them of an enormous size and astraddle his back, two on his legs, and what felt like two more on his head and shoulders.

"Where's he at, Kilborn?" a voice asked Pack, close to his ear.

"Find him yourself, you sonofabitch." There were tears in Pack's eyes, and he drew himself up inside, waiting for the kick, the clout from some iron bar or blackjack that would crack his ribs, shatter his skull, dim his life forever. Success saved his life, the success of the mob, for just as Pack rasped out his hoarse and defiant cry, another yell went up as the heavy door to the cells came open.

They surged into the jail by the dozens, but a knot of fifteen or so took the lead. The rest made carnival a few paces behind, echoing, mocking, encouraging to frenzy. Up the stairs they went—the same iron stairs down which Uncle Tom, Pack, and Marshall Ratliff had tumbled the night before—yelling and howling like a pack of monkeys.

"Ratliff . . . where are you, Ratliff?" they called, like children involved in a game of hide-and-seek.

"Come on out, Santa Claus . . . we see you, Santa Claus . . ." Laughter rang through the jail corridors, volleying off the rusty-looking, iron walls of the cellblock.

A scream went up. It was from a woman.

"Here he is! Here's the beast!"

A roar greeted her words. It started on the floor where they were, then like a tidal wave it traveled through the crowd, down the stairs, to the office, out the door and across the mob that pushed and urged its way forward. The roar was deep and furious, greedy, lusty, full of dark significance; not for the man whom it acclaimed, but for the humans that formed the sound.

By now the jail was pressed full, and some were even on the top floor. The other prisoners were as far back in their cells as they could get, some cowering under their bed coverings, others hiding their faces. Thompson, the double murderer who now shared the short corridor on the second floor with Ratliff, lay like a human log, his face toward the wall, while some of the mob pounded on his cell bars and called to him to wake up and see what they done brung Santa. Nobody in the mob knew who Thompson was.

They pushed hard against Ratliff's cell while the keys were being tried. Hands reached into the cell, straining toward the prisoner. Spit flew at him from a dozen mouths, and oaths and profanity were thick.

"Hurry up," voices yelled, "we want him . . . we want him . . ."

A hairy arm with a long knife in its fist was pushed through toward Ratliff, who was tensed, upright against his bunk.

"I'm gonna cut your balls off, Santy Claus," the arm wagged the knife. "Cut 'em off and make you eat 'em, Santy Claus. Better get ready, Santy Claus . . ."

The only woman in the corridor immediately in front of his cell—the woman who had shouted his discovery—was screaming at the top of her lungs, but her face was contorted in what looked to be as much a smile as a fury. She kept yelling, between screams, "I've got a daughter, too . . . I've got a daughter, too . . . ," as though Ratliff were a rapist or a child molester.

The cell door lock gave way and they entered to take him. But only one man at a time could get at him, and Ratliff reared back and bellowed with fear, slashing and beating the air in front of him. He danced around the narrow cell, dodging, kicking, clawing, but gradually the first three men inside the cell were pushed against him, and the sheer weight of the pressure from behind them overcame him. Hands grabbed his legs, others grabbed arms, any part of his body fingers could claw into and grasp. Someone yelled, "Don't carry him. Don't carry. Drag. Drag him!" His head was dropped and feet stumbled over his body as he was being pulled from the cell by his legs, his clothes ripped from him so that he was naked except for the bandages wrapped around his head.

Down the iron stairs he was dragged, bumping down each step, through the office and then outside, they shoved and hauled him. Now and then he would kick frantically, but it only brought a laugh of triumph from the people who crowded around him. In the passage through the office his body was carried so that his genitals were exposed, and some-one bellowed out, "Hey, Bubba. Bring that knife. Where's ol' Bubba?" But no one appeared.

Outside the crowd had increased to two thousand persons. Cars, full of spectators, were parked at the curbs, some of them with their headlights on, creating sharp shadow-work that moved in giant figures, and the air was cut into light and black cubes and triangles. There were a number of women and girls to be seen, some pushing forward frantically to view the man as he was dragged out of the jail and along the side-walk. A large, fat woman in a fur coat was leaping up on the backs of those nearest him, bouncing high into the air with each leap, screaming, "Oh, that darling . . . oh, that darling . . ."

"Take him to the square," a voice decreed. The jail sat by itself in the center of a quarter block, just one block south from the square. But in dragging Ratliff out of the jail, the mob had pulled him off toward the west, and now was proceeding down an alley that ran behind the Connellee Theater. Directly behind the theater was a large vacant lot where several tall utility poles supported transformers and other heavy power line equipment. Dragging Ratliff was a knot of boys and men, some fifteen or twenty, each holding on to some part of the man until his grasp slipped, then dancing back into the pack, attempting to grab again. The rest of the foot crowd came along behind a few yards, stopping when the leaders stopped, moving forward again when they moved. They were in the alley directly behind the theater itself when someone began shouting, "Let's hang him here . . . let's don't wait . . . hang him here!"

A chorus of approval rose from the spectators.

The leaders stopped dragging Ratliff and looked around them. Two poles stood about twenty feet apart with a heavy cable between them that acted as a supporting guy.

"How'd this work?" one man asked, pointing to the cable.

"It'll hold him," another one said.

Ratliff, lying on the pavement where the procession had stopped, began threshing and kicking. Several of the men rushed over and kicked him, yelling at him to be still, but he continued fighting.

"Get something to tie this sonofabitch up with," a big man called. He began clubbing Ratliff with his fists, forcing him to fall back down on the road.

"Here," a hand reached from the surrounding crowd and gave the big man a length of rope.

"Somebody help me hold him while I tie him up," the big man asked. Half a dozen men fell on Ratliff, and the man with the rope wrapped it tightly around his ankles, tied a square knot in it, and said, "There's his legs."

Another rope appeared. Ratliff was rolled over on his stomach, and his wrists were pulled together behind his back. They, too, were secured tightly. A cheer went up, and the cars parked at the curbs took up the excitement, honking in the night, although most of those in the cars couldn't see what was taking place or know what the cheer was about.

With the prostrate man tightly tied and unable to cause any physical commotion, the leaders stepped back from his form, and for the first time the others could get a good look at the Santa Claus bandit. He was stretched out, almost in a coma from the pummeling given him and the long, dragging journey. Miraculously, the bandage was still on his head, brown with dirt and bloody mud.

"Where's the rope?" a man yelled. A signal was given to someone on the edge of the crowd, and another man came forward with several loops of hemp wrapped around his shoulder.

It was taken to where Ratliff lay.

"Anyone know how to tie a hangman's noose?" someone shouted, and the man with the rope glanced around the crowd.

"Hell no. It takes too long," someone else yelled.

There was laughter. Another voice, a young one, cried out, "Use a slip knot!"

An older man, dressed in a gray suit with a dark bowtie under his chin—a man who might well have been some public official from his looks—came forward and asked in a low voice of the leaders:

"We've got quite a few ladies among the spectators. This man is exposed, er, quite a bit. I think it would be better if we could wrap him in something—a blanket or an old pair of pants."

"Hell, give the ladies a treat," one of the men said.

"They deserve something for coming out tonight," another laughed.

"There's decency even in this," the white-haired, older man said. His face was furious but his voice was well controlled. "You know that quite often, when you hang a man, there will be an erection, and a considerable emission . . ."

"I ain't hanged nobody before, but I'm willing to watch," someone said. It brought a laugh.

A woman screeched, "Quit fiddling around and hang him."

Dozens joined her, "Yeah—hang him!"

The white-haired, dignified man, his fury abated, said, "Please, let's cover his loins. Let's be decent."

"How about his pecker, too, judge?" a man said, bringing more laughter.

A tow sack was thrust through the nearby wall of humans. "Here's the best we can do," a man said.

Two of the men wrapped the tow sack around Ratliff's waist as best they could, and someone kicked him in the back of the head, saying, "Hey, Santa Claus. Should have worn your pretty red suit so we could hang you in it."

Ratliff's mouth was working, but the words were too low to hear. Someone near him said, "Shhhh. He's trying to confess." But not much attention was paid him. His hoarse whispers were about the Holy Ghost and Christ the Redeemer, and one man, who had lowered his face to Ratliff's to pick up his words, stood up and said, "Hell, he's just talking religion."

The long rope was tied around his neck. It was wrapped twice, but the knot was a slip knot.

The other end of the rope was tossed over the taut guy wire that ran between the poles, and the man holding the rope turned to the crowd, yelling:

"All right. Ever'body that wants to have a hand, come a-runnin!"

A pack of men and boys numbering forty or fifty quickly assembled along the rope, which rode up over the guy wire and down to the neck of Marshall Ratliff.

"All right," the leader called, "when we yell GO, you hit it."

The crowd held its breath for precisely two seconds. The big man with the booming voice bellowed: "Hit him!" and the mob surged against the rope.

Ratliff's fallen body was jerked high into the air, swinging out in an obscene, unexpected arc, so sudden was the snap of the pullers on the hemp. At the top of the swing the rope parted and the bound body crashed back to earth. An immense intake of breath created a sigh that flew over the whole pack of humanity like a flight of loosened birds.

"Jesus God . . ." one of the spectators said, recoiling at the sound of the heavy *whump* Ratliff's form made dropping to the dirt. A gasp followed.

"Quit screaming, you silly bitches," a young man turned, giving a shrill comment to three girls who were standing behind him.

"Quit screaming yourself, nancy," one of the girls said. The others giggled.

"Did you see nancy's tongue get hard when that tow sack come off Santa Claus just now?" one of the girls asked.

The young man turned back and spat out, "Whores!"

"How come you're never up to see us, nancy? 'Fraid you'll learn something embarrassing?"

"He don't like ol' nasty girls," one of the whores said. "He likes boys. He likes great big boys like Santa Claus there." The young man walked rapidly around the crowd and disappeared. The three whores giggled and put their arms around each other, swaying in time as the crowd chanted, "Get a rope . . . get a rope . . . get a rope . . ."

Ratliff lay where he had fallen in the dirt beneath the guy wire. The tow sack, which had fallen off him as his body was jerked upward by the rope, had been thrown back across his loins but not tied.

Back at the jail, they let Pack Kilborn loose about then. One of the men, one of those whom he didn't recognize, told him to go look at the prisoner.

"See what should have been done two years ago to the sonofabitch," the man said.

"I've seen hangings," Pack told him, after hearing what was being done to Ratliff. "I've seen legal hangings. They're bad enough. I don't need this."

"Hell, we're just saving the state money," the man said.

Pack Kilborn refused to go out where the mob was.

Someone asked if that was Ratliff who had yelled when the rope broke. A man on the forward edge of the crowd turned around and said, "Yes. He said, 'God have mercy on me for I am a sinner.'"

"That sounds more like a sermon to me," the man said who had asked the question.

His wife laughed and said to the woman who was with her, "He better give his heart to God because his ass belongs to us."

The woman with her didn't smile. "I've heard that before," she said, "Gene says it all the time." It miffed the first woman and she turned back to watching Ratliff, looking straight ahead. Her husband winked at the other woman behind her back and the other woman smiled.

"Where's a new rope?" a voice yelled. A few automobile horns honked the same question with impatience. Two men had gone on the run to a hardware store on the square to get a new rope. The owner had volunteered to unlock his place for them.

Out in the cars some of the boys and girls could be seen necking. An older woman from Cisco, who was in Eastland visiting her daughter and son-in-law, pointed to a Dodge touring car near where she and her daughter were standing, and whispered, cupping a hand to her daughter's ear:

"Eunice, I want you to watch how that boy and girl are carrying on in the front seat of that car. That girl's got her dress up to here. You can see ever'thing she's got."

Her daughter looked at the car and saw a boy and girl embracing. It was easy to look into the open car and see the girl's bare legs where the boy had pushed her dress up from her knees, and although people were leaning on the Dodge and were standing close around it, the couple didn't seem to find it inhibiting to their lovemaking. They would kiss a while, then look out to where Ratliff lay, then go back to kissing.

"Mama, they're just smooching, as Bonnie calls it," the married daughter told the older woman.

"Well, I hope you don't let Bonnie carry on like that."

"I don't do nothing about Bonnie except to tell her what can happen to her in a car, and she don't believe that. Clarence threatened to take his razor strop to her the other night when he caught her lettin' that Wimp Hughes boy feel of her. She just laughed at Clarence and told him to go right on if it made him feel bigger than she was. That girl's a pure-dee mess."

"My Lord, Eunice. You sound right proud of it. You oughten to let a fifteen-year-old girl run around the way Bonnie does."

"Mama, you've forgot how old I was when me and Clarence married, ain't you? I wasn't but fifteen myself, and you wasn't any too happy about it, neither."

"Yes, but Clarence turned out to be so steady. He was a dependable boy even then."

The daughter nodded, "Yeah, he was." She looked toward where the little cluster of men stood who had pulled the rope. "Where's Clarence at? I don't see him out there."

The mother-in-law looked over the group and said, "Maybe he was the one that went for a new rope."

THEY HAD TO WAIT fifteen minutes for the new rope. When the messengers got back with it, it was stiff and bright yellow: brand-new.

"That's the best anchor test there is," the hardware store employe who had unlocked for them said. "You can't get better manila hemp in Texas."

The stiff coil of rope was dragged over to where Ratliff

lay on the ground. He had kicked and twitched several times during the long wait for a new rope, but had not yelled or talked. Once again one end of the rope was tossed over the guy wire. This time the knot at his neck was huge and clumsy, because the rope was so stiff. It was a ratty collection of three or four simple overhand bends jammed together.

"I always have wondered how they tied them fancy hangman's nooses," one of the men said. "Well, it's damn complicated," someone else answered. "Besides, I don't know what difference it makes. You just want to kill the sonofabitch, you don't want to decorate him."

The same man who had counted cadence before shouted again:

"Okay. Ever'body wants to help, let's get ready."

There was another scramble to get a place along the end of the new rope. At two or three spots, fathers were reserving a small piece of the hemp so their young sons could help and could say later that they had had a hand in it.

"Now this time don't jerk it all at once," the big voice boomed. "Take him up easy."

"Won't this rope hold?" a teenaged boy asked the farmer who stood holding it beside him.

"It looks to me to be about as stout a line as you could get," the farmer said, rubbing his callused thumb over the stiff strands. "Sure is nice and hard."

Someone on the rope suggested they stand Ratliff on his feet this time. "It was the jerk up off the ground so sudden that broke the other rope."

The leader nodded his approval and three men ran to the figure in the dust and lifted him to his knees; then two of them propped him between them on his feet.

"Okay, he's ready," they said to the leader.

"All right, boys," he yelled out, "when I say GO, well I want you all to go. You ready now?"

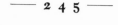

There were scattered shouts of agreement.

The leader paused, looked at them, then cried out: "Go!"

Just as he started his shout, a high, screaming wail burst from Ratliff's lips. The body jerked up again, the new, yellow hemp coming sliding over the guy wire, but a yell went up at the same time from the crowd: "Down, down . . . he wants to talk. Let him down!"

The hangmen stopped, then as others yelled to let him down, they eased their upward pull, and Ratliff was lowered to earth a second time.

"Did you want to say something, Santy Claus?" one of the leaders asked him. Ratliff's head bobbed around as if to say yes, and hands tore at the rope around his neck. The knots pulled apart sufficiently for him to gasp out a word that sounded like an affirmative.

"He wants to talk," several people shouted.

"Loosen that knot a little more there and let's hear what he has to say," the leader said.

Two men tussled briefly with the knot and slipped it away from Ratliff's throat a few inches. His lips moved but only a harsh sound, without words, came from his mouth.

"Stand him up. Let's hear him." Several of the crowd were leaning forward, but not moving, as if restrained by some invisible barrier between them and the condemned man.

The same three men raised Ratliff to his feet again, and suddenly he spoke:

"Yes, I've got something to say. I want to speak."

They waited. Someone yelled nervously, "Speak out!"

Ratliff stared around him wildly, turning his head as far to each side as he could, then slowly gazing at the faces before him before he swept his eyes out over the mob.

"Honorthyfatheran'moth . . ." It was a mumbled, unintelligible stream of noise, "Dayslongearthspiritbridesays-come . . ."

There was a horror to it, the sounds droning too soft to be understood, but penetrating the hearing with the shape of their tones. The whole crowd was silent. Even the November night winds sweeping through the wires and tangle of circuits above them seemed to drone an accompaniment to his eerie recital.

"What's he saying, honey? Can you tell?" a woman whispered to her husband.

He took her hand. "He's praying," he told her.

"What kind of a prayer is it?"

"I can't tell, he's mumbling so. He may be speaking in the unknown tongue."

A slow intake of breath, collected from the night wind, seemed to be swelling up the crowd to an enormous size so that the sudden scream of a voice was like a balloon bursting, releasing the pressure in a fury of words:

"Hell! He doesn't want to talk!" the voice screamed, and then:

"String him up!"

"And make a good job of it this time."

"FORGIVE . . . ME."

The words burst from Ratliff's throat. The mob moaned at the sound, and the men on the rope, without waiting for a signal from the leader, took that as their sign and threw themselves against the end of the hemp, fifty strong, jerking Ratliff into the air with all the power of their combined muscles like a huge, perfectly coordinated many-horse hitch untracking a heavily loaded wagon in a pulling contest.

High into the air the body twirled. The men on the rope held it there for an instant, all of their eyes watching it, then they moved back and around the nearest utility pole with the rope, wrapping the line so that the body remained suspended. The slow gasp of his strangulation could be heard as the slip knot tightened off the air, a gasp which continued for so long that the watchers and listeners shivered with incredulity, marking the seconds which seemed to be turning into minutes as the inhuman sound endured.

Then the gasp ceased, and the body, naked to the cold winds, spun slowly at the end of the new hemp.

The mob watched, silently, waiting; some mouths bitten tightly shut, others gaping up at the slowly turning corpse. The face looked to the north, staring with bulging, sightless eyes over their heads, then slowly swung—westward, southward, eastward—not blinking or seeing, but staring into the dark beyond, pausing a moment at the end of its circuit, then reversing, and slowly making its staring, circular inspection again, making a dead inventory of all the humans gathered, face up, below it—eastward, southward, westward, and north again.

Only the faintest sound could be heard: a soft whimper, a moan in some throat, or not even in the throat, but in the mind; a sound that never passed the lips of any who made it but passed out through the skin of the moaners and made its way around and around the mob in time with the movement of the uplifted corpse.

No one moved until the turning stopped, and the face's gaze was fixed on some uninhabited point on the black horizon well beyond the limits and the numbers of the crowd. It swayed, but ceased to turn. Then a cry, a shout, a roar went up, the movement was an eruption, and laughter mixed with turning, waving, exclamations.

Santa Claus was dead.

13 / DESPITE THE EARLIER OPTIMISM of the day, Uncle Tom Jones was going fast. He had had an operation several hours earlier in which doctors had attempted to tie off some of the vessels in his body and stop the bleeding, but it had not been a success.

Pack Kilborn stood in the hospital room looking at his friend.

"They ganged up on me, Tom," he said. "There was too many of them."

The dying man nodded weakly, "I'm sorry I wasn't there to help," he whispered.

One of his family spoke sharply, "Uncle Tom, they done it for you." The man on the bed whispered words. Heads were bent to hear, and later one of the family quoted him as saying, " 'That's good. I'm glad they did it.' " But others swore he had said, " 'It's bad. They shouldn't have done it.' "

Tom Jones reached out a hand, and Pack took it.

"Pack," he whispered, "I've stayed with you to the last, but I've got to leave you now." His eight-year-old son leaned over and kissed his father. Tom said, "Be a good boy, Billie." And at 10:50 P.M. on the same night, Uncle Tom Jones departed this world, leaving a roomful of weeping family members and fellow officers to remember his end.

OVER ON THE SQUARE, portions of the mob, which had broken up, were drifting around in the darkness. A newsman recognized County Judge Clyde Garrett and ran to him.

"Did you know they got Ratliff?" he asked the official.

"Yes," Judge Garrett replied, "I guess the county will have to bury him."

"Were you there?" the newsman asked. The judge moved away and disappeared in the dark.

Several men stood at the bottom of the utility pole which anchored the line from which Ratliff's body hung. Now and then a woman or a girl would come tiptoeing over to look up toward the yellowish corpse, which was spotlighted by a portable electric lamp someone had rigged up. Once in a while one of the women would involuntarily raise her hand to point at something, but another woman would push it down, causing an embarrassed ripple of giggles.

Suddenly, it seemed, the men around the pole and on the sidewalks began recognizing one another.

"Sam—Sam Heather. Why, how in the world are you? Haven't seen you in a coon's age."

"Hello, Blakley. Well, me and the missus was coming over to Eastland to the picture show and got in on the tail end of this . . ." Both men would glance up, quickly, then go to talking to each other again.

Two Eastland merchants stood exchanging greetings as if they had been parted from each other for years, then asking cautiously, "Did you recognize any of the leaders?"

"Why, no. I don't think it was Eastland people, though. I figure it was outsiders. From Cisco, maybe, or some of them oil camp roughs come in here and done it."

All the Eastland people agreed that it hadn't been anybody from Eastland who did it.

The Cisco contingent was numerous. Before long the people were gathering in groups, almost by neighborhoods, there were so many of them; laughing and waving at one another.

"Claude . . . you and Helen. What are you doing over here?"

"Why, we come over every week for the Bible study class at the First Baptist. We used to be members here, you know."

"Why no, I never remembered that. I forgot you all used to live in Eastland, didn't you?"

"Yes, Claude's daddy and mother still run a little store, over behind the bank."

Then there would be the comparisons made, especially among the men, who would slowly separate from the women and talk among themselves.

"I didn't get in on the first of it," each would say, the others joining in quickly to qualify and record their own late arrivals.

"I didn't see who it was went into the jail after him," the Cisco man would say to the other Cisco man, "but I did get a good look at the ones that got on the rope, and I looked pretty carefully, and I couldn't see a single face I knew."

"None of them looked to be from Cisco," the others agreed.

The three whores gave each other silent signals as they happened to pass each other going in opposite directions. They all had dates, and one of them, a seventeen-year-old girl named Carmine, thought hers was that big boy who had done all the hollering and giving out of orders. "Just be sure you get his five dollars first," one of the older girls warned her. "Don't worry," Carmine said. "He's gonna give me ten."

The other girl whistled, "Well, in that case, bring him to me when you're through." Carmine giggled, "For ten dollars he says he won't be through till tomorrow."

JUDGE GARRETT SENT WORD for Dr. F. T. Isbell, the Eastland County health officer, to go render a coroner's verdict when they took Ratliff's body down. Justice of the Peace Jim Steele took charge, ordering that the body be taken afterward to the undertaker's place around on the square.

The body had been turning in the night for twenty minutes when Dr. Isbell arrived at the pole and asked that it be lowered for him to certify it was dead.

"You going to stick something in his side to see if he's dead for sure?" a man asked the doctor. The medical man frowned at the man, "Are you trying to be funny?"

"No, doc, but I've always heard that was the way you could tell. Like they done Jesus?"

Dr. Isbell didn't answer but said to two men who were standing near the rope that anchored the corpse, "Let it down, if you don't mind."

Ratliff's body was laid out on the ground and the doctor took his stethoscope and listened for any vital signs, then folded the instrument and stuck it in his coat pocket.

"He's dead," he said, and looked at his watch, which he pulled out of his vest. "You want the time now or the time I figure he died?"

"Time now's good enough," the justice said. "We know for sure he's dead."

"All right," the doctor said, "put down he died at 9:55 P.M., of strangulation—or suffocation."

The justice of the peace wrote the data down, then said to a deputy who was standing by him, "Get one of the boys to call the ambulance and take him to Brown's." The deputy went away.

Steele looked at the lifeless form on the ground and shook his head.

"What do you think, Judge?" someone asked him.

"He looks younger than I thought," Steele said.

"Ain't you ever seen him before?"

"Just in pictures," the justice replied.

He looked around. "Well, can you boys take care of things now?"

Nobody answered. Some of the men looked alarmed at his words.

Steele spoke again, "I just meant, can you take care of gettin' this body over to the undertaker? I guess the county will pay for it."

Someone finally said, "Oh, sure. We'll see it gets took care of."

After Steele walked away one of the men said, "Why don't we get a can of gasoline and burn it?"

Another agreed. "I got a can right in the rumble seat of my Ford. It's just parked over there." He pointed out into the dark.

But a third man said, "We better not start nothing now. Steele knows who all's here. He said he was leaving it up to us."

"Well hell, that's what we can decide."

"No, but he won't want that. There'll be enough hell raised about tonight as it is."

The first man said, "Why should there be? Seems to me like everybody'll think we done the only thing there was to be done."

"Was you one of the guys that drug him out of the jail?" a voice asked.

"Oh hell, no. I didn't get here until he was already about swinging off that rope."

"I thought sure I seen you back there at the jail door, when the jailer's boy was rushing out there to help his dad."

The man got mad, "Hell no, I told you. I didn't come up until he was already dead."

One of the others asked, slowly and deliberately, "What was it like, there in the jail?"

The man who had mentioned Kilborn's son quickly shook his head. "I come running up just as they were breaking in. And when I seen what was happening, I turned and hightailed it. I sure didn't want no part of a lynching."

Nobody else said anything except to grunt something that sounded like agreement with the statement.

THE AMBULANCE HADN'T ARRIVED after nearly ten minutes, and then some of the men voted to drag Ratliff's body over to the morgue by themselves. They removed the rope from his neck and untied his hands and feet, then each man took a limb. It was only a short distance around the corner of the theater and across the street to the morgue.

Pack Kilborn, after he left Tom Jones's hospital room, went back to the jail. There were several deputies there, and the lights were on all over the building. The prisoners were still awake, except for Thompson, who remained with his face to the wall as he had been when the lynching party came and took out Ratliff.

One of the deputies, a young man who had accompanied Ratliff to Eastland from Huntsville, asked:

"You recognize any of them, Pack?"

The jailer nodded. "Sure. Knew half a dozen or more of them."

"Where were they from?"

"They were from ever'where. Some from Cisco, some from around here."

"Did you know the ringleaders?" the young deputy asked.

Pack shook his head, "There weren't any ringleaders. Just people."

"Seems to me like somebody had to plan it; getting in the jail and finding the right keys," the deputy said.

"You don't plan a lynching. It plans itself," Pack said,

"and as for my keys—hell, that was no trouble. Sooner or later one of them had to fit the lock. There wasn't any planning involved."

"Yeah, but it seems like to me there still had to be a ringleader to tell 'em how to do things."

Pack Kilborn leaned back in the old Morris chair he kept in the jail office.

"They didn't have to be told. They didn't even have to care about Ratliff and what he had done. Hell, he wasn't important. There was half a dozen times tonight, before it happened, I could have stopped it. I can see how, now. I should have gone right out into the crowd, for one thing, and picked out that old bullfrog-voiced boy. Should have asked him his name and where he come from. Should have made it personal 'tween me and him, right then before it got going good."

"That wouldn't have stopped 'em," the young deputy said. "They was determined to get Ratliff. I knew what was going to happen as soon as Uncle Tom started dropping during the afternoon."

Pack disagreed, nodding his head.

"They didn't care anything about Uncle Tom. Hell, he wasn't even dead yet when they got Ratliff. Far as they knew, Uncle Tom wasn't going to die. Last word the crowd got, he was doing better. Most of 'em didn't even know him, anyway."

"You think it's human nature, then? Get a crowd together like that anytime and they get mean?"

"I think you have lynchings because people think they can get away with it," Pack said. "You set up a couple of machine guns and put a Texas Ranger behind them with orders to shoot—I guarantee you, you won't have no lynching."

"Now Pack," the deputy said, "you know, they burned

that jail down, up in North Texas, gettin' to one of the prisoners. They were that determined."

"They didn't burn the jail down because they wanted to get to some prisoner. They burned the jail down because they wanted to burn the jail. It was a chance to get a little arson in they wouldn't otherwise get. They already knew they were going to get their prisoner. Burnin' the jail was just like a second helping of dessert."

The deputy frowned, "There's a streak of law and order in us that don't like to see justice thwarted."

Pack curled his lip.

"Son, you believe that and you've got a lot of goddam learning to do."

Out on the streets the groups broke up into couples and individuals, and these began drifting home. By eleven o'clock the highway back to Cisco was a solid line of headlights from cars returning home, and lonely farm houses still had lamps lit where the families were just getting in from Eastland.

One by one the lights in the jail were turned off until only the Kilborn living quarters remained bright.

In the undertaker's establishment where Ratliff's body was taken, the owner and two assistants worked on the body.

"Judge Garrett said just to embalm it. Don't try to make him look pretty," the older man told his helpers.

The body showed the signs of what the mortal had gone through. Scars from his gunshot wounds were glistening white, rope marks and bruises showed vividly on the whitish-yellow cadaver.

"I wish I was a doctor," one of the young men said, "I'd like to cut into that brain and see what's wrong with it. I'll bet you would find something abnormal about it."

"You might not find one at all," the owner said.

In his office on the other side of the square, the Eastland

newspaper editor was taking long distance calls from all over the Southwest, repeating the same story to each of the callers and making sure they got his name correctly for his stringer fee. He just told them the news as he had it, and he didn't try to make it sound any better or any worse than it was. To one or two of the more indignant callers he simply said, "Well, you can make whatever of it you want to, I'm just telling you all the facts I have." During one lull in the calling he looked out the window of his office and saw two cars full of men going around the square. The next time he had a chance to look the clock showed midnight, and the streets of the city were deserted.

EARLY WEDNESDAY MORNING it was announced that due to an expression of concern on the part of so many people, the public would be allowed to see Ratliff's body. After three or four hundred persons had pushed into line in a matter of minutes following the announcement, the body was moved from the small morgue to the larger Barrow Furniture Store which adjoined it, so that the remains might be more accessible to the huge crowds passing by.

The lynching drew blistering editorial comment in the larger cities of Texas. The Dallas and Houston newspapers pointed out that this was the kind of thing that kept Texas from being accepted as part of the modern industrial society of America by eastern investors. The Dallas papers also noted that a recent attempt to lynch two men from the Dallas County jail had been firmly rebuffed by the law enforcement agencies and the fire department of the city.

"The determination that there shall not be a lynching is what marks the difference between success and failure of this illegal and immoral act," one editor proclaimed. The Houston papers, located several hundred miles from the area, were scornful of all West Texas, and said this was the sort of action one might expect from that backward section.

A few of the West Texas papers in the smaller towns defended the mob, or blamed the slowness of the courts and the official red tape for what happened. "Had Ratliff been sentenced and that sentence executed at a reasonable time, this would not have been necessary," said one editor. Frank Grimes, editor of the Abilene *Reporter,* said sadly, "Of Ratliff's lynching, the law is the real victim."

A grand jury was immediately empaneled by Eastland County to investigate the circumstances of the assault on the jail. Tom Jones's nephew, County Attorney Joe Jones, promised he would prosecute to the fullest extent of the law anyone the grand jury indicted for taking part in the lynching. The family of Uncle Tom issued a statement regretting the lynching and denying that their father had said, "I'm glad they did it." Tom Jones, they pointed out, had spent a great many years of his life enforcing the law. He could never accept a mob taking the law into its own hands.

An enterprising newspaper photographer went over to Eastland, the morning after the lynching, and found the tow sack Ratliff had worn lying at the foot of one of the utility poles. He took a picture of it, the two poles and the guy wire, with a couple of white arrows drawn in to make sure all the readers understood. The picture was circulated all over the United States, but there were enough lynchings that it was only a short time until another one had taken over public interest.

Joe Jones issued statements about the investigation almost daily, following the appointment of the grand jury. Governor Dan Moody offered state aid in case Eastland County needed outside help, but the county officials declined the offer. Pack Kilborn was never asked exactly who it was he had seen that he knew, although several officials told him to get a list ready for when the time came. Eventually the investigation into the lynching disappeared from the front page of the papers, then disappeared from the papers altogether, and no names were published and no results made public.

ROBERT HILL, STILL AT LARGE the day Ratliff was lynched, was caught the week after and returned to Huntsville. He escaped yet a third time, leaving a note which read: "If you want me you'll have to come to Paris, France," but they picked him up in Houston a week or so later.

That time, when he was brought back to the prison, the warden sent for him and gave him a talk.

"Hill," he said, "you're still a young man, but you're going to pay out your whole life, it looks like, just because you're sore at the world. You're still telling yourself you never had a chance and you're just about to eliminate any chance you do have or ever will have."

Hill scowled and looked at his shoes.

"You better make up your mind right now that if there's going to be a chance for you, it's going to be you that makes it," the warden said. "One more time that you leave here and it will be the last, you understand? You really will be the boy that never had a chance."

Bob Hill settled down after that last escape. He grew older and as he did so he became a model prisoner. Early in the 1940's, after he had applied for pardon two times, he was granted parole on his ninety-nine year sentence. When he got out he got permission to change his name and he moved to a new part of the state. He reportedly became a valuable citizen of the little town where he chose to live.

.   .   .

AFTER SEVERAL THOUSAND PERSONS had passed by the improvised bier for Ratliff's body in the Barrow Furniture Store Wednesday morning, Judge Garrett ordered the corpse locked up so that the curious might no longer view the remains.

Later that afternoon he received a telegram from Corsicana from Mrs. Rilla Carter saying she would be coming to claim her son's body.

She arrived Thursday and was taken in to see Marshall. She stood looking at the pale face, shaking her head and whispering his name to herself. She wanted Lee to be there when they buried Marshall, but Lee was serving a long sentence for robbery. She telegraphed Governor Moody, asking him to let Lee attend his brother's funeral, but the governor refused to allow him to leave prison. It was held to be too big a risk.

Thursday night, Mrs. Carter and a daughter took the body of their son and brother to Fort Worth where he was to be buried in Mount Olivet Cemetery. They arranged with a downtown Fort Worth funeral home to use its chapel so that the service would be private and the curious crowds would not overflow a public place such as a church.

Mrs. Carter talked to a Church of Christ minister about conducting the funeral. He had not known Marshall but he agreed to perform the service.

"But I must tell you," he said to Rilla Carter, "he died from his sins. I cannot say your son lived a good life."

"No," she said, "you don't need to say that."

They met Saturday to bury him. The family was there and a group of plainclothesmen, looking for the escapee, Robert Hill (who was still at large) in case some strange loyalty caused him to show up at the funeral. The cheap coffin, its lid raised so that the head and shoulders of the dead boy were visible, was embellished with a few red and yellow flowers.

A quartet, unaccompanied in accordance with the musical beliefs of the Church of Christ, sang a hymn Rilla Carter herself picked out:

> *Not now, but in the coming years,*
> *It may be in a better land;*
> *We'll read the meaning of our tears,*
> *And there, sometime, we'll understand.*

> *We'll know why clouds instead of sun*
> *Were over many a cherished plan.*
> *Why song has ceased when scarce begun:*
> *'Tis there; sometime we'll understand.*

The newspaper reporters at the funeral found only a few things to call attention to. One of the mourners was a pretty young girl, and they called her Ratliff's sweetheart and stated she was from Dallas. She broke down in tears as, in the little line of relatives and friends, she moved past the open casket where his body lay.

"Something could have been done . . . done better," she sobbed to the undertaker, who stood at the head of the casket.

"No, Miss Tellet, we tried. Believe me, we truly tried."

Ratliff's mother became uncontrollable as, for the last time, she looked at her son's features which still bore the marks of the mob's violence. She was led away by her daughters, and the undertaker closed the coffin's lid.

Just as the chapel door was opened for the mourners to file out and get in their cars to follow the body to the cemetery, a final irony blared by. A big parade with a band, heralding the opening of the Christmas season at a large Fort Worth department store, came marching along the street, right by the front door and holding up the mourners. The parade was led by a make-believe Santa Claus, waving and ho-hoing to the crowds.

THE GRAVESIDE SERVICE was brief.
"The wages of sin is death," the young minister read.
And they laid the body of Marshall Ratliff to rest.

Epilogue

THE FIRST NATIONAL BANK OF CISCO is still in business on Avenue D. Now it has spread out to include twice as much space as it had in 1927, but the alley is still there, and so are most of the utility poles which furnished shelter for some who fled the bank that December day.

The people, of course, have changed. More than the town. That year was a long time ago, and many of the people are dead. Even Marion Olson, who was a student. He went on to be a successful Texas lawyer in San Antonio, but he died in 1966. Alex Spears was president of the First National when he passed away in 1945.

Jewell Poe left the bank in 1946 to go into business for himself. Freda Stroebel, who became Mrs. Paul Weiser not long after the hold-up, was the last bank employe who had lived through that fateful day when she retired in the 1960's. Woodrow Harris remained in Rising Star, and Laverne Comer, at last report, was a happy grandmother.

In 1967, on the fortieth anniversary of the robbery, the Texas State Historical Survey Committee placed an official medallion on the bank building making it a state historical shrine. A small plaque gives some of the story.

At first the bank tried to let the episode die by neglect. During the 1930's when banks everywhere faced troubles, the First National carefully avoided mentioning the hold-up. But as the years passed and the bitter events lost their sharpness of memory, the institution began collecting various accounts of the robbery, the chase, even the lynching—newspaper clippings, magazine articles (of which there have been several), a few of the items actually used during the robbery.

For years there were hundreds of Cisco citizens who took part in the downtown gun battle, and a few dozens more who gradually came to believe they did. Facts became blurred, of course, and even today there are those in West Texas who take exception to any account which does not include precisely what Father or Grandfather claimed he was doing during the long chain of events. One survivor kept his story in metal to show anyone at any time: Woodrow (Woody) Harris was given a gold pocket watch by the bank's insurance company; a hunting case with an engraved recital of the young boy's heroism in walking off with the car keys right under the guns of the bandits—and thus causing them to leave the loot behind.

Lloyd London, a vice president of the bank whose desk sits very near the spot up front where Charlie Fee's was, has become the institution's expert on the Santa Claus affair. He was forced to become one, he says, because his is the first official face the visitors see when they walk in the bank.

Quite a few people, strangers, drop in just to see what it looks like inside from reading the historical plaque by the door.

"Do you mind?" they ask Mr. London, glancing around the modern lobby. He can tell when they come in what they are wanting. Most of the time he can satisfy them with half a dozen simple answers. And then they usually say something like, "Thank you very much, Mr. London. You know, I've been coming through Cisco for twenty years and I've always intended to come by here and see this place, but this is the first time I ever have."

He understands, and assures them that the bank really is happy not only for them to drop in out of curiosity, but is happy to have him answer their questions about the Santa Claus robbery, and show them around.

Now and then, of course, someone wants more detailed information, someone like a feature writer for a newspaper or a magazine. Every few years some newspaper rewrites the tale for a new generation of readers. For these professional writers, Mr. London keeps a special cabinet of old newspaper files—protected by a plastic coating, because they get used a great deal—and other mementoes of that time. Two revolvers used in the hold-up, said to be Marshall Ratliff's, are kept in a framed box but not on display. The bank, several years afterward, published a brief, but well written, account of things, with photographs of the town and some of the people as they looked when it happened. The pictures are beginning to appear quaint to us now.

Some of the visitors are old enough to remember the day of the robbery itself and recall what they were doing. One gray haired man hesitated after he had entered the glass double doors. Mr. London knew what he wanted. He introduced himself and asked if he could assist him.

The man smiled and shook his head, "Oh, just thought I'd come in and look around, if you folks don't mind."

Mr. London nodded, "Make yourself at home. Would you like for me to point out where some of the things took place?"

The man frowned, "You mean the robbery? The Santa Claus hold-up?"

"Yes, sir."

The man looked around the bank lobby, then said, "Where is that back door? You brick it up?"

"No, it's still there but it's now the drive-in deposit window," the vice president said.

The man's eyes turned to a large painting which hung on the north wall of the bank lobby.

"That's a painting the bank had done by Randy Steffens.

He's a pretty well known painter. Used to live in Cisco. It's very good, don't you think?"

"Got lots of detail," the man said. He looked closely at the painted figures. "That's the way the lobby was, isn't it?"

"As accurately as he could make it," Mr. London said.

"Even to the calendar on the wall there."

"Yes sir, Mr. Poe, who was a teller here for many years, said the bank calendar always hung right there by the cashier's desk."

The man put his finger on one of the painted figures. "Who's this fellow with his back turned, holding two guns?"

Mr. London shook his head. "That's either Davis or Hill, two of the bandits. The accounts are confusing. I think it's Hill, myself."

"He's wearing a cowboy hat, looks like," the man said.

Mr. London smiled, "Well, Mr. Steffens, the painter, did mostly western pictures, and I guess he figured a West Texas hold-up ought to have at least one Stetson in it."

The man looked at Lloyd London: "You're not old enough to remember much about that day, are you?"

The banker laughed and said, "I wasn't even born when the Santa Claus bank robbery took place."

The man turned around to look over the lobby again.

"Would you like to see the rest of the bank?" Mr. London asked him. "I'd be glad to show you our vault, and our electronic posting equipment. It's pretty fancy for a small town bank."

The man shook his head. "No, I reckon I'd better be getting back to my car. I was driving through Cisco and had tire trouble. Had to buy a new one. Saw this building and thought I'd come over and take a look. I guess they've got my tire on the wheel by now."

"Are you from around here?" Lloyd London asked.

"No, I'm from up in the Panhandle. Haven't been through

this part of the world in a long, long time. Be a good many years before I get back again, I imagine."

Mr. London told him goodbye and went back to his desk.

The old man walked out of the bank and stood for a moment on the sidewalk by the alley. He heard the whine of the bullets and the skidding shriek of the tires on the brick pavement, and the wild music that rose and fell as a blind man tried desperately to fiddle down the terror that was singing around him, and there were tears in the old man's eyes as he lowered his head and went quickly toward the automobile that was waiting in the service station driveway, ready for him to drive off.

A. C. Greene was born in Abilene, Texas, in 1923. After service in World War II and graduation from college, he was on the staff of the Abilene *Reporter-News* for several years. In 1960 he joined the Dallas *Times Herald*, where he served as book editor, editorial page editor, and editorial page columnist. He resigned in 1968 to accept a Dobie-Paisano writing fellowship from the University of Texas in Austin. Later he was an editor there for *Southwestern Historical Quarterly*. In 1970–71 he wrote and produced his own television show for the Public Broadcasting Station in Dallas. He now lives in Dallas with his wife and children, and is a historical consultant.

A NOTE ON THE TYPE

The text of this book is set in Caledonia, a type face designed by W(illiam) A(ddison) Dwiggins for the Mergenthaler Linotype Company in 1939. Dwiggins chose to call his new type face Caledonia, the Roman name for Scotland, because it was inspired by the Scotch types cast about 1833 by Alexander Wilson & Son, Glasgow type founders. However, there is a calligraphic quality about Caledonia that is totally lacking in the Wilson types. Dwiggins referred to an even earlier type face for this "liveliness of action"— one cut around 1790 by William Martin for the printer William Bulmer. Caledonia has more weight than the Martin letters, and the bottom finishing strokes (serifs) of the letters are cut straight across, without brackets, to make sharp angles with the upright stems, thus giving a "modern face" appearance.

This book was composed, printed and bound by The Haddon Craftsmen, Inc., Scranton, Pennsylvania. The typography and binding design are by Christine Aulicino.